✧✧✧✧✧✧✧✧✧

EMERSON'S TRUTH,
EMERSON'S WISDOM

✧✧✧✧✧✧✧✧✧

BOOKS BY LEN GOUGEON

VIRTUE'S HERO: EMERSON, ANTISLAVERY, AND REFORM

EMERSON'S ANTISLAVERY WRITINGS
(Edited with Joel Myerson)

EMERSON AND EROS: THE MAKING OF A CULTURAL HERO

EMERSON'S TRUTH,

EMERSON'S WISDOM:

TRANSCENDENTAL ADVICE FOR EVERYDAY LIFE

RALPH WALDO EMERSON

AND

LEN GOUGEON

American Transcendental Books
2010

Copyright © 2010 by Len Gougeon
All rights reserved

Cover Artist: Jannah Brown
Mandala—pink lotus
http://www.jannahbrown.com
Copyright © 2010

Cover design & book format: Lynn A. Scramuzza

Printed in the United States of America

ISBN: 978-0-615-34845-2.

1. Emerson, Ralph Waldo, 1803-1882— Philosophy
2. Emerson, Ralph Waldo, 1803-1882— Knowledge and Learning
3. Emerson, Ralph Waldo, 1803-1882— Religion
4. Authors, American— 19th century— Biography
5. Transcendentalists (New England)— Biography
6. United States— Intellectual Life— 19th century
7. Spiritual Life in Literature
8. Religion in Literature
9. Spiritual Life
10. Self-help

*For
Deborah
and
Lidian*

TABLE OF CONTENTS

PROLOGUE
(ix)

HISTORICAL INTRODUCTION
(xi)

CHAPTER ONE: DISCOVERING SPIRITUAL TRUTH
(1)

The Transcendental Unity of Life; Human Divinity; The Search
for Faith; Discovering Divinity in Nature;
The Failure of Formal Religion

CHAPTER TWO: SELF-RELIANCE
(73)

Listening to the Voice Within;
Discerning Truth; Vanquishing Fear and Anxiety;
Character Formation and Personal Integrity

CHAPTER THREE: PERSONAL LOVE AND COSMIC LOVE
(113)

The Awakening of Spiritual Life;
Cosmic Love and Personal Love;
Marriage and Family; Transcendental Sex;
Dealing with Bereavement and Loss;
The Meaning of Suffering

CONTENTS...

CHAPTER FOUR: SOCIETY AND SELF
(167)

Vocation and Life Changes; Friendship;
Social Engagement;
The Responsibilities of Citizenship;
Transcendental Politics

CHAPTER FIVE: FATE AND POWER
(249)

Dealing with Life's Limitations;
Bearing Up Under the Weight of the World;
Preserving Personal Freedom; Developing Personal Power

CHAPTER SIX: WEALTH AND SUCCESS
(297)

You were Born to be Rich; The Responsibilities of Wealth;
Intellect, Imagination, and Creativity

EPILOGUE
(361)

PROLOGUE

This book has been forty years in the making. It results from a lifetime of teaching Emerson and writing about his life and the society in which he lived. I have two goals here. The first is to provide an introduction to Emerson's Transcendental philosophy that can be understood by the average person. Emerson's writings often appear to be excessively abstract and, therefore, difficult for the average reader to understand. Over the years, however, I have discovered that even Emerson's most abstract philosophical speculations are, more often than not, grounded in the actual experience of his everyday life. In his lectures and published writings he simply distilled from that experience what he considered to be its universal, transcendent truth.

In light of this, it should not be surprising that in teaching Emerson I found he is more easily comprehended when his thought is reconnected with the experience that gave rise to it. Therefore, in the pages that follow I have traced the evolution of some of Emerson's most profound and moving insights as they grew out of the personal experiences of his life. In short, what is presented here is a biographically inspired reading of several of Emerson's most important works. The spectrum covered is broad, ranging from the purely spiritual—the search for faith and meaning, to the more practical—finding one's vocation in life. Emerson's thoughts on politics and social justice are also treated.

The second goal of this book is to suggest how Emerson's wisdom can be deployed to meet the challenges of our own everyday lives. As a means towards this end, I have organized some of his most essential writings into chapters that deal with specific issues of importance to every person. These include finding a spiritual basis for life, the importance of self-reliance and the means of achieving it, the relationship between cosmic love and personal love, the spiritual mystery of sexuality, dealing with death and bereavement, and others. In each instance I have presented lengthy selections from Emerson's writings— often whole essays, poems, or addresses— in thematic units. Each unit is then divided into brief subtopics that invite thoughtful contemplation. The reason for this subdividing grows out of a consideration both of Emerson's unique writing style and the profound depth of his thought. Emerson's primary genre is the sentence. His aphorisms are world famous. He gives us a lot to think about in a small space and, therefore, he is best read in small doses over time. As readers' aids, I have provided brief introductions to each thematic chapter, as well as biographical and historical information that helps to unfold Emerson's meaning. Along the way, I present brief editorial commentary that helps to explain key points, and I have also included in the text brief definitions of unusual or archaic words. Finally, on occasion I have offered personal reflections on Emerson's wisdom, its relevance to contemporary society, and its impact on my own life.

The works by Emerson that are presented and discussed in their entirety or nearly so include the essays **"The Over-Soul," "Self-Reliance," "Love," "Friendship," "Fate," "Wealth," and "Success,"** and the **"Address on the Fugitive Slave Law"** as well as the poems **"Give All to Love," "Threnody," "Terminus," and "Eros-October."** Works that are substantially represented and discussed include *Nature* (1836), **"The Divinity School Address," "The American Scholar," "Politics," "The Conservative," "Experienc**e," and **"Spiritual Laws."**

Len Gougeon

HISTORICAL INTRODUCTION

Ralph Waldo Emerson (1803-1882) suffered a great deal in his lifetime. Although he is known today for the optimistic and idealistic tone of his Transcendental philosophy, his was a hard-won optimism. His father, a prominent Boston Unitarian minister, died when Ralph Waldo was only eight. He left behind a substantial reputation, but little else. His widow and six children began a life of genteel poverty, dependent on the generosity of relatives and friends in the community. Emerson's only sister, Mary Caroline, died three years later and his mentally challenged brother, Bulkeley, would require custodial care for his entire life. Despite these hardships, Waldo (as he preferred to be called) as well as his three brothers, Charles, Edward, and William, all managed to graduate from Harvard, which at the time was more of an academy for young men than what we would consider a college today.

While Waldo was only an average student, graduating in the middle of his class, his two younger brothers, Charles and Edward, were outstanding students, and great things were expected of them. Both, however, were cut down early in life by the disease that was a veritable plague throughout the nineteenth century, tuberculosis. They called this mysterious killer "consumption," undoubtedly because it slowly consumed the lives of its victims. Charles was just 28, Edward only 29. Waldo was devastated by these losses. His brothers were not only brothers, they were also his closest friends.

After completing a degree in divinity (also at Harvard) in 1829, Waldo married a beautiful, young woman, Ellen Tucker. She was just eighteen. He was twenty-six. A little more than a year later, Ellen, too, was dead from consumption. Her death drove Emerson into a deep depression. Some describe it as a nervous breakdown. During this dark time, he experienced a period of intense soul-searching wherein he questioned his faith, his church, and the value and purpose of his life. Before long, he made a critical decision to resign from the ministry, to abandon his church and with it the entire structure of his once highly-structured life. Very soon he closed up his house, put his furniture

Historical Introduction

in storage, bid good-bye to friends and family, and sailed for Europe on Christmas Day, 1832. Setting out on a long outward and inward journey while in a deep state of depression, he would eventually discover a profoundly significant source of power, light, and life that resided within himself. A belief in this "Divinity within," would very soon become the basis for his Transcendental faith.

    Life would continue to challenge Emerson, and he experienced more than his share of what Shakespeare once called, "the thousand natural shocks that flesh is heir to." After remarrying (to Lydia Jackson) in 1835, he suffered the devastating loss (to scarlet fever) of his first-born son, Waldo. The child was only five, and he occupied the center of his father's world. His death was a truly bitter blow from which Emerson struggled to recover, as we shall see later. Additionally, from time to time Emerson would himself be plagued by symptoms of tuberculosis, the disease that took the lives of so many of those he loved. At one point, he began to lose his vision and feared that he would become completely blind, a fate that he dreaded above all others.

    In addition to the sufferings that were visited upon Emerson as a result of painful personal losses and his own ill health, he also had the unwelcome experience of being publicly reviled in his early career because of his unorthodox views. Conservative authorities were outraged by his criticisms of the sacred institutions of church and state. In response to his sharp and incisive critiques of the failings of the Unitarian church, his former home, Emerson was bitterly castigated by prominent church officials and their supporters in the popular press. The leaders of what Emerson would eventually call "the establishment" were incensed by his criticism. They condemned his Transcendental teachings as "the latest form of infidelity." Emerson himself was personally vilified. One contemporary recorded in his journal in the late 1830s, that Boston conservatives had come "to abhor and abominate R. W. Emerson as a sort of mad dog."

Emerson's Truth, Emerson's Wisdom

Despite all of these challenges and difficulties, however, Emerson eventually prevailed, both personally and in his public life. In the first half of the nineteenth century he emerged as the leader of a group of unorthodox New England thinkers who became known as the Transcendentalists. The name was derived from their association with the German philosopher Immanuel Kant. Kant used the term "transcendental" to describe knowledge that was beyond the realm of conventional reason. Today this term is also frequently associated with various Eastern religions, especially Hinduism, Buddhism, and Confucianism. All of these, especially the first, had an influence on American Transcendentalism. Emerson read and admired the *Bhagavad-Gita*, the *Upanishads*, and the *Veda*, as well as the writings of the Persian poets, Saadi and Hafiz. However, his own thinking was well-developed by the time he made their acquaintance. Ultimately, Emerson found many representations of divinity in human experience. Among these were Jesus Christ, Buddha, Moses, the Hebrew Prophets, Plato, and Mohammed, as well as others.

In the period before the Civil War, approximately 1830-1860, American Transcendentalists developed a new way of understanding human potential and its ability to meet the many challenges of life. The group included both women and men. Most are little remembered today except by cultural historians and other such scholars. The most famous, in addition to Emerson, are Henry David Thoreau, author of the classics **Walden** and "Civil Disobedience," Margaret Fuller, whose **Woman in the Nineteenth Century** stands as America's first feminist manifesto, and Bronson Alcott, a man who published very little in his lifetime but a person whom Emerson felt possessed one of the most brilliant minds of the age. For the most part, Alcott is only remembered today as the father of Louisa May Alcott, the author of the children's classic **Little Women**.

Although opinions have varied over the years, many scholars today believe that the Transcendentalists have had a profound impact on the development of what is sometimes called "American consciousness," that set of ideas, beliefs, and values that constitutes our collective national identity. This impact, however, did not come about by the issuance of dramatic, nation-

Historical Introduction

changing declarations. Instead, the Transcendentalists sought to bring about change one person at a time. Their movement was largely aimed at individuals. Their primary goal was to encourage the development of a deep sense of personal self-reliance that would enable individuals to meet the many challenges of everyday life.

The key to this development, these Transcendentalists believed, was the fact that every human being possesses an element of divinity. Because of this every life could, and ideally should, present an ongoing process of self-improvement that was simultaneously moral, ethical, and practical. This improvement would come about largely by acknowledging and embracing the inward divinity that is the ultimate source of our personal power and potential. Rather than being impractical dreamers, the Transcendentalists wanted to help people succeed in the world in their personal, social, and material lives. Their approach was necessarily holistic. They referred to this regimen of evolutionary improvement as "self-culture."

The essential element and the starting point for this process was accessing the deep, spiritual, and psychic energy that they believed was the source of all life, all truth, and all that is meaningful in human experience. Emerson called this spiritual dynamic by various names such as the "Over-Soul," the "great Soul," "Love," and sometimes simply "God" or "the God within." Something like the ubiquitous but invisible "Black Matter" that scientists today believe constitutes the vast majority of substance in the cosmos, the Emersonian Over-Soul is pervasive, but in a spiritual rather than a material sense. However, because the Over-Soul can only be perceived through feeling and intuition, most "practical" people in Emerson's time scoffed at the idea of such a transcendent spiritual power and the idealism that it engendered. In an 1862 lecture titled "Perpetual Forces" Emerson offers a description of this spiritual force and the skepticism it often elicited.

> *We are made of it, the world is built by it, things endure as they share it; all beauty, all health, all intelligence, exist by it; yet we shrink to speak it, or to range*

> *ourselves on its side. Nay, we presume strength of him or them who deny it. Cities go against it, the college goes against it, the courts snatch at any precedent, at any vicious form of law, to rule it out; legislatures listen with appetite to declamations against it, and vote it down. Every new assertor of the right surprises us, like a man joining the church, and we hardly dare believe he is in earnest.*

Despite such general skepticism, Emerson believed this spiritual dynamic to be the bed rock of our individual identity and personal strength. It is the power behind the "moral sentiment," which allows us to discern good from bad and right from wrong. It also provides the confidence and courage we need to stand on our own two feet, especially when we make important decisions that place us in opposition to others. Sadly, because practical people, like those Emerson describes above, only believe in what they can see, touch, or taste, they are deprived of access to this dynamic and potentially life-changing force. Also, as Emerson learned very early on, society often takes a dim view of self-directed individuals who think for themselves and act in accordance with their own personal sense of what is right. Most people prefer those who affirm the status quo, who believe what they believe and who agree to see only what they see. Any contrary belief is perceived as a threat and a violation of what is inevitably defined as "common sense." In his classic essay *"Self-Reliance"* Emerson summarizes this wide-spread "corporate" social attitude.

> *Society is a joint-stock company, in which the members agree, for the better securing of his bread to each shareholder, to surrender the liberty and culture of the eater. The virtue in most request is conformity. Self-reliance is its aversion. It loves not realities and creators, but names and customs.*

Historical Introduction

Regardless of such opposition, Emerson always insisted that people must believe in themselves. This is the only acceptable course in life for those who truly wish to be anything other than a rubber stamp for the majority view.

Whoso would be a man, must be a non-conformist. He who would gather immortal palms must not be hindered by the name of goodness, but must explore if it be goodness. Nothing is at last sacred but the integrity of your own mind.

Emerson came to know of the "divinity within" as a result of deep personal trauma in his own life. His first-hand experience with family tragedies, which included painful losses, led to his discovery of the "great Soul" that resides in all people. His belief in the transforming power of this dynamic Over-Soul became the basis for his Transcendental philosophy. It is this truth, this philosophy that has had a dramatic, life-changing effect on a multitude of people since Emerson's time. These include industrial genius Henry Ford, poet Robert Frost, football coach Woody Hayes, visionary architect Frank Lloyd Wright, civil rights martyr Martin Luther King, Jr., Latin American revolutionary Jose' Marti', philosopher William James, psychologist Carl Jung, mythologist Joseph Campbell, mythic writer and moralist C. S. Lewis, composer Charles Ives, Existential philosopher Albert Camus, and, most recently, President Barack Obama. All of these individuals have testified to being touched by Emerson. But in addition to these famous examples, there are many, many common folks who, over the years, have benefited from his sound, sage, and often profound advice.

By the time of his death in 1882, Emerson had become a veritable American icon, a national treasure, revered and celebrated by religious, social, and political leaders alike. His poems and essays placed him in the first rank of American authors. His Transcendental philosophy provided guidance and insight to a multitude of adoring readers. The one hundredth anniversary of Emerson's birth in 1903 was celebrated in one form or another in virtually every major American city. He was memorialized by the President of Harvard and the President of the United States. By the end of the decade, his works had been translated into all major western European languages, as well as Swedish, Russian, and Japanese.

By the mid-twentieth century Emerson's popularity with general readers had fallen off considerably. His writings came to be seen by many as too obtuse and philosophical for general audiences. His deep thinking and somewhat oracular style of expression seemed abstract and remote from everyday life. Serious readers and scholars, however, continued to be attracted to Emerson. As the once mighty reputations of his illustrious contemporaries faded to near oblivion, Emerson stood with even sharper clarity as the dominant cultural figure of his age. Iconic writers such as Oliver Wendell Holmes, John Greenleaf Whittier, James Russell Lowell, William Cullen Bryant, and Henry Wadsworth Longfellow, once constituted the American literary pantheon. But their writings now, with a few notable exceptions, are seen as quaint literary artifacts, while Emerson's works pulse with ardent life. Legions of scholars continue to mine Emerson's prolific writings (almost fifty volumes in modern editions of his essays, poems, journals, letters, sermons, etc.) for insights into the human condition. The historian Arthur Schlesinger, Jr. named Emerson's **Essays** as one of the ten essential books that define American character (along with **The Federalist Papers** and Franklin's **Autobiography**). In the decade of the nineties alone, nearly one thousand articles and books were published discussing his life, ideas, and influence.

Despite such continuing and wide-spread interest among scholars and creative thinkers of all types, Emerson is not what one might call "popular" with general readers. Part of the problem is that you have to get to know Emerson a bit before you become attuned to his thought. Another issue is the apparent abstractness of his expression. Often, to modern readers, it doesn't seem that Emerson has his feet firmly on the ground. To those willing make the effort, however, there are great rewards. One quickly discovers that Emerson's writing style is at once both a challenge and a delight. Cuban revolutionary poet José Martí described the unorthodox nature of Emerson's writing in a memorial essay published shortly after the bard's death in 1882. "He followed no system," says Martí , "for that struck him as the

Historical Introduction

act of a blind man or a servant; he believed in no system, for that struck him as the act of a weak, low, and envious mind. He plunged into nature and emerged from her radiant. He felt himself to be a man, and, as such, God. He said what he saw; and where he could not see, he said nothing. . . . He knew the ineffable sweetness of ecstasy."

Reading Emerson, whatever the level of difficulty, can be a supremely exciting and even profound experience, as Martí and so many others have testified over the years. "There is a sense of vertigo," he says, "as if we were riding on the back of a lion in flight. He himself felt it, and emerged from it strengthened. . . . He thought of all that is profound. He wanted to penetrate the mystery of life, to discover the universal laws of existence." Like Martí, those who have made the effort to engage Emerson soon discover that his expressions of Transcendental truth are deeply meaningful and related closely to everyday life. They are the hard-won products of his own, often traumatic, experiences. Once these connections are made, and one becomes attuned to Emerson's expression and the central tenants of his thought, his often profound insights into the human condition are revealed with compelling power.

Emerson sought throughout his lifetime to offer practical guidance in meeting the challenges of everyday life. He dealt with everything from discovering the sources of an authentic faith, to finding the right career, to maintaining a personal sense of self-reliance and self-worth, to navigating the sometimes rough seas of personal relationships, to making money and finding success in a highly competitive society while maintaining a sense of dignity and moral self-worth. That advice is still relevant in our modern world. When reading Emerson's words today it should be noted that he, like most writers of his time, routinely used the word "man" to refer to all of humanity. Emerson's wisdom is not directed exclusively to males.

One final note, it is imperative to keep in mind that the best way to read Emerson is in small doses. C. S. Lewis learned this lesson early. In a letter to a friend, written when he was still a young man, Lewis observed, "I often pick [Emerson] up here for an odd quarter of an hour, and go away full of new ideas. Every sentence is weighty: he puts into paragraphs what others, seeking charm, expand into whole essays or chapters. At the same time his tense concentration makes him painful reading, he gives you no rest. I don't know why you object to his style— it seems to me admirable." Emerson himself appears to have anticipated this problem, and in his journals he offers the following advice to readers.

> *I would have my book read as I have read my favorite books, not with explosion and astonishment, a marvel and a rocket, but a friendly and agreeable influence stealing like the scent of a flower; or the sight of a new landscape on a traveller.*

CHAPTER ONE: DISCOVERING SPIRITUAL TRUTH

The Transcendental Unity of Life; Human Divinity; The Search for Faith; Discovering Divinity in Nature; The Failure of Formal Religion

CONFRONTING ANXIETY AND ALIENATION

Alienation is one of the worst and yet most common sources of personal pain and depression. It often involves a feeling of estrangement from what was once familiar and comforting. This may be due to the loss of a job, a hurtful disagreement with family, friends, or members of our community, or the breakdown of a marriage or other close personal relationship. Sometimes we experience a sense of alienation from God and our own better selves. This used to be called sin. In each of these instances our sense of personal harmony and oneness with the world is shattered. We lose our grasp of what Hawthorne called "the magnetic chain of humanity." We feel like aliens, literally "others," strangers in a strange land, disconnected and drifting fragments.

Emerson was familiar with these maladies through first-hand, personal experience. He lived in a time, somewhat like our own, when dramatic downturns in the economy frequently brought suffering and hardship. Fear and anxiety were common. Emerson reached his intellectual maturity in the period 1830-1860. Throughout this time, dramatic changes in American society led to social tensions and alienation. Many people felt oppressed by what they saw as a growing emphasis on material wealth, often at the cost of human dignity, meaning, and self-worth. Emerson captured the mood of the times in an 1846 poem where he observed,

Emerson's Truth, Emerson's Wisdom

'Tis the day of the chattel,
Web to weave, and corn to grind;
Things are in the saddle,
And ride mankind.

The result of this situation was that individuals often felt disconnected from the world and from the human family itself. Instead of enjoying the beauty and harmony of life, they saw themselves as mere functionaries, tiny, anonymous cogs being churned by the iron gears of life. Under such oppressive circumstances, people seemed to be mere "bugs," or "things." This is how Emerson described life in America in his **"American Scholar"** address, delivered at Harvard in 1837.

Man is thus metamorphosed into a thing, into many things. The planter, who is Man sent out into the field to gather food, is seldom cheered by any idea of the true dignity of his ministry. He sees his bushel and his cart, and nothing beyond, and sinks into the farmer, instead of Man on the farm. The tradesman scarcely ever gives an ideal worth to his work, but is ridden by the routine of his craft, and the soul is subject to dollars. The priest becomes a form; the attorney a statute-book; the mechanic a machine; the sailor a rope of the ship.

All of these workers felt alienated from their labor and from one another. One of the reasons for this unfortunate situation was that the early stages of the American Industrial Revolution were just beginning to be felt. The rapid development of commercial enterprise was also accelerating the pace of life and creating enormous wealth for some but misery for others. In other words, the world as we know it today was beginning to emerge. The American economy was shifting dramatically from a largely agrarian-based, home-centered enterprise to a market-based structure. Before this, most Americans worked for themselves on family farms.

Spiritual Truth

Earlier generations of Americans bartered or traded home-grown produce for services or goods such as shoes from the local cobbler or perhaps flour from the miller. Labor, for the most part, was not considered a commodity, and trade was primarily local. By the end of the period, however, on the threshold of the Civil War, manufacturing had become the major source of consumer goods. Factories now provided many products once made in the home. Agriculture became profit-based and men and women sold their labor on the open market. Commercial enterprise and manufacturing developed rapidly. Fortunes were made and lost as the economy churned through cycles of boom and bust, a phenomenon all too familiar to us at the present time. Several major financial panics occurred in this period. The evolution of the market economy was clearly a great stimulant to growth.

On the down side, however, the rise of competition and the persistent pursuit of material gain often brought about the subordination of humane values. This led to an alienating environment. It seemed to many, like Emerson's friend Henry Thoreau, that "men have become the tools of their tools." The tail was wagging the dog. Material worth often seemed to outweigh human worth. Indeed, to many at the time humanity appeared to be more the victim than the beneficiary of the new economic order. Thoreau expressed this notion succinctly in **Walden** when he observed with chagrin that "We do not ride on the railroad; it rides upon us." We might feel the same way today about the multitude of electronic devices that seem to demand so much of our time and attention.

Emerson felt this anxiety acutely at various times in his life. He made his living largely as a lecturer. His income was mostly seasonal, and hard times were always looming just over the horizon. Much of his correspondence with his older brother, William, is concerned with finances. The wolf, it seems, was always near if not yet actually at the door. In the same year that Emerson gave his American Scholar address, the nation experienced a severe economic depression, similar to the traumatic situation that many of us are now facing. It brought economic ruin to many and frightened just about everyone. The entire economy appeared to be collapsing. Emerson recorded the following in his journal at the time.

> *Cold April; hard times; men breaking who ought not to break; banks bullied into the bolstering of desperate speculators; all the newspapers a chorus of owls. "Tobacco, cotton, teas, indigo, & timber all at tremendous discount & the end not yet."*
> *... Loud cracks in the social edifice.— Sixty thousand laborers, says rumor, to be presently thrown out of work, and these make a formidable mob to break open banks & rob the rich & brave, the domestic government. In New York the president (Fleming) of the Mechanics Bank resigns, & the next morning is found dead in his bed "by mental excitement," according to the verdict of the Coroner. Added bitterness from the burning of the Exchange in New Orleans by an incendiary; the Park mobs, & the running on banks for specie in N.Y.*

In addition to these social and economic stresses and strains, at various times in his life Emerson experienced more personal forms of alienation and loss. The death of his first wife, Ellen, within a year of their marriage, the crisis of faith and abandonment of the ministry that followed, as well as his later commitment to a radical social reform agenda, all served to challenge Emerson's personal resiliency. Amidst all of this tribulation, however, he managed to hold onto a strong lifeline connecting him with a source of stability and strength that answered the needs of the moment. He found this divine power at the end of a long and sometimes painful inward journey. It was the "Over-Soul." As we shall later see, Emerson's personal experience of divinity became the central element, the very cornerstone of his Transcendental philosophy. In one of his most challenging and profound essays, *"The Over-Soul,"* Emerson articulates both the nature and the power of this divinity. The answer to alienation and anxiety, he discovered, is Transcendental unity, and the source of that unity lies within. In

Spiritual Truth

the pages that follow, this magnificent rumination on man and God is presented in its entirety.

TRANSCENDENTAL FAITH

Emerson begins *"The Over-Soul"* by observing the surprising persistence of hope as an aspect of human nature. This hopefulness contradicts the "meanness" of everyday experience, which for many often leads to both hopelessness and anxiety. Nevertheless, there is something inside of us, Emerson insists, that enables us to triumph over the tribulations of the moment, as distressing as they may be. This "divinity within" appears as an island of tranquility in a vast sea of troubles. Our awareness of it comes, however, in brief, intuitive flashes that only hint at its enduring presence. This vital spirit is the source of all true faith, hope, and love, transcendent qualities that stand in sharp contrast to the drudgery of everyday life. We feel at these special moments an unspoken certainty that there is more to us than what is contained between our hats and our boot soles. We know this intuitively. We also know that anxiety and misery are not our normal condition. We were born to experience a higher and more complete and joyful state. Like faith itself, there is an element of mystery in this notion, one that goes beyond formal philosophy and *"books of metaphysics."* It cannot be comprehended by reason alone.

There is a difference between one and another hour of life in their authority and subsequent effect. Our faith comes in moments; our vice is habitual. Yet there is a depth in those brief moments which constrains us to ascribe more reality to them than to all other experiences. For this reason the argument which is always forthcoming to silence those who conceive extraordinary hopes of man, namely the appeal to experience, is for ever invalid and vain. We give up the past to the objector, and yet we hope. He must explain this hope. We grant that human life is mean, but how did we find out that it was mean? What is the ground of this uneasiness of ours; of this old discontent? What is the universal sense of want and ignorance, but the fine innuendo by which the soul makes its enormous claim? Why do men feel that the natural history of man has never been written, but he is always leaving behind what you have said of him, and it becomes old, and books of metaphysics worthless? The philosophy of six thousand years has not searched the chambers and magazines of the soul. In its experiments there has always remained, in the last analysis, a residuum it could not resolve. Man is a stream whose source is hidden. Our being is descending into us from we know not whence. The most exact calculator has no prescience [i.e. fore-knowledge] that some[thing] incalculable may not balk the very next moment. I am constrained every moment to acknowledge a higher origin for events than the will I call mine.

Emerson's point here is that our lives are infused with a benevolent force that is largely unknown to us, and yet it is the very source of our life and our hope.

THE RIVER OF LIFE AND THE WISDOM WITHIN

When we are suffering from the ravages of alienation and depression, our world often appears to be a wasteland, arid and lifeless. And yet, if we open ourselves to it, there is a wellspring within us that can renew and revitalize this world. Emerson insists that the hopefulness we feel, even when facing life's many disappointments and challenges, derives from a "river" of divine energy that flows into us from an unknown source. It is the foundation of human fortitude in times of need. But we must open ourselves to this spiritual influx in order to benefit from it.

As with events, so is it with thoughts. When I watch that flowing river, which, out of regions I see not, pours for a season its streams into me, I see that I am a pensioner [i.e. a beneficiary]; not a cause but a surprised spectator of this ethereal water; that I desire and look up and put myself in the attitude of reception, but from some alien energy the visions come.

This transcendent energy is also the origin of all *"wisdom, and virtue, and power, and beauty."* It is the power of the Over-Soul, the Great Soul. It testifies to the presence of a living divinity within us that permeates and unites all things. It is this beneficent, unifying, and divine force that overwhelms, finally, our feeling of alienation, the painful byproduct of modern life, as described earlier. It fills us with its strength and unites us through its force. The Over-Soul is "our common heart." It not only inspires but directs. It is the bond that makes the human family one. It is the ultimate source of all our better thoughts, feelings, and instincts. It provides us with a knowledge that passes understanding, a knowledge that exceeds the power of mere words to express. Indeed, words can only hint at its true meaning. It is the divine hum of life that emanates from our souls. It provides both strength and direction in our lives. It connects us with the universe and the human family because it is the primal source of the life we all share.

Spiritual Truth

The Supreme Critic on the errors of the past and the present, and the only prophet of that which must be, is that great nature in which we rest as the earth lies in the soft arms of the atmosphere; that Unity, that Over-Soul within which every man's particular being is contained and made one with all other; that common heart of which all sincere conversation is the worship, to which all right action is submission; that overpowering reality which confutes our tricks and talents, and constrains every one to pass for what he is, and to speak from his character and not from his tongue, and which evermore tends to pass into our thought and hand and become wisdom and virtue and power and beauty. We live in succession, in division, in parts, in particles. Meantime within man is the soul of the whole; the wise silence; the universal beauty, to which every part and particle is equally related; the eternal ONE. And this deep power in which we exist and whose beatitude is all accessible to us, is not only self-sufficing and perfect in every hour, but the act of seeing and the thing seen, the seer and the spectacle, the subject and the object, are one. We see the world piece by piece, as the sun, the moon, the animal, the tree; but the whole, of which these are the shining parts, is the soul. Only by the vision of that Wisdom can the horoscope of the ages be read, and by falling back on our better thoughts, by yielding to the spirit of prophecy which is innate in every man, we can know what it saith. Every man's words who speaks from that life must sound vain to those who do not dwell in the same thought on their own part. I dare not speak for it. My words do not carry its august sense; they fall short and cold. Only itself can inspire whom it will, and behold! their speech shall be lyrical, and sweet, and universal as the rising of the wind. Yet I desire, even by profane words, if I may not use sacred, to indicate the heaven of this deity and to report what hints I have collected of the transcendent simplicity and energy of the Highest Law.

If we consider what happens in conversation, in reveries, in remorse, in times of passion, in surprises, in the instructions of dreams, wherein often we see ourselves in masquerade,—the droll disguises only magnifying and enhancing a real element and forcing it on our distant notice,—we shall catch many hints that will broaden and lighten into knowledge of the secret of nature. All goes to show that the soul in man is not an organ, but animates and exercises all the organs; is not a function, like the power of memory, of calculation, of comparison, but uses these as hands and feet; is not a faculty, but a light; is not the intellect or the will, but the master of the intellect and the will; is the background of our being, in which they lie,—an immensity not possessed and that cannot be possessed. From within or from behind, a light shines through us upon things and makes us aware that we are nothing, but the light is all. A man is the façade of a temple wherein all wisdom and all good abide. What we commonly call man, the eating, drinking, planting, counting man, does not, as we know him, represent himself, but misrepresents himself. Him we do not

Spiritual Truth

respect, but the soul, whose organ he is, would he let it appear through his action, would make our knees bend. When it breathes through his intellect, it is genius; when it breathes through his will, it is virtue; when it flows through his affection, it is love. And the blindness of the intellect begins when it would be something of itself. The weakness of the will begins when the individual would be something of himself. All reform aims in some one particular to let the soul have its way through us; in other words, to engage us to obey.

TRANSCENDING THE TYRANNY OF TIME

We feel the power of the Over-Soul every day, every time we respond to something that is beautiful, every time we do something good, and decent, and generous for no other reason except that it is good, and decent, and generous. The Over-Soul is eternal, timeless. And because it is ubiquitous, that is, everywhere and always, the power and presence of the Over-Soul "abolishes time and space" and with them the anxiety they engender. By opening ourselves to the power of this divine force that dwells within, we are able to transcend the seemingly endless worries that plague us when thinking about what we did yesterday, what we must do today, and what we absolutely have to do tomorrow. Our external senses reveal to us a world that is limited, but our internal sense reveals eternity.

The sovereignty of this nature whereof we speak is made known by its independency of those limitations which circumscribe us on every hand. The soul circumscribes all things. As I have said, it contradicts all experience. In like manner it abolishes time and space. The influence of the senses has in most men overpowered the mind to that degree that the walls of time and space have come to look real and insurmountable; and to speak with levity of these limits is, in the world, the sign of insanity. Yet time and space are but inverse measures of the force of the soul. The spirit sports with time,—

"Can crowd eternity into an hour,
Or stretch an hour to eternity."

We are often made to feel that there is another youth and age than that which is measured from the year of our natural birth. Some thoughts always find and keep us so. Such a thought is the love of the universal and eternal beauty. Every man parts from that contemplation with the feeling that it rather belongs to ages than to mortal life. The least activity of the intellectual powers redeems us in a degree from the conditions of time. In sickness, in languor, give us a strain of poetry or a profound sentence, and we are refreshed; or produce a volume of Plato or Shakespeare, or remind us of their names, and instantly we come into a feeling of longevity. See how the deep divine thought reduces centuries and millenniums, and makes itself present through all ages. Is the teaching of Christ less effective now than it was when first his mouth was opened? The emphasis of facts and persons in my thought has nothing to do with time. And so always the soul's scale is one, the scale of the senses and the understanding is another. Before the revelations of the soul, Time, Space, and Nature shrink away. In common speech we refer all things to time, as we habitually refer the immensely sundered stars to one concave sphere. And so we say that the Judgment is distant or near, that the Millennium approaches, that a day of certain political, moral, social reforms is at hand, and the like, when we mean that in the nature of things one of the facts we contemplate is external and fugitive, and the other is permanent and connate [i.e. born together] with the soul. The things we now esteem fixed shall, one by one, detach themselves like ripe fruit from our experience, and fall. The wind shall blow them none knows whither. The landscape, the figures, Boston, London, are facts as fugitive as any institution past, or any

> *whiff of mist or smoke, and so is society, and so is the world. The soul looketh steadily forwards, creating a world before her, leaving worlds behind her. She has no dates, nor rites, nor persons, nor specialties nor men. The soul knows only the soul; the web of events is the flowing robe in which she is clothed.*

Emerson's point here is clear. Something in us, a spiritual constant, endures, while the events of the day and their related anxieties slide away like yesterday's breaking news.

Spiritual Truth

DIVINITY AND PERSONAL EMPOWERMENT

Once we establish a sympathetic relationship with the Over-Soul, we become filled with it and empowered by it. We are no longer mere temporal and spatial fragments, bits of cosmic flotsam and jetsam. Nor are we simply parts of an equation of someone else's making. No. We will occupy the commanding center of our own world, a firm and fixed position from which we are able to absorb *"particular knowledges and powers"* that will enable us to deal with the many challenges of everyday life. This *"certain wisdom"* has a divine source, *"which lives in all of us."* The Over-Soul provides both meaning and direction in our lives. It is an endless source of innate knowledge and insight. If we are willing to listen, it will tell us what we need to know and what we have to do.

Like a lover who has found a true soul mate, we find our true completion as we abandon our individual hearts to unity with the "Supreme Mind" that is the source of our being and our understanding. This, in turn, connects us to the entire human family through our common nature and the shared pulse of life. From this still and serene point, we grow in wisdom, knowledge, and light. Eventually, we lay claim to our authentic selves, no longer mere actors or animated statistics. We sense the divine in one another. In all earnest and sincere conversation on serious matters, matters such as love, friendship, truth, and justice, conversations in which we express what is truly in our hearts and not just our heads, we become aware that something larger and more godlike is at work. We express what we feel, and what we feel is prompted by the God within. All of us, both the highest and the lowest, share in this divine wisdom. In our earnest conversation with others our hearts pulse with truth, and *"Jove nods to Jove from behind each of us."*

> **Within the same sentiment is the germ of intellectual growth, which obeys the same law. Those who are capable of humility, of justice, of love, of aspiration, stand already on a platform that commands the sciences and arts, speech**

and poetry, action and grace. For whoso dwells in this moral beatitude already anticipates those special powers which men prize so highly. The lover has no talent, no skill, which passes for quite nothing with his enamored maiden, however little she may possess of related faculty; and the heart which abandons itself to the Supreme Mind finds itself related to all its works, and will travel a royal road to particular knowledges and powers. In ascending to this primary and aboriginal sentiment we have come from our remote station on the circumference instantaneously to the centre of the world, where, as in the closet of God, we see causes, and anticipate the universe, which is but a slow effect.

One mode of the divine teaching is the incarnation of the spirit in a form,— in forms, like my own. I live in society; with persons who answer to thoughts in my own mind, or express a certain obedience to the great instincts to which I live. I see its presence to them. I am certified of a common nature; and these other souls, these separated selves, draw me as nothing else can. They stir in me the new emotions we call passion; of love, hatred, fear, admiration, pity; thence come conversation, competition, persuasion, cities and war. Persons are supplementary to the primary teaching of the soul. In youth we are mad for persons. Childhood and youth see all the world in them. But the larger experience of man discovers the identical nature appearing through them all. Persons themselves acquaint us with the impersonal. In all conversation between two persons tacit

Spiritual Truth

reference is made, as to a third party, to a common nature. That third party or common nature is not social; it is impersonal; is God. And so in groups where debate is earnest, and especially on high questions, the company become aware that the thought rises to an equal level in all bosoms, that all have a spiritual property in what was said, as well as the sayer. They all become wiser than they were. It arches over them like a temple, this unity of thought in which every heart beats with nobler sense of power and duty, and thinks and acts with unusual solemnity. All are conscious of attaining to a higher self-possession. It shines for all. There is a certain wisdom of humanity which is common to the greatest men with the lowest, and which our ordinary education often labors to silence and obstruct. The mind is one, and the best minds, who love truth for its own sake, think much less of property in truth. They accept it thankfully everywhere, and do not label or stamp it with any man's name, for it is theirs long beforehand, and from eternity. The learned and the studious of thought have no monopoly of wisdom. Their violence of direction in some degree disqualifies them to think truly. We owe many valuable observations to people who are not very acute or profound, and who say the thing without effort which we want and have long been hunting in vain. The action of the soul is oftener in that which is felt and left unsaid than in that which is said in any conversation. It broods over every society, and they unconsciously seek for it in each other. We know better than we do. We do not yet possess ourselves, and we know at the same time that we are much more. I feel the same truth how often in my trivial conversation with my neighbors, that some[thing] higher in each of us overlooks this by-play, and Jove nods to Jove from behind each of us.

KNOWING TRUTH THROUGH INTUITION

In order to navigate successfully in this world, we must rely upon the truth and wisdom that we were born with. The Great Soul, of which we are all a part, is the source of that essential truth. It allows all of us to live with dignity, discretion, and confidence. We know this truth intuitively and instinctively. We were born with it. We feel it in our gut. We know it when we see it.

> *The soul is the perceiver and revealer of truth. We know truth when we see it, let skeptic and scoffer say what they choose. Foolish people ask you, when you have spoken what they do not wish to hear, 'How do you know it is truth, and not an error of your own?' We know truth when we see it, from opinion, as we know when we are awake that we are awake. It was a grand sentence of Emanuel Swedenborg, which would alone indicate the greatness of that man's perception,— "It is no proof of a man's understanding to be able to affirm whatever he pleases; but to be able to discern that what is true is true, and that what is false is false,— this is the mark and character of intelligence." In the book I read, the good thought returns to me, as every truth will, the image of the whole soul. To the bad thought which I find in it, the same soul becomes a discerning, separating sword, and lops it away. We are wiser than we know. If we will not interfere with our thought, but will act entirely, or see how the thing stands in God, we know the particular thing, and every thing, and every man. For the Maker of all things and all persons stands behind us and casts his dread omniscience through us over things.*

But beyond this recognition of its own in particular passages of the individual's experience, it also reveals truth. And here we should seek to reinforce ourselves by its very presence, and to speak with a worthier, loftier strain of that advent. For the soul's communication of truth is the highest event in nature, since it then does not give somewhat from itself, but it gives itself, or passes into and becomes that man whom it enlightens; or in proportion to that truth he receives, it takes him to itself.

Spiritual Truth

MORAL FEELINGS AND MORAL ACTIONS

The perception of truth through the power within is characterized by feeling. Like all of our intuitions, truth is felt before it is understood. These feelings, which direct us towards that which is right and good, are often subtle, like *"the faintest glow of virtuous emotion."* We experience such feelings when we are running an errand for a sick friend, donating blood so that others might be healed, helping the kids with their homework, or defending someone who has been unfairly criticized. At other times, we are moved more deeply by the resonating reception of divine truth, perhaps when we hear an inspiring leader speaking out against injustice, or when we testify to the sacrifices that others have made in the name of truth.

Sometime this influence is more dramatic and might include *"the performance of a great action"* as when those spontaneous heroes who, in times of natural disasters and local emergencies, selflessly rush to aid others in need. There were also heroes in America's past who suffered legal persecution and physical violence to protest against such evils as slavery, segregation, racial bigotry, or the denial of the vote to women. There is a common virtue in all such acts that serves to identify us as members of the same human family. We love and care about one another.

In each instance we become our truest selves by stepping out of a narrow and singular identity to join the divine circle of humanity. By selflessly acting for the good of others, we affirm the goodness of the divinity that dwells within all of us. What we feel on these occasions is the subtle influence of the Over-Soul, which is the source of all virtue as well as the power behind it.

> *A thrill passes through all men at the reception of new truth, or at the performance of a great action, which comes out of the heart of nature. In these communications the power to see is not separated from the will to do, but the insight proceeds from obedience, and the*

> *obedience proceeds from a joyful perception. Every moment when the individual feels himself invaded by it is memorable. By the necessity of our constitution a certain enthusiasm attends the individual's consciousness of that divine presence. The character and duration of this enthusiasm vary with the state of the individual, from an ecstasy and trance and prophetic inspiration,—which is its rarer appearance,—to the faintest glow of virtuous emotion, in which form it warms, like our household fires, all the families and associations of men, and makes society possible.*

If we live each day as we feel it should be lived, if we live each day in harmony with the *"moral sentiment"* within us, then we will be fulfilled. We will live in harmony with ourselves and with others. The universal law of *"cause and effect"* applies in the moral as well as in the physical realm. It assures a moral equilibrium and a positive outcome. We need not be anxious about tomorrow. If we do what is right today, if we treat others as we wish to be treated ourselves, tomorrow will take care of itself. Our obligation is simply to *"work and live."* We should not bother ourselves with idle questions about future things. Such questioning only shows the weakness and shallowness of our vision.

> *[The] questions which we lust to ask about the future are a confession of sin. God has no answer for them. No answer in words can reply to a question of things. It is not in an arbitrary "decree of God," but in the nature of man, that a veil shuts down on the facts of tomorrow; for the soul will not have us read any other cipher than that of cause and effect. By this veil which curtains events it instructs the children of men to live in today. The only mode of obtaining an*

answer to these questions of the senses is to forego all low curiosity, and, accepting the tide of being which floats us into the secret of nature, work and live, work and live, and all unawares the advancing soul has built and forged for itself a new condition, and the question and the answer are one.

FORMING A NOBLE CHARACTER WHILE LIVING AN EVERYDAY LIFE

When we allow ourselves to be possessed by our own better angels, by the divine spirit that is within us, and when we allow that spirit to inform and direct our lives, then we will succeed in forming a positive and even noble character. And it is through this character that the world will come to know us, and we shall know the world.

> *We are all discerners of spirits. That diagnosis lies aloft in our life or unconscious power. The intercourse of society, its trade, its religion, its friendships, its quarrels, is one wide judicial investigation of character. In full court, or in small committee, or confronted face to face, accuser and accused, men offer themselves to be judged. Against their will they exhibit those decisive trifles by which character is read. But who judges? and what? Not our understanding. We do not read them by learning or craft. No; the wisdom of the wise man consists herein, that he does not judge them; he lets them judge themselves and merely reads and records their own verdict.*
>
> *By virtue of this inevitable nature, private will is overpowered, and, maugre [i.e. in spite of] our efforts or our imperfections, your genius will speak from you, and mine from me. That which we are, we shall teach, not voluntarily but involuntarily. Thoughts come into our minds by avenues which we never left open, and thoughts go out of our minds through avenues which we never voluntarily opened. Character teaches over our head. The infallible index of true*

progress is found in the tone the man takes. Neither his age, nor his breeding, nor company, nor books, nor actions, nor talents, nor all together can hinder him from being deferential to a higher spirit than his own. If he have not found his home in God, his manners, his forms of speech, the turn of his sentences, the build, shall I say, of all his opinions will involuntarily confess it, let him brave it out how he will. If he have found his centre, the Deity will shine through him, through all the disguises of ignorance, of ungenial temperament, of unfavorable circumstance. The tone of seeking is one, and the tone of having is another.

The power of the spirit that informs a strong and virtuous character is not showy or ostentatious. It does not make a spectacle of itself. It is not reserved only for the high and the mighty, but it comes to the *"lowly and the simple"* as insight or understanding. It brings serenity and the kind of quiet and subtle dignity that comes with simply being a good person. No matter what our career path in life might be, there is nothing more important than being the best person that we can be. It is this effort that that will lead to the truest kind of success in life. This is not a superficial success. It does not depend on what you have or who you know. It's a matter of who and what you are. It's a deeply personal disposition and inward sense of worth that brings with it *"serenity and grandeur."*

I saw in my own parents a confirmation of Emerson's insight. A lower, middle-class couple, they worked hard every day to raise five children under what must have been, at times, very trying circumstances. My father was a factory worker. My mother was, in the truest sense, "a homemaker." The most important thing that they did with their lives was not just providing food, shelter, and clothing for us all, although that was certainly important. More significant, by far, was the sense of character that they expressed, quietly, throughout their lives. You always knew that they stood for something meaningful and real. Without ever being spoken, that something expressed itself in the loving care they showed to us and in the sincerity of their relations with the larger community. It showed itself in the simple honesty and integrity of their everyday lives, and their unquestioning commitment to friends, neighbors, and community. Although they never had more than the minimum in terms of material things, they nevertheless led beautiful and worthwhile lives that eloquently expressed an Emersonian *"serenity and grandeur."* They were, in short, real people.

> **This energy does not descend into individual life on any other condition than entire possession. It comes to the lowly and simple; it comes to whomsoever will put off what is foreign and proud; it comes as insight; it comes as serenity and grandeur. When we see those whom it inhabits, we are apprised of new degrees of greatness. From that inspiration the man comes back with a changed tone. He does not talk with men with an eye to their opinion. He tries them. It requires of us to be plain and true. The vain traveller attempts to embellish his life by quoting my lord and the prince and the countess, who thus said or did to him. The ambitious vulgar show you their spoons and brooches and rings, and preserve their cards and compliments. The more cultivated, in their account of their own experience, cull out the pleasing, poetic circumstance,—the visit to Rome, the man of genius they saw, the brilliant friend they know; still further on perhaps the gorgeous landscape, the mountain lights, the mountain thoughts they enjoyed yesterday,—and so seek to throw a romantic color over their life. But the soul that ascends to worship the great God is plain and true; has no rose-color, no fine**

friends, no chivalry, no adventures; does not want admiration; dwells in the hour that now is, in the earnest experience of the common day,—by reason of the present moment and the mere trifle having become porous to thought and bibulous [i.e. absorbent] of the sea of light.

BECOMING ONE WITH THE DIVINE

By opening ourselves to the divine spirit that dwells within all of us, we become one with the spirit of God, the great Soul, the Over-Soul that pervades, animates, and unifies all of creation. Most of us were raised with a notion of God as a kind of "Supreme Other," an entity that is infinitely superior to anyone or anything that we could ever personally know, an elevated being that resides in a sublime, heavenly mansion who ultimately judges the rightness and the wrongness of our actions, dispensing rewards or punishments in the great and somewhat misty hereafter. For Emerson, God, the Great Soul, the Over-Soul, the Divine One, is anything but remote. As noted earlier, God is the very essence of what we are. This divinity not only dwells within us, but actually is us. It is the same divine force that binds the human family together, holds the stars in the heavens, the planets in their orbits and guides the galaxies in their serene drift across the cosmos. This is not a traditional god, a god of words, a *"God of rhetoric."* This is a dynamic divinity that takes many forms. It is the source of our being, of all life, and all meaning. When we acknowledge this spirit of God within and allow the influx of that divine spirit to empower us, then we *"become God,"* part and particle, united with all of creation. And when this happens, our will becomes one with the will of God, and our fulfillment emerges in the natural evolution of events that are woven into the fabric of our lives.

Ineffable is the union of man and God in every act of the soul. The simplest person who in his integrity worships God, becomes God; yet for ever and ever the influx of this better and universal self is new and unsearchable. It inspires awe and astonishment. How dear, how soothing to man, arises the idea of God, peopling the lonely place, effacing the scars of our mistakes and disappointments! When we have broken our god of tradition and ceased from our god of rhetoric, then may God fire the heart with his presence. It is the doubling

Spiritual Truth

of the heart itself, nay, the infinite enlargement of the heart with a power of growth to a new infinity on every side. It inspires in man an infallible trust. He has not the conviction, but the sight, that the best is the true, and may in that thought easily dismiss all particular uncertainties and fears, and adjourn to the sure revelation of time the solution of his private riddles. He is sure that his welfare is dear to the heart of being. In the presence of law to his mind he is overflowed with a reliance so universal that it sweeps away all cherished hopes and the most stable projects of mortal condition in its flood. He believes that he cannot escape from his good. The things that are really for thee gravitate to thee. You are running to seek your friend. Let your feet run, but your mind need not. If you do not find him, will you not acquiesce that it is best you should not find him? for there is a power, which, as it is in you, is in him also, and could therefore very well bring you together, if it were for the best. You are preparing with eagerness to go and render a service to which your talent and your taste invite you, the love of men and the hope of fame. Has it not occurred to you that you have no right to go, unless you are equally willing to be prevented from going? O, believe, as thou livest, that every sound that is spoken over the round world, which thou oughtest to hear, will vibrate on thine ear! Every proverb, every book, every byword that belongs to thee for aid or comfort, shall surely come home through open or winding passages. Every friend whom not thy fantastic [i.e. imaginary] will but the great and tender

> *heart in thee craveth, shall lock thee in his embrace. And this because the heart in thee is the heart of all; not a valve, not a wall, not an intersection is there anywhere in nature, but one blood rolls uninterruptedly an endless circulation through all men, as the water of the globe is all one sea, and, truly seen, its tide is one.*

Emerson ends this magnificent meditation on the divine with the following exhortation to all, especially *"the lowly"* of the earth, to embrace the immortal divinity that is theirs, and the *"divine unity"* that is life.

> *Great is the soul, and plain. It is no flatterer, it is no follower; it never appeals from itself. It believes in itself. Before the immense possibilities of man all mere experience, all past biography, however spotless and sainted, shrinks away. Before that heaven which our presentiments foreshow us, we cannot easily praise any form of life we have seen or read of. We not only affirm that we have few great men, but, absolutely speaking, that we have none; that we have no history, no record of any character or mode of living that entirely contents us. The saints and demigods whom history worships we are constrained to accept with a grain of allowance. Though in our lonely hours we draw a new strength out of their memory, yet, pressed on our attention, as they are by the thoughtless and customary, they fatigue and invade. The soul gives itself, alone, original and pure, to the Lonely, Original and Pure, who, on that condition, gladly inhabits, leads and speaks through it. Then is it glad, young*

Spiritual Truth

*and nimble. It is not wise, but it sees through all things. It is not called religious, but it is innocent. It calls the light its own, and feels that the grass grows and the stone falls by a law inferior to, and dependent on, its nature. Behold, it saith, I am born into the great, the universal mind. I, the imperfect, adore my own Perfect. I am somehow receptive of the great soul, and thereby I do overlook the sun and the stars and feel them to be the fair accidents and effects which change and pass. More and more the surges of everlasting nature enter into me, and I become public and human in my regards and actions. So come I to live in thoughts and act with energies which are immortal. Thus revering the soul, and learning, as the ancient said, that "its beauty is immense," man will come to see that the world is the perennial miracle which the soul worketh, and be less astonished at particular wonders; he will learn that there is no profane history; that all history is sacred; that the universe is represented in an atom, in a moment of time. He will weave no longer a spotted life of shreds and patches, but he will live with a divine unity. He will cease from what is base and frivolous in his life and be content with all places and with any service he can render. He will calmly front the morrow in the negligency [*i.e. without care or anxiety*] of that trust which carries God with it and so hath already the whole future in the bottom of the heart.*

For Emerson, this "divine unity" is the ultimate and ever-enduring answer to the alienation of his age, and ours.

(RE) DISCOVERING DIVINITY

Now, most people, I have found, are inclined to be skeptical regarding any notion of a divinity or spiritual power within, a power that many have never consciously felt but unconsciously yearned for. As a result, the world lies before such saddened souls like a heap of broken fragments, heavy, ponderous, and suffocating, an alien place filled with deceptions, disappointments, and failed hopes. I have felt that way myself, and so did Emerson, many times. But he did not let that stand as the dominant tone of his life. His life's motto was, *"I am defeated all the time, yet to victory I am born."* How did Emerson discover this Over-Soul, this Divinity Within and how can we open ourselves to a similar discovery?

Whether we believe it or not, all of us were once fully possessed by the divine power that Emerson describes. This was during the pre-conscious stage in our development, before the ego— our sense of individual self— separated us from the rhythms of life that reflect its essential harmony and unity. This ideal stage is associated with early childhood. Unfortunately, for most of us childhood is but a dim memory. We have matured into adults and instead of seeing the world as a great playground and other people as potential playmates, we now see a vast and somewhat oppressive workplace filled with competitors. Even in our closest personal relationships we seem to be painfully aware that the world consists of two apparently opposing entities. These Emerson defined as "the me and the not me."

This attitude, of course, reflects a state of alienation. Instead of acting naturally and spontaneously, as we did in childhood, we are now acutely self-conscious. It seems necessary to hide our true selves from the world. Like T. S. Eliot's "Prufrock," each morning we "prepare a face to meet the faces that we meet." In the process of hiding our true selves, we subordinate our finer inclinations and instead submit to following the ways of the world, assuming that everyone else does the same. But we also sense the wrongness of this deception. The resulting disjunction between our inner and outer selves is sometimes painful. We are no longer in rapport with our inner divinity; the better angels of our being are silenced. We begin to experience a

Spiritual Truth

sense of unease and even quiet guilt, which Emerson calls *"the mumps and measles of the soul."* Well, the damage has been done. Our primal innocence has been lost. Like Adam and Eve, we have been expelled from the Garden and now live in a fallen world. As Emerson observes in **"*Experience,*"** *"It is very unhappy, but too late to be helped, the discovery we have made that we exist. That discovery is called the Fall of Man."* But all is not lost forever. We can recover that primal sense of unity, on a conscious level, by reconnecting with its source, a source that still dwells within us. That inner voice will yet speak to us, if we are willing to listen.

DISCOVERING DIVINITY IN THE NATURAL WORLD

In order to re-open the pathway to the Divinity Within, to reconnect with the life-renewing power of the Over-Soul, we must look both inwardly, into ourselves, and outwardly, towards nature and the natural world. Emerson observes in his *"American Scholar"* address that *"nature is the opposite of the soul, answering to it part for part. One is seal and one is print. Its beauty is the beauty of [our] own mind. Its laws are the laws of [our] own mind."* The divinity that is within us is both reflected in and symbolized by the natural world around us which, like ourselves, is the product of divine creation. You may recall how, when you were a child, nature was a place of endless delight. If you were lucky enough to grow up in a suburban or rural area, as I was, there were woods with brooks and streams to be explored, and that's where you headed every sunny day. Trees were there to be climbed, brooks to be dammed, fields to be traversed, hills to be conquered. Rivers and ponds were for swimming. There was no end to the delicious, sensuous experience of what Wordsworth called "splendor in the grass," and "glory in the flower." Urban kids might experience the slightly tamer version of nature that is present in city parks and playgrounds. Also, family trips into the countryside and Sunday picnics could provide occasional but intense pleasure.

During these special times, our inward and outward senses were in delight-filled harmony. Immersion in nature was literal. Who could distinguish the swimmer from the lake or the climber from the tree? At some sad point, unfortunately, we seem to lose this innocent spontaneity and closeness to nature, as well as contact with the divine spirit that is the source of both. Most of us are eventually expelled from this idyllic Garden of Eden as we mature. Emerson, however, believed we can recover that lost spirit by opening ourselves, once again, to the beauty and the glory and the wonder of the natural world, of which we were once so happily and fully a part. Because the spirit in nature is the same spirit that is within us, and because *"the Universe is the externalization of the soul,"* this re-connection becomes simultaneously an inward and an outward journey.

Spiritual Truth

Here is the idea as Emerson describes it in his appropriately titled work, **Nature** (1836). The process begins with self-awareness, which leads to awareness of the natural world, which, in turn, culminates with a conscious perception of the "sublime," that is, the presence of God in nature.

To go into solitude, a man needs to retire as much from his chamber as from society. I am not solitary whilst I read and write, though nobody is with me. But if a man would be alone, let him look at the stars. The rays that come from those heavenly worlds will separate between him and what he touches. One might think the atmosphere was made transparent with this design, to give man, in the heavenly bodies, the perpetual presence of the sublime. Seen in the streets of cities, how great they are! If the stars should appear one night in a thousand years, how would men believe and adore; and preserve for many generations the remembrance of the city of God which had been shown! But every night come out these envoys of beauty, and light the universe with their admonishing smile.

The stars awaken a certain reverence, because though always present, they are inaccessible; but all natural objects make a kindred impression, when the mind is open to their influence. Nature never wears a mean appearance. Neither does the wisest man extort her secret, and lose his curiosity by finding out all her perfection. Nature never became a toy to a wise spirit. The flowers, the animals, the mountains, reflected the wisdom of his

best hour, as much as they had delighted the simplicity of his childhood.

Emerson's emphasis on the child-like state is important and deliberate. This is no fairy tale wish to return to childhood. It is instead a sincere effort to break down the barriers between us and the Divinity Within that have arisen since that time.

The lover of nature is he whose inward and outward senses are still truly adjusted to each other; who has retained the spirit of infancy even into the era of manhood. His intercourse with heaven and earth becomes part of his daily food. In the presence of nature a wild delight runs through the man, in spite of real sorrows. Nature says,—he is my creature, and maugre all his impertinent griefs, he shall be glad with me. Not the sun or the summer alone, but every hour and season yields its tribute of delight; for every hour and change corresponds to and authorizes a different state of the mind, from breathless noon to grimmest midnight. Nature is a setting that fits equally well a comic or a mourning piece. In good health, the air is a cordial of incredible virtue.

Spiritual Truth

EXPERIENCING GOD, NATURE, AND DIVINE ECSTASY

On rare occasions the experience of the Divinity Without, as it resonates with the Divinity Within, can be dramatic and even mystical. Sometimes for Emerson this experience reached the level of spiritual ecstasy. He suddenly felt as if he were merged into a divine union where he became, quite literally, *"part or parcel of God."*

> *Crossing a bare common, in snow puddles, at twilight, under a clouded sky, without having in my thoughts any occurrence of special good fortune, I have enjoyed a perfect exhilaration. I am glad to the brink of fear. In the woods, too, a man casts off his years, as the snake his slough, and at what period soever of life is always a child. In the woods is perpetual youth. Within these plantations of God, a decorum and sanctity reign, a perennial festival is dressed, and the guest sees not how he should tire of them in a thousand years. In the woods, we return to reason and faith. There I feel that nothing can befall me in life,—no disgrace, no calamity (leaving me my eyes), which nature cannot repair. Standing on the bare ground,—my head bathed by the blithe air and uplifted into infinite space,—all mean egotism vanishes. I become a transparent eyeball; I am nothing; I see all; the currents of the Universal Being circulate through me; I am part or parcel of God. The name of the nearest friend sounds then foreign and accidental: to be brothers, to be acquaintances, master or servant, is then a trifle and a disturbance. I am the lover of uncontained and immortal beauty. In the wilderness, I find something more*

dear and connate [i.e. congenial] than in streets or villages. In the tranquil landscape, and especially in the distant line of the horizon, man beholds some[thing] as beautiful as his own nature.

Emerson's image of a *"transparent eyeball"* is particularly apt. As noted earlier, he recognized that the source of the anxiety plaguing his society (and ours), was a feeling of alienation, a painful divide between the me and the not me. By describing himself as a transparent eyeball, Emerson closed that gap, healed that division. The perceiver and the perceived are now one. The relationship is literally transparent. The swimmer becomes a drop of water in the pond. The climber becomes a limb of the tree. We are what we see.

The greatest delight which the fields and woods minister is the suggestion of an occult relation between man and the vegetable. I am not alone and un-acknowledged. They nod to me, and I to them. The waving of the boughs in the storm is new to me and old. It takes me by surprise, and yet is not unknown. Its effect is like that of a higher thought or a better emotion coming over me, when I deemed I was thinking justly or doing right.

Yet it is certain that the power to produce this delight does not reside in nature, but in man, or in a harmony of both.

The miraculous delight and spiritual joy to be found in nature, which Emerson here describes so beautifully, was once quite natural to us all. Occasionally, we are reminded of that fact. I recall an experience that occurred when I was a freshman in college. I lived in a dorm that was part of a quadrangle of buildings. It was an evening in early December, and I was alone in my room. Suddenly I heard a raucous sound coming from the yard below. When I glanced out the window, I noticed that a gentle snow was falling, the first of the winter season. Having grown up in New England, I didn't think much about it. Snow is snow. I was about to return to my studies when I noticed that the noise I was hearing, loud laughter mixed with shrieks of childish delight, was coming from a small group of young men. They were bounding through the falling flakes and bubbling over with exuberance and spontaneous glee.

Upon closer inspection I realized that the young men were my dorm mates. They were all from West Africa, and they had never seen snow before. To them, this snow shower was a first-rate miracle, and they just couldn't get enough of it. They responded with child-like joy because this natural miracle was new to them, and their spirits were deeply moved by it. For my part, the beauty of a snowstorm was apparently something I left behind in my youth. I recalled for a moment my childhood and how delightful it had been to awaken on a school day morning to discover that a storm was in progress and school had been cancelled! How delicious to learn that the demanding discipline of life was halted, at least temporarily, by an act of nature so supremely powerful that it could suspend the iron routine of life. And suddenly we were all free simply to have fun and enjoy a world made new by a blanket of snowy whiteness. The once familiar world without had been miraculously transformed overnight into a fairyland of strange and beautiful shapes that were, *"the frolic architecture of the snow."* This is how Emerson described just such a day.

THE SNOW-STORM

Announced by all the trumpets of the sky,
Arrives the snow, and, driving o'er the fields,
Seems nowhere to alight: the whited air
Hides hills and woods, the river, and the heaven,
And veils the farm-house at the garden's end.
The sled and traveller stopped, the courier's feet
Delayed, all friends shut out, the housemates sit
Around the radiant fireplace, enclosed
In a tumultuous privacy of storm.

Come see the north wind's masonry.
Out of an unseen quarry evermore
Furnished with tile, the fierce artificer
Curves his white bastions with projected roof
Round every windward stake, or tree, or door.
Speeding, the myriad-handed, his wild work
So fanciful, so savage, nought cares he
For number or proportion. Mockingly,
On coop or kennel he hangs Parian wreaths;
A swan-like form invests the hidden thorn;
Fills up the farmer's lane from wall to wall,
Maugre the farmer's sighs; and at the gate
A tapering turret overtops the work.
And when his hours are numbered, and the world
Is all his own, retiring, as he were not,
Leaves, when the sun appears, astonished Art
To mimic in slow structures, stone by stone,
Built in an age, the mad wind's night-work,
The frolic architecture of the snow.

Many of us who live where snow and winter are synonymous no longer feel the joy of this miracle. It is, no doubt, a sad sign of our spiritual lethargy. Like the majestic stars that shine down upon us from a serene evening sky, the familiarity of this magnificent beauty renders us insensitive to it. (A phenomenon that can, unfortunately, also occur in our relationships with those we love the most.) The tyrannizing cares of the workaday world can contribute to this numbness. However, if we were newly arrived from West Africa or the tropics, the miraculous quality of a snow storm would fill us with voluptuous delight, and we would become, for a time, children again.

Sometimes, even as adults, we have an experience that reminds us of the transcendent beauty of the world. This beauty is a sublime reflection of the spirit that created both it and us, and we resonate in spontaneous response to it. I recall just such an experience. Some years ago, when my children were young, my wife and I decided to drive across the country just to see what was there. From eastern Pennsylvania we drove west through Ohio, Indiana, and Illinois, across the Mississippi and down into

Spiritual Truth

Missouri. In St. Louis we ascended the apex of the great stainless steel arch, the symbolic "Gateway to the West." From St. Louis we continued through Oklahoma, the Texas Panhandle, and into New Mexico where we crossed the Rockies, the great Continental Divide. We then descended into the Petrified Forest of Arizona. From there it was on to southern California, then north to San Francisco, then east on Interstate 80, across the Rockies again, and the Utah Salt Flats, all the way back to Pennsylvania. While on this trip we saw many awesome sights that caused us to breath deeply and stare in wonderment. The mighty Mississippi River, the endless plains of Oklahoma and the Texas Panhandle, the barren majesty of the deserts of the great southwest, the imperial poise of the Rocky Mountains, the stark, blanc beauty of the Utah Salt Flats, the endless green farmlands of Iowa and Nebraska.

The most thrilling moment in the trip for me, however, came in Arizona as I gazed upon the vast, majestic beauty of the aptly named Grand Canyon. Upon arriving, we parked our family van in an area adjacent to the canyon's rim. From there we had to make our way through some tall shrubs, as we followed the path that led to the lookout point. When we emerged from behind this natural curtain, we found ourselves gazing upon one of the most magnificent vistas that human eyes have ever beheld. I don't have the words to express exactly what I felt at that instant.

I do know that it was very much like Emerson's spontaneous moment of ecstasy as he crossed the Boston Commons on a star-filled winter's night. In the presence of the awesome beauty and magnitude of the expansive scene that opened before me, my sense of self seemed to fade to the point of transparency. I truly felt that I had been, in some mysterious way, absorbed into the scene that I observed. I had become "part or parcel" of that vast beauty. It seemed for a moment as if I were nothing and everything, simultaneously. My sense of self, my personal ego, dissolved into harmony with the *"sublime of the beautiful."* My soul was touched and resonated to the very core of my being. The experience was breathtaking, inspiring, and unforgettable.

RECONNECTING WITH THE SPIRIT IN NATURE

Unfortunately, because most of us are caught up in the hectic busyness of our lives, we have no time, it seems, to meditate on the beauties of nature. Also, for many who live in an urban environment there appears to be scant opportunity for immersion in the natural world. Nevertheless, there are still possibilities. Even in an urban setting, there is ever a sky overhead, and clouds, and warm breezes in the summer as well as frosty chills in the winter. And often there are the glorious stars at night alternating with the varied beauty of clouds and patchy blueness of day.

On occasion we experience the somber darkness of storms, at times rent with sharp lightening then healed by muffled rumbles of thunder. And there is the never failing glory of sunrise and sunset. On nice days, for the fortunate, there may be a park of some sort nearby, alive with flowers, and trees, and grass in season. Intermingled with all this beauty and life, there is humanity, that special part of nature that we seldom consider as such. If we allowed just a few solitary moments at the beginning or the end of each day to quietly contemplate nature, even from our door stoops, we might thereby reconnect with the Divine Power that is the author of it all.

Living in a suburban environment, I have found that the most serene moments in my day happen when I make the short walk from my front door to the mail box to retrieve my morning paper. This is normally sometime between 5 and 6 am. At this early hour, the neighborhood is silent and still. In the summer, the dawn is just beginning to break. In the winter, the black sky overhead is alit with a myriad of stars. On other mornings, there are grey and pink clouds sweeping across the sky. When I first moved into this area, more often than not I would simply rush out to the mail box and back, the object being simply to retrieve my paper.

Soon, however, it dawned on me that this is such a perfect and delicious moment, I should take the time to relish it. And so now I actually stop along the way and turn slowly about,

Spiritual Truth

just to take in the beauty and serenity of the moment. Often at this time I am moved to silent prayer, usually in thanksgiving for all that I see and feel. In this way, I prepare myself, mentally and spiritually, for the day ahead. I now know why ancient priests never missed their "matins," their morning prayers. Reminding ourselves of the beauty, meaning, and purpose of our existence is a fine way to begin or end a day. In *Nature* (1836), Emerson describes the beauty that he found just outside his door in the small town of Concord, Massachusetts.

> *But in other hours, Nature satisfies by its loveliness, and without any mixture of corporeal benefit. I see the spectacle of morning from the hilltop over against my house, from daybreak to sunrise, with emotions which an angel might share. The long slender bars of cloud float like fishes in the sea of crimson light. From the earth, as a shore, I look out into that silent sea. I seem to partake its rapid transformations; the active enchantment reaches my dust, and I dilate and conspire with the morning wind. How does Nature deify us with a few and cheap elements! Give me health and a day, and I will make the pomp of emperors ridiculous. The dawn is my Assyria; the sunset and moonrise my Paphos, and unimaginable realms of faerie; broad noon shall be my England of the senses and the understanding; the night shall be my Germany of mystic philosophy and dreams.*
>
> *Not less excellent, except for our less susceptibility in the afternoon, was the charm, last evening, of a January sunset. The western clouds divided and subdivided themselves into pink flakes modulated with tints of unspeakable softness, and the air had so much life and*

> *sweetness that it was a pain to come within doors. What was it that nature would say? Was there no meaning in the live repose of the valley behind the mill, and which Homer or Shakespeare could not re-form for me in words? The leafless trees become spires of flame in the sunset, with the blue east for their background, and the stars of the dead calices of flowers, and every withered stem and stubble rimed with frost, contribute something to the mute music.*

Like all Transcendentalists, Emerson saw his world as positively infused with a dynamic and divine spirit that gives meaning and purpose to all things. By reconnecting with this spirit, we can emerge from the ruin and rubble of everyday life and take possession of our true selves. We can be so much more than we have settled for, if we could only clear our eyes and our minds of the fog that obscures this beatific vision. We are, indeed, *"gods in ruin,"* and it is up to us to reclaim our divine birthright. If we are open to them, our instincts will show the way.

> *The foundations of man are not in matter, but in spirit. But the element of spirit is eternity. To it, therefore, the longest series of events, the oldest chronologies are young and recent. In the cycle of the universal man, from whom the known individuals proceed, centuries are points, and all history is but the epoch of one degradation.*

> *We distrust and deny inwardly our sympathy with nature. We own and disown our relation to it, by turns. We are like Nebuchadnezzar, dethroned, bereft of reason, and eating grass like an ox. But who can set limits to the remedial force of spirit?*

Spiritual Truth

A man is a god in ruins. When men are innocent, life shall be longer, and shall pass into the immortal as gently as we awake from dreams. Now, the world would be insane and rabid, if these disorganizations should last for hundreds of years. It is kept in check by death and infancy. Infancy is the perpetual Messiah, which comes into the arms of fallen men, and pleads with them to return to paradise.

'Man is the dwarf of himself. Once he was permeated and dissolved by spirit. He filled nature with his overflowing currents. Out from him sprang the sun and moon; from man the sun, from woman the moon. The laws of his mind, the periods of his actions externized themselves into day and night, into the year and the seasons. But, having made for himself this huge shell, his waters retired; he no longer fills the veins and veinlets; he is shrunk to a drop. He sees that the structure still fits him, but fits him colossally. Say, rather, once it fitted him, now it corresponds to him from far and on high. He adores timidly his own work. Now is man the follower of the sun, and woman the follower of the moon. Yet sometimes he starts in his slumber, and wonders at himself and his house, and muses strangely at the resemblance betwixt him and it. He perceives that if his law is still paramount, if still he have elemental power, if his word is sterling yet in nature, it is not conscious power, it is not inferior but superior to his will. It is instinct.

Emerson's Truth, Emerson's Wisdom

REUNION AND REDEMPTION: (RE) BUILDING OUR WORLD

By engaging the divinity that was present both within himself and his world, Emerson was able to assert the dignity and the power that is humanity's birthright. He lived his life according to a "higher law" that allowed him to discern what was important and what was unimportant. Because his faith and self-confidence rested on the power of the God within, Emerson was not only able to live a rich and meaningful life but, by drawing on that power, he also became a redeemer, oracle, and prophet to his age. He challenges us to see through our shortcomings to our true potential. We can redeem ourselves from the moral and mental lethargy that has prevented our personal fulfillment. Our spiritual needs are as important as our material needs. Rational thought must always be informed by spirit and affection as Emerson reminds us in *Nature* (1836).

The problem of restoring to the world original and eternal beauty is solved by the redemption of the soul. The ruin or the blank that we see when we look at nature, is in our own eye. The axis of vision is not coincident with the axis of things, and so they appear not transparent but opaque. The reason why the world lacks unity, and lies broken and in heaps, is because man is disunited with himself. He cannot be a naturalist until he satisfies all the demands of the spirit. Love is as much its demand as perception. Indeed, neither can be perfect without the other. In the uttermost meaning of the words, thought is devout, and devotion is thought. Deep calls unto deep. But in actual life, the marriage is not celebrated. There are innocent men who worship God after the tradition of their fathers, but their sense of duty has not yet extended to the use of all their faculties. And there are patient naturalists, but they freeze their

> *subject under the wintry light of the understanding [i.e. mere logic]. Is not prayer also a study of truth,—a sally of the soul into the unfound infinite? No man ever prayed heartily without learning something. But when a faithful thinker, resolute to detach every object from personal relations and see it in the light of thought, shall, at the same time, kindle science with the fire of the holiest affections, then will God go forth anew into the creation.*

Once we have opened ourselves to the divine spirit within us, our lives acquire a spiritual force and vitality. We discover that the world is "not fixed but fluid," and everything is subject to change. By acting through the spirit, we will be empowered to build our own world and manage our own lives in a way that reflects our true potential, whatever it may be.

> *So shall we come to look at the world with new eyes. It shall answer the endless inquiry of the intellect,—What is truth? and of the affections,—What is good? by yielding itself passive to the educated Will. Then shall come to pass what my poet said: 'Nature is not fixed but fluid. Spirit alters, moulds, makes it. The immobility or bruteness of nature is the absence of spirit; to pure spirit it is fluid, it is volatile, it is obedient. Every spirit builds itself a house, and beyond its house a world, and beyond its world a heaven. Know then that the world exists for you. For you is the phenomenon perfect. What we are, that only can we see. All that Adam had, all that Caesar could, you have and can do. Adam called his house, heaven and earth; Caesar called his house, Rome; you perhaps call yours, a cobbler's trade; a hundred acres*

of ploughed land; or a scholar's garret. Yet line for line and point for point your dominion is as great as theirs, though without fine names. Build therefore your own world. As fast as you conform your life to the pure idea in your mind, that will unfold its great proportions.

LOOKING FOR FAITH IN ALL THE WRONG PLACES

The reason that Emerson felt compelled to apprise people of the presence of the great spiritual force that pulsed within them and their world is because most of the organized, formal religions of his time did not. They were so consumed with maintaining the formality of religion, with its dry, dusty dogmas and doctrines, that they were blind to the very spirit that once gave those doctrines life. In their preoccupation with intellectual commentaries on Biblical texts and religious debates regarding such arcane matters as the nature of the divine trinity and the authenticity of Christ's miracles, they completely ignored the sublime life of the spirit that transcends all such petty concerns. In their focus on the head, they forgot the heart, which is where the true religious spirit resides. In their study of the manifestations of the divine spirit in the past, they completely neglected the manifestations of that spirit in the present. At the outset of **Nature** (1836), Emerson describes this tendency as backwards looking and pernicious.

> *Our age is retrospective. It builds the sepulchres of the fathers. It writes biographies, histories, and criticism. The foregoing generations beheld God and nature face to face; we, through their eyes. Why should not we also enjoy an original relation to the universe? Why should not we have a poetry and philosophy of insight and not of tradition, and a religion by revelation to us, and not the history of theirs? Embosomed for a season in nature, whose floods of life stream around and through us, and invite us, by the powers they supply, to action proportioned to nature, why should we grope among the dry bones of the past, or put the living generation into masquerade out of its faded wardrobe? The sun shines today also. There is more wool and flax in the fields. There are new*

lands, new men, new thoughts. Let us demand our own works and laws and worship.

It was this blindness, in large part, that drove Emerson from the church of his fathers. The comic Lenny Bruce once observed sardonically, that "people are leaving the church and going back to God every day." More or less, that's what Emerson did. Some years after his departure, he was invited to speak at Harvard to the graduating class of the Divinity School, the chilly center of what he once called that "ice-house, Unitarianism." In his address to the young, would-be ministers, Emerson made it very clear that if they were to truly communicate the love of God to those who looked to them as the designated intermediaries of that great Soul, some major changes would have to be made in how they approached the task.

Emerson's ***"Divinity School Address"*** proved to be the most controversial of his career. Influential Unitarian leaders, all highly regarded in the community, were deeply offended by his criticisms of their church. One of them, a major figure in the Divinity School where Emerson spoke, called his talk "the latest form of infidelity," and argued that Emerson should be shunned as a heretic. Fortunately, he survived the storm, all the while recording in his journals ruminations on the importance of self-reliance. Some of these insights would later emerge in one of his most profound essays dealing with that very subject.

Emerson begins his address, which was delivered in July of 1838, with a striking description of the beauty and vitality of a natural world radiant with the spiritual life of the great Soul.

In this refulgent summer, it has been a luxury to draw the breath of life. The grass grows, the buds burst, the meadow is spotted with fire and gold in the tint of flowers. The air is full of birds, and sweet with the breath of the pine, the balm-of-Gilead, and the new hay. Night brings no gloom to the heart with its welcome shade. Through the transparent

Spiritual Truth

darkness the stars pour their almost spiritual rays. Man under them seems a young child, and his huge globe a toy. The cool night bathes the world as with a river, and prepares his eyes again for the crimson dawn. The mystery of nature was never displayed more happily.

Clearly, Emerson's intention here is to remind his young audience that the world is full of life and that natural life is a manifestation of the great Spirit whom they seek to serve. If they wish to communicate with this spirit, that goal is more likely to be accomplished in the bosom of nature, not the dusty confines of the library where they spent the last few years of their lives. The images that he presents here are deliberately chosen to reflect spiritual as well as physical life. Phrases such as "breath of life," "breath of pine," "fire," "heart," and "new hay,"— and kinetic symbols such as "refulgent" (from the Latin, shining brightly), "grass grows," and "buds burst," as well as fluid images such as "pour," "draw," "bathes," and "river," all suggest flowing movement, growth, vitality, and regeneration.

Expressions such as "balm-of-Gilead," and "spiritual rays" have a strong religious connotation that serves to reinforce the notion that it is God's power, the power of the Over-Soul, that is represented in this dramatic display of cosmic energy. One might also note that the observer here, in his spontaneous response to this marvelous display of natural and spiritual life, becomes "a young child" again.

All of this reflects Emerson's constant belief that spiritual redemption can be enacted through a return to nature where we seek to recover the spontaneous innocence of childhood. The "huge globe" itself becomes a "toy" and a plaything to the person/child who is in harmony with this natural and divine world. Emerson's concern here is that the young ministers-in-training that sat before him have somehow failed to connect with the very spirit that once gave life to the religion they hoped to serve. Their training had been directed almost exclusively at their heads and not their hearts. As a result, they were, as the poet Milton once put it, "deep versed in books, but shallow in themselves." They were out of touch (literally) with the natural world and the "moral sentiment" manifested in it. Ironically, it is this moral sentiment that provides the connecting link to the great Soul, the ultimate divinity. As Emerson himself came to realize some years earlier, the true spirit of religion must be felt. It cannot *"be written out on paper or spoken by the tongue."* This divine sentiment, in turn, becomes the basis for all moral and ethical behavior. Our actions always speak for themselves and by these the world shall know us.

The sentiment of virtue is a reverence and delight in the presence of certain divine laws. It perceives that this homely game of life we play, covers, under what seem foolish details, principles that astonish. The child amidst his baubles is learning the action of light, motion, gravity, muscular force; and in the game of human life, love, fear, justice, appetite, man, and God, interact. These laws refuse to be adequately stated. They will not be written out on paper, or spoken by the tongue. They elude our persevering thought; yet we read them hourly in each other's faces, in each other's actions, in our own remorse. The moral traits which are all globed into every virtuous act and thought,—in speech we must sever, and describe or suggest by painful enumeration of many particulars. Yet, as this sentiment is the essence of all religion, let me guide your eye to the precise objects of the sentiment, by an enumeration of some of those classes of facts in which this element is conspicuous.

The intuition of the moral sentiment is an insight of the perfection of the laws of the soul. These laws execute themselves. They are out of time, out of

Spiritual Truth

space, and not subject to circumstance. Thus in the soul of man there is a justice whose retributions are instant and entire. He who does a good deed is instantly ennobled. He who does a mean deed is by the action itself contracted. He who puts off impurity, thereby puts on purity. If a man is at heart just, then in so far is he God; the safety of God, the immortality of God, the majesty of God do enter into that man with justice. If a man dissemble, deceive, he deceives himself, and goes out of acquaintance with his own being. A man in the view of absolute goodness, adores, with total humility. Every step so downward, is a step upward. The man who renounces himself, comes to himself.

See how this rapid intrinsic energy worketh everywhere, righting wrongs, correcting appearances, and bringing up facts to a harmony with thoughts. Its operation in life, though slow to the senses, is at last as sure as in the soul. By it a man is made the Providence to himself, dispensing good to his goodness, and evil to his sin. Character is always known. Thefts never enrich; alms never impoverish; murder will speak out of stone walls. The least admixture of a lie,— for example, the taint of vanity, any attempt to make a good impression, a favorable appearance,—will instantly vitiate the effect. But speak the truth, and all nature and all spirits help you with unexpected furtherance. Speak the truth, and all things alive or brute are vouchers, and the very roots of the grass underground there do seem to stir and move to bear you witness. See again the perfection of the Law as it applies itself to the affections, and becomes the law of society. As we are, so we associate. The good, by affinity, seek the good; the vile, by affinity, the vile. Thus of their own volition, souls proceed into heaven, into hell.

MORAL SENTIMENT AND MORAL LIFE

The Over-Soul is the source of all moral laws. These laws are revealed to us through intuitions, or what Emerson sometimes calls "moral sentiment." The rejection or repression of this moral sentiment is the source of all evil. Such willful blindness cuts us off from the very spirit of life and love that imparts dignity and meaning to human existence. The sign of such laws is that they are always universal. Indeed, universality is the very essence of all moral principles. Either they apply to all or to none. There is no middle ground. There are no moral laws that apply to some, but not to others. For example, take the notion that *"All people are created equal."* When you attempt to deny equal rights to others, for whatever reason, the fraud is made manifest immediately. The moral voice refuses to be silenced in the presence of such bigotry.

Over time, the truth will, indeed, set us free. This explains the Civil Rights Movement, the Women's Movement, and the protests and debates that led to the passage of the Americans with Disabilities Act. The latest area of contention involves gender relationships. Can anyone doubt that we will eventually have equality of choice in sexual relationships, including the choice of whom we shall marry? Emerson believed that the principle of freedom should rule in all questions of social policy. He insists in his **"Lecture on Slavery"** (1855), that *"No citizen will go wrong who on every question leans to the side of general liberty."* The objections to same-sex marriages today are more often than not based on the presumed authority of scripture and/or historically sanctioned traditions (as were most of the arguments that sought to justify slavery). But Emerson refused to acknowledge such second-hand authority when it violated his own intuitive sense of universal moral truth. As he notes in **"Self-Reliance,"**

> *It must be that when God speaketh he should communicate, not one thing, but all things; should fill the world with his voice; should scatter forth light, nature, time, souls, from the centre of the present thought; and new date and new create the*

whole. Whenever a mind is simple and receives a divine wisdom, old things pass away,—means, teachers, texts, temples fall; it lives now, and absorbs past and future into the present hour. All things are made sacred by relation to it,—one as much as another. All things are dissolved to their centre by their cause, and in the universal miracle petty and particular miracles disappear. If therefore a man claims to know and speak of God and carries you backward to the phraseology of some old mouldered nation in another country, in another world, believe him not.

Another obvious example of universal truth is the notion that *"All people must be treated with dignity and respect, even in war."* And so you cannot profess your commitment to the Geneva Convention, for example, when it is convenient to do so, and then torture people when it suits you. The world will not be fooled. In Emerson's time, slavery was accepted as a fact of life by many, but today we see it as morally reprehensible and an appalling denial of basic human decency. Emerson always knew it to be such, as did others who were willing to listen to the dictates of the moral sentiment. He was convinced that the institution would most certainly be abolished because, as he noted in his address on the **"Fugitive Slave Law"** in 1854, "the inconsistency of slavery with the principles on which the world is built guarantees its downfall."

The same could be said at a later time regarding segregation and the lack of equal rights for women. All injustice will eventually be exposed, both in the wide world and in our own lives. The inner voice that speaks from the collective heart of humanity will always demand justice. Emerson makes this point emphatically in his **"Divinity School Address."** Here he insists that moral laws, like the laws of physical science, permeate our universe. We derive our greatest and truest strength when our thoughts and actions are aligned with these laws. Conversely, our negative actions are "balked and baffled" by them. Persistence in evil-doing is self-destructive and ultimately suicidal.

These facts have always suggested to man the sublime creed that the world is not the product of manifold power, but of one will, of one mind; and that one mind is everywhere active, in each ray of the star, in each wavelet of the pool; and whatever opposes that will is everywhere balked and baffled, because things are made so, and not otherwise. Good is positive. Evil is merely privative, not absolute: it is like cold, which is the privation of heat. All evil is so much death or nonentity. Benevolence is absolute and real. So much benevolence as a man hath, so much life hath he. For all things proceed out of this same spirit, which is differently named love, justice, temperance, in its different applications, just as the ocean receives different names on the several shores which it washes. All things proceed out of the same spirit, and all things conspire with it. Whilst a man seeks good ends, he is strong by the whole strength of nature. In so far as he roves from these ends, he bereaves himself of power, or auxiliaries; his being shrinks out of all remote channels, he becomes less and less, a mote, a point, until absolute badness is absolute death.

The perception of this law of laws awakens in the mind a sentiment which we call the religious sentiment, and which makes our highest happiness. Wonderful is its power to charm and to command. It is a mountain air. It is the embalmer [i.e. preserver] of the world. It is myrrh and storax, and chlorine and rosemary. It makes the sky and the hills sublime, and the silent song of the stars is it. By it is the universe made safe and habitable, not by science or power. Thought may work cold and intransitive in things, and find no end or unity; but the dawn of the sentiment of virtue on the heart, gives and is the assurance that Law is sovereign over all natures; and the worlds, time, space, eternity, do seem to break out into joy.

This sentiment is divine and deifying. It is the beatitude of man. It makes him illimitable. Through it, the soul first knows itself. It corrects the capital mistake of the infant man, who seeks to be great by following the great, and hopes to derive advantages from another,—by showing the fountain of all good to be in himself, and that he, equally with every man, is an inlet into the deeps of Reason [i.e. intuitive truth]. When he says, "I ought;" when love warms him; when he chooses, warned from on high, the good and great deed; then, deep melodies wander through his soul from Supreme Wisdom.—Then he can worship, and be enlarged by his worship; for he can never go behind this sentiment. In the sublimest flights of the soul, rectitude is never surmounted, love is never outgrown.

Spiritual Truth

TRUE FAITH AND TRUE RELIGION

For Emerson, it is the sentiment of virtue and intuition of truth that stand at the center of all true religions as they have expressed the presence of the great Soul throughout human history, in every culture, and in all parts of the world. When formal churches attempt to codify this spirit into rigid doctrine and dogma, however, the result is often perverse. It was this very condition that drove Emerson from his own Unitarian church, as he reminds his audience of young ministers in his *"Divinity School Address."*

> *This sentiment lies at the foundation of society, and successively creates all forms of worship. The principle of veneration never dies out. Man fallen into superstition, into sensuality, is never quite without the visions of the moral sentiment. In like manner, all the expressions of this sentiment are sacred and permanent in proportion to their purity. The expressions of this sentiment affect us more than all other compositions. The sentences of the oldest time, which ejaculate this piety, are still fresh and fragrant. This thought dwelled always deepest in the minds of men in the devout and contemplative East; not alone in Palestine, where it reached its purest expression, but in Egypt, in Persia, in India, in China. Europe has always owed to oriental genius its divine impulses. What these holy bards said, all sane men found agreeable and true. And the unique impression of Jesus upon mankind, whose name is not so much written as ploughed into the history of this world, is proof of the subtle virtue of this infusion.*

Meantime, whilst the doors of the temple stand open, night and day, before every man, and the oracles of this truth cease never, it is guarded by one stern condition; this, namely, it is an intuition. It cannot be received at second hand. Truly speaking, it is not instruction, but provocation, that I can receive from another soul. What he announces, I must find true in me, or reject; and on his word, or as his second, be he who he may, I can accept nothing. On the contrary, the absence of this primary faith is the presence of degradation. As is the flood, so is the ebb. Let this faith depart, and the very words it spake and the things it made become false and hurtful. Then falls the church, the state, art, letters, life. The doctrine of the divine nature being forgotten, a sickness infects and dwarfs the constitution. Once man was all; now he is an appendage, a nuisance. And because the indwelling Supreme Spirit cannot wholly be got rid of, the doctrine of it suffers this perversion, that the divine nature is attributed to one or two persons, and denied to all the rest, and denied with fury. The doctrine of inspiration is lost; the base doctrine of the majority of voices usurps the place of the doctrine of the soul. Miracles, prophecy, poetry, the ideal life, the holy life, exist as ancient history merely; they are not in the belief, nor in the aspiration of society; but, when suggested, seem ridiculous. Life is comic or pitiful as soon as the high ends of being fade out of sight, and man becomes nearsighted, and can only attend to what addresses the senses.

Spiritual Truth

Christianity for Emerson was but one expression of this truth, and Jesus Christ was one of its true prophets. His most important miracle and the truest sign of his divinity was the revelation of the power of the great Soul that resides within all of us and within our world. This revelation of the divine life goes far beyond multiplying loaves and fishes.

> *These general views, which, whilst they are general, none will contest, find abundant illustration in the history of religion, and especially in the history of the Christian church. In that, all of us have had our birth and nurture. The truth contained in that, you, my young friends, are now setting forth to teach. As the Cultus, or established worship of the civilized world, it has great historical interest for us. Of its blessed words, which have been the consolation of humanity, you need not that I should speak. I shall endeavor to discharge my duty to you on this occasion, by pointing out two errors in its administration, which daily appear more gross from the point of view we have just now taken.*

The first of the "two errors" of modern Christianity that Emerson identifies is the tendency to focus on the historical person of Jesus as a unique manifestation of divinity, rather than his revelation of the divinity of *all* humankind. The second error is placing too much emphasis on Christ's unique miracles rather than emphasizing the fact that daily life itself is a divine miracle.

> *Jesus Christ belonged to the true race of prophets. He saw with open eye the mystery of the soul. Drawn by its severe harmony, ravished with its beauty, he lived in it, and had his being there. Alone in all history he estimated the greatness of man. One man was true to what is in you and me. He saw that God*

incarnates himself in man, and evermore goes forth anew to take possession of his World. He said, in this jubilee of sublime emotion, 'I am divine. Through me, God acts; through me, speaks. Would you see God, see me; or see thee, when thou also thinkest as I now think.' But what a distortion did his doctrine and memory suffer in the same, in the next, and the following ages! There is no doctrine of the Reason [i.e. the soul] which will bear to be taught by the Understanding [i.e. logic]. The understanding caught this high chant from the poet's lips, and said, in the next age, 'This was Jehovah come down out of heaven. I will kill you, if you say he was a man.' The idioms of his language and the figures of his rhetoric have usurped the place of his truth; and churches are not built on his principles, but on his tropes [i.e. figures of speech]. Christianity became a Mythus [i.e. ancient belief], as the poetic teaching of Greece and of Egypt, before. He spoke of miracles; for he felt that man's life was a miracle, and all that man doth, and he knew that this daily miracle shines as the character ascends. But the word Miracle, as pronounced by Christian churches, gives a false impression; it is Monster. It is not one with the blowing clover and the falling rain.

He felt respect for Moses and the prophets, but no unfit tenderness at postponing their initial revelations to the hour and the man that now is; to the eternal revelation in the heart. Thus was he a true man. Having seen that the law in us is commanding, he would not suffer it to be commanded. Boldly, with hand,

Spiritual Truth

> *and heart, and life, he declared it was God. Thus is he, as I think, the only soul in history who has appreciated the worth of man.*

For Emerson, religion should always be a matter of personal faith, something that truly lives within your own soul. The mystical power that stimulates this inward feeling is the very essence of true religion. It ennobles us by revealing the divine presence in all of our lives. This divine spirit is not narrow and exclusive, unique to one church or sect, but natural and all encompassing. Through it, the divinity of all of humanity is made manifest.

> *That is always best which gives me to myself. The sublime is excited in me by the great stoical doctrine, Obey thyself. That which shows God in me, fortifies me. That which shows God out of me, makes me a wart and a wen. There is no longer a necessary reason for my being. Already the long shadows of untimely oblivion creep over me, and I shall decease forever.*

> *The divine bards are the friends of my virtue, of my intellect, of my strength. They admonish me that the gleams which flash across my mind are not mine, but God's; that they had the like, and were not disobedient to the heavenly vision. So I love them. Noble provocations go out from them, inviting me to resist evil; to subdue the world; and to Be. And thus, by his holy thoughts, Jesus serves us, and thus only. To aim to convert a man by miracles is a profanation of the soul. A true conversion, a true Christ, is now, as always, to be made by the reception of beautiful sentiments. It is true that a great and rich soul, like his, falling among the simple, does so preponderate,*

that, as his did, it names the world. The world seems to them to exist for him, and they have not yet drunk so deeply of his sense as to see that only by coming again to themselves, or to God in themselves, can they grow forevermore. It is a low benefit to give me something; it is a high benefit to enable me to do somewhat of myself. The time is coming when all men will see that the gift of God to the soul is not a vaunting, over-powering, excluding sanctity, but a sweet, natural goodness, a goodness like thine and mine, and that so invites thine and mine to be and to grow.

The injustice of the vulgar tone of preaching is not less flagrant to Jesus than to the souls which it profanes. The preachers do not see that they make his gospel not glad, and shear him of the locks of beauty and the attributes of heaven. When I see a majestic Epaminondas, or Washington; when I see among my contemporaries a true orator, an upright judge, a dear friend; when I vibrate to the melody and fancy of a poem; I see beauty that is to be desired. And so lovely, and with yet more entire consent of my human being, sounds in my ear the severe music of the bards that have sung of the true God in all ages. Now do not degrade the life and dialogues of Christ out of the circle of this charm, by insulation and peculiarity. Let them lie as they befell, alive and warm, part of human life and of the landscape and of the cheerful day.

WHY MOST FORMAL RELIGIONS FAIL THE TEST OF FAITH

The revelation of the power of the Over-Soul is ongoing and liberating. It is the very essence of the true religious spirit. Unfortunately, it is not this doctrine of imminent divinity that is normally preached today. Most frequently, instead of looking within to find God, preachers look back to the utterances of prophets long dead. The living God cannot be found this way. Therefore, we are left only with the residue of the past, a God who came and went. Such preachers speak, says Emerson, *"as if God were dead."* Instead of this moribund musing, the ideal preacher should always present a vibrant and vital *"conversation with the beauty of the soul."*

Men have come to speak of the revelation as somewhat long ago given and done, as if God were dead. The injury to faith throttles the preacher; and the goodliest of institutions becomes an uncertain and inarticulate voice.

It is very certain that it is the effect of conversation with the beauty of the soul, to beget a desire and need to impart to others the same knowledge and love. If utterance is denied, the thought lies like a burden on the man. Always the seer is a sayer. Somehow his dream is told; somehow he publishes it with solemn joy: sometimes with pencil on canvas, sometimes with chisel on stone, sometimes in towers and aisles of granite, his soul's worship is builded; sometimes in anthems of indefinite music; but clearest and most permanent, in words.

The man enamored of this excellency becomes its priest or poet. The office is coeval [i.e. the same age] with the world. But observe the condition, the

> *spiritual limitation of the office. The spirit only can teach. Not any profane man, not any sensual, not any liar, not any slave can teach, but only he can give, who has; he only can create, who is. The man on whom the soul descends, through whom the soul speaks, alone can teach. Courage, piety, love, wisdom, can teach; and every man can open his door to these angels, and they shall bring him the gift of tongues. But the man who aims to speak as books enable, as synods use, as the fashion guides, and as interest commands, babbles. Let him hush.*

Emerson ends his address at the Divinity School with a special message for the young ministers before him and for all who would come after. He tells them that they should follow their spiritual vocation with *"throbs of desire."* He speaks in particular of preaching the truth of Christ, but his concern with a true, living faith obviously transcends the narrow limitations of any denomination. It is the life of the "infinite Soul," shared by all people, that concerns him.

> *To this holy office you propose to devote yourselves. I wish you may feel your call in throbs of desire and hope. The office is the first in the world. It is of that reality that it cannot suffer the deduction of any falsehood. And it is my duty to say to you that the need was never greater of new revelation than now. From the views I have already expressed, you will infer the sad conviction, which I share, I believe, with numbers, of the universal decay and now almost death of faith in society. The soul is not preached. The Church seems to totter to its fall, almost all life extinct. On this occasion, any complaisance would be criminal which told you, whose hope and commission it is*

Spiritual Truth

to preach the faith of Christ, that the faith of Christ is preached.

It is time that this ill-suppressed murmur of all thoughtful men against the famine of our churches;—this moaning of the heart because it is bereaved of the consolation, the hope, the grandeur that come alone out of the culture of the moral nature,—should be heard through the sleep of indolence, and over the din of routine. This great and perpetual office of the preacher is not discharged. Preaching is the expression of the moral sentiment in application to the duties of life. In how many churches, by how many prophets, tell me, is man made sensible that he is an infinite Soul; that the earth and heavens are passing into his mind; that he is drinking forever the soul of God? Where now sounds the persuasion, that by its very melody im-paradises my heart, and so affirms its own origin in heaven? Where shall I hear words such as in elder ages drew men to leave all and follow,— father and mother, house and land, wife and child? Where shall I hear these august laws of moral being so pronounced as to fill my ear, and I feel ennobled by the offer of my uttermost action and passion? The test of the true faith, certainly, should be its power to charm and command the soul, as the laws of nature control the activity of the hands,—so commanding that we find pleasure and honor in obeying. The faith should blend with the light of rising and of setting suns, with the flying cloud, the singing bird, and the breath of flowers. But now the priest's Sabbath has lost the splendor of nature; it is unlovely; we are glad when it is done; we can make, we do make, even sitting in our pews, a far better, holier, sweeter, for ourselves.

In Emerson's day, as in ours, there is no more compelling evidence of the deadness of religion than the sermonizing of a "formalist" preacher. In his effort to articulate and support the dear, old doctrines of the church, the preacher speaks from his head, not his heart. As a result, he does not present himself as a representative of a living God. He is more like a retained attorney who argues the case for the institution that employs him. Such preachers inevitably fail to meet the most important obligation of their profession, namely, "to convert life into truth." The deadness of this sermonizing contrasts with the spiritual vitality of the natural world without.

Whenever the pulpit is usurped by a formalist, then is the worshipper defrauded and disconsolate. We shrink as soon as the prayers begin, which do not uplift, but smite and offend us. We are fain to wrap our cloaks about us, and secure, as best we can, a solitude that hears not. I once heard a preacher who sorely tempted me to say I would go to church no more. Men go, thought I, where they are wont to go, else had no soul entered the temple in the afternoon. A snow-storm was falling around us. The snow-storm was real, the preacher merely spectral, and the eye felt the sad contrast in looking at him, and then out of the window behind him into the beautiful meteor of the snow. He had lived in vain. He had no one word intimating that he had laughed or wept, was married or in love, had been commended, or cheated, or chagrined. If he had ever lived and acted, we were none the wiser for it. The capital secret of his profession, namely, to convert life into truth, he had not learned.

Spiritual Truth

Not one fact in all his experience had he yet imported into his doctrine. This man had ploughed and planted and talked and bought and sold; he had read books; he had eaten and drunken; his head aches, his heart throbs; he smiles and suffers; yet was there not a surmise, a hint, in all the discourse, that he had ever lived at all. Not a line did he draw out of real history. The true preacher can be known by this, that he deals out to the people his life,— life passed through the fire of thought. But of the bad preacher, it could not be told from his sermon what age of the world he fell in; whether he had a father or a child; whether he was a freeholder or a pauper; whether he was a citizen or a countryman; or any other fact of his biography. It seemed strange that the people should come to church. It seemed as if their houses were very unentertaining, that they should prefer this thoughtless clamor. It shows that there is a commanding attraction in the moral sentiment, that can lend a faint tint of light to dulness and ignorance coming in its name and place. The good hearer is sure he has been touched sometimes; is sure there is somewhat to be reached, and some word that can reach it. When he listens to these vain words, he comforts himself by their relation to his remembrance of better hours, and so they clatter and echo unchallenged.

✿✿✿✿✿✿✿✿✿

Let me not taint the sincerity of this plea by any oversight of the claims of good men. I know and honor the purity and strict conscience of numbers of the clergy. What life the public worship retains, it owes to the scattered company of pious men, who minister here and there in the churches, and who, sometimes accepting with too great tenderness the tenet of the elders, have not accepted from others, but from their own heart, the genuine impulses of virtue, and so still command our love and awe, to the sanctity of character. Moreover, the exceptions are not so much to be found in a few eminent preachers, as in the better hours, the truer inspirations of all,—nay, in the sincere moments of every man. But, with whatever exception, it is still true that tradition characterizes the preaching of this country; that it comes out of the memory, and not out of the soul; that it aims at what is usual, and not at what is necessary and eternal; that thus historical Christianity destroys the power of preaching, by withdrawing it from the exploration of the moral nature of man; where the sublime is, where are the resources of astonishment and power. What a cruel injustice it is to that Law, the joy of the whole earth, which alone can make thought dear and rich; that Law whose fatal sureness the astronomical orbits poorly emulate;— that it is travestied and depreciated, that it is behooted and behowled, and not a trait, not a word of it articulated. The pulpit in losing sight of this Law, loses its reason, and gropes after it knows not what. And for want of this culture the soul of the community is sick and faithless. It wants nothing so much as a stern, high, stoical, Christian discipline, to make it know itself and the divinity that speaks through it. Now man is ashamed of himself; he skulks and sneaks through the world, to be tolerated, to be pitied, and scarcely in a thousand years does any man dare to be wise and good, and so draw after him the tears and blessings of his kind.

WHAT CAN WE DO?

Emerson insists that the answer to the unfortunate failure of formal religion is to open ourselves to the divine, to the power and spirit of God that is within every one of us. If we do this, we will become *"newborn bard[s] of the Holy Ghost,"* a living representation of the God that created and loves us. Then, and only then, will religion resume its true place in the living world. This bold thought can prompt a revolutionary awakening. Why can't we minister to one another, bring comfort and love to one another, as the spirit brings comfort and love to us? Each of us could and should become God's designated hitter, an imperial emissary of divine truth, an embodiment of Godliness, virtue, and justice. We all have the potential be so much more than we are. The door stands open before us and there is no reason why we cannot begin this very day to live lives of beauty, benevolence, and joy.

CHAPTER TWO: SELF-RELIANCE

*Listening to the Voice Within;
Discerning Truth; Vanquishing Fear and Anxiety;
Character Formation and Personal Integrity*

The linchpin of Transcendentalism is self-reliance. Emerson knew that there's no point in speaking of a dynamic divinity within if people lack the self-confidence to act upon its promptings. While we are all gifted with insights and intuitions that serve to point us in a certain direction in life, few have the courage to follow them. We are all too easily intimidated by the opinions of others, and what they might think of us. What is far more important, however, is what we think of ourselves. When we listen to the voice of divinity within us, when we speak what we truly feel, then our lives are in sync with the pulse of the universe. Our authentic feelings, Emerson insists, are a reflection of what everyone, in their heart of hearts, truly feels. As noted in Chapter One, he makes this point clearly in *"The Over-Soul."*

> *The soul is the perceiver and revealer of truth. We know truth when we see it, let skeptic and scoffer say what they choose. Foolish people ask you, when you have spoken what they do not wish to hear, 'How do you know it is truth, and not an error of your own?' We know truth when we see it, from opinion, as we know when we are awake that we are awake.*

While Emerson's assertion may appear to be naïve or simply wishful thinking to a conservative mind, the concept of intuitively perceived, universal truth actually provides the foundation for all civilized life. At the time of the Civil War, Lincoln referred to this divinely-inspired truth as "the better angels of our natures," and James Russell Lowell defined it as the "universal sentiment of mankind." It is reflected in the Declaration of Independence, the

Emerson's Truth, Emerson's Wisdom

foundational document of our national character. When Thomas Jefferson wrote that that "all men are created equal" and endowed with certain "inalienable rights," he described this truth as "self-evident." There was no tangible proof for it. No mathematical equation, no scientific experiment, no historical example, no process of pure reason could possibly prove that all men are created equal or that they have any rights whatsoever. Either you believe it or you don't.

Clearly, Jefferson, like Emerson, was confident that decent people know truth when they see it. Indeed, all of the Founding Fathers who signed the Declaration of Independence were willing to pledge their lives, their fortunes, and their sacred honor that this proposition was right. This same notion of self-evident truth underlies the "Universal Declaration of Human Rights" proclaimed by the United Nations in its founding charter. That document declares that a "recognition of the inherent dignity and of the equal and inalienable rights of all members of the human family is the foundation of freedom, justice and peace in the world." Our ability to get along as a world community of over six billion human beings is dependent upon our intuitive "recognition" of the universal values that inform our lives, both individually and collectively.

The common source for these truths, Emerson believed, was the "great Soul," the divine spirit that resides in all of us. The same spirit that guides nations and civilizations is at work in each of us individually. Obviously, nations, like the global community of which they are a part, are made up of a variety of people. But these people share a common human nature that is informed by common human values. We must look within ourselves to find these values and apply them in our relations with the larger community. We must be units before we can be united. We must connect with ourselves before we can connect with others. Emerson expresses this concept in ***"New England Reformers,"*** a lecture that he directed specifically to those who hoped to reform the world.

The world is awaking to the idea of union, and these experiments [at reform] show what it is thinking of. It is and will

Self-Reliance

be magic. Men will live and communicate, and plough, and reap, and govern, as by added ethereal power, when once they are united; as in a celebrated experiment, by expiration and respiration exactly together, four persons lift a heavy man from the ground by the little finger only, and without sense of weight. But this union must be inward, and not one of covenants, and is to be reached by a reverse of the methods they use. The union is only perfect when all the uniters are isolated. It is the union of friends who live in different streets or towns. Each man, if he attempts to join himself to others, is on all sides cramped and diminished of his proportion; and the stricter the union the smaller and the more pitiful he is. But leave him alone, to recognize in every hour and place the secret soul; he will go up and down doing the works of a true member, and, to the astonishment of all, the work will be done with concert, though no man spoke. Government will be adamantine without any governor. The union must be ideal in actual individualism.

Emerson's point here is that we discover our true selves by connecting with the spirit within us. Once we have acknowledged and embraced our own individuality, we can then add something special and unique to the larger community of which we are a part. The tragedy is that most of us do not take the first step of looking within to find truth and meaning. We simply conform to the standards of society, even when they are not satisfying, or agreeable, or just. The result is a constant state of frustration, discontent, or quiet desperation. If we are not true to ourselves, a price will be paid for this infidelity. Emerson was fully aware of how difficult self-reliance can be in a world that demands conformity. But he was also confident that we all have the necessary resources to be the individuals that we were born to be.

He begins his essay *"Self-Reliance"* with the observation that we all have access to universal truth, a truth that is operative in both the smallest and the greatest matters of human conduct. To follow this truth is to follow the "genius," the spirit, that informs our individual being.

> **To believe your own thought, to believe that what is true for you in your private heart is true for all men,—that is genius. Speak your latent conviction, and it shall be the universal sense; for the inmost in due time becomes the outmost, and our first thought is rendered back to us by the trumpets of the Last Judgment.**

Once we have acquainted ourselves with this inner truth, we are then prepared to take our proper place in the world.

Self-Reliance

WE ALL HAVE SOME SPECIAL WORK TO DO

Emerson believed that if we fail to trust ourselves and instead simply "go with the flow," adapting and conforming to the ideas and styles of others, we cease to be true individuals. We forgo the unique personality that we were born with and thereby deprive the world of the special gifts that were ours and ours alone to give. People are like their fingerprints. No two are exactly the same. We are unique for a reason. Each has a specific role to play and the failure to play that role would constitute a cowardly betrayal of God and the life and power that was given us. It is tantamount to suicide.

There is a time in every man's education when he arrives at the conviction that envy is ignorance; that imitation is suicide; that he must take himself for better for worse as his portion; that though the wide universe is full of good, no kernel of nourishing corn can come to him but through his toil bestowed on that plot of ground which is given to him to till. The power which resides in him is new in nature, and none but he knows what that is which he can do, nor does he know until he has tried. Not for nothing one face, one character, one fact, makes much impression on him, and another none. This sculpture in the memory is not without preëstablished harmony. The eye was placed where one ray should fall, that it might testify of that particular ray. We but half express ourselves, and are ashamed of that divine idea which each of us represents. It may be safely trusted as proportionate and of good issues, so it be faithfully imparted, but God will not have his work made manifest by cowards. A man is relieved and gay when he has put his heart into his work and done his best; but what he has said or done otherwise shall give him no peace. It is a deliverance which does not deliver. In the attempt his genius deserts him; no muse befriends; no invention, no hope.

Trust thyself: every heart vibrates to that iron string. Accept the place the divine providence has found for you, the society of your contemporaries, the connection of events. Great men have always done so, and confided themselves childlike to the genius of their age, betraying their perception that the absolutely trustworthy was seated at their heart, working through their hands, predominating in all their being. And we are now men, and must accept in the highest mind the same transcendent destiny; and not minors and invalids in a protected corner, not cowards fleeing before a revolution, but guides, redeemers and benefactors, obeying the Almighty effort and advancing on Chaos and the Dark.

What pretty oracles nature yields us on this text in the face and behavior of children, babes, and even brutes! That divided and rebel mind, that distrust of a sentiment because our arithmetic has computed the strength and means opposed to our purpose, these have not. Their mind being whole, their eye is as yet unconquered, and when we look in their faces we are disconcerted. Infancy conforms to nobody; all conform to it; so that one babe commonly makes four or five out of the adults who prattle and play to it. So God has armed youth and

Self-Reliance

puberty and manhood no less with its own piquancy and charm, and made it enviable and gracious and its claims not to be put by, if it will stand by itself. Do not think the youth has no force, because he cannot speak to you and me. Hark! in the next room his voice is sufficiently clear and emphatic. It seems he knows how to speak to his contemporaries. Bashful or bold then, he will know how to make us seniors very unnecessary.

Emerson observes that in our youth we naturally possess a self-confidence that allows us to see ourselves as the equals of anyone. Indeed, at one time this very sense of natural equality was seen by some as the essence of our youthful national and democratic identity. Walt Whitman once described Americans as having "the air . . . of persons who never knew how it felt to stand in the presence of superiors." Kings and princes don't intimidate us. They live by the same spirit that gives life to all of us, each one the same.

While this attitude has served us well in our national life, at some point in our individual lives, most of us seem to lose this youthful self-confidence. We are frequently cowed and intimidated by the appearance of a superior authority or by any expression of self-confidence in others. These others seem to know something that we don't, but actually they are simply fortified by having the courage of their convictions. Additionally, there is the fear that if we ever did manage to express an opinion clearly and forcefully, the world would expect us to adhere to that opinion forever. By saying something with certainty and conviction, we define ourselves in the eyes of the world. Henceforth, we will be known as conservative, or liberal, pro-life or pro-choice, feminist or antifeminist, etc. At this sad point we are *"clapped into jail by our consciousness."* We become reluctant to express any contrary or alternative opinion out of fear that it might disappoint the expectations of others.

The nonchalance of boys who are sure of a dinner, and would disdain as much as a lord to do or say aught to conciliate one, is the healthy attitude of human nature. A boy is in the parlor what the pit is in the playhouse; independent, irresponsible, looking out from his corner on such people and facts as pass by, he tries and sentences them on their merits, in the swift, summary way of boys, as good, bad, interesting, silly, eloquent, troublesome. He cumbers himself never about consequences, about interests; he gives an independent, genuine verdict. You must court him; he does not court you. But the man is as it were clapped into jail by his consciousness. As soon as he has once acted or spoken with éclat he is a committed person, watched by the sympathy or the hatred of hundreds, whose affections must now enter into his account. There is no Lethe for this. Ah, that he could pass again into his neutrality! Who can thus avoid all pledges and, having observed, observe again from the same unaffected, unbiased, unbribable, un-affrighted innocence,—must always be formidable. He would utter opinions on all passing affairs, which being seen to be not private but necessary, would sink like darts into the ear of men and put them in fear.

Self-Reliance

RESISTING THE PRESSURE TO CONFORM

Emerson well knew from his own painful experience that society is a tyrant. If you look around, you will notice that we very readily separate ourselves into groups wherein just about everybody looks like everybody else. We tend to dress the same way, eat the same foods, attend the same churches, watch the same programs, and go to the same schools. We all want to "fit in." Children excuse or explain their conduct by insisting that "Everyone does it." Often adults follow the same principle, albeit silently. Like most animals, we are inclined to be imitators, and our conduct falls easily into fixed patterns. Obviously, much of this imitative behavior is fairly benign. It is either unavoidable or it's simply convenient.

No one wants to be "out of style." Adult men stopped wearing hats when John F. Kennedy chose to forgo the formality. Young men stopped wearing white socks when they became associated with the "greaser look." The polyester leisure suit went out shortly after LSD became a banned substance. Young women no longer wear Poodle skirts or Bobby socks. Crew cuts gave way to long hair, which gave way to no hair. The mullet is passé. No big deal. The inclination towards sameness and imitation becomes pernicious, however, when it causes us to violate our own intuitive sense of right and wrong, or when it discourages our own creativity and uniqueness. It is easy for this to happen. Society encourages conformity and punishes individualism. Sometimes this is overt. Most of the time it is subtle. If you oppose an unjust war, or take a stand for human rights, condemn bigotry and narrow-mindedness, or question the policies of church or state, society becomes defensive.

People who are comfortable with the status quo tend to see free thinkers or "protesters" as a threat. In fact, anyone who is "different" is potentially a threat, no matter how insignificant that difference may be. Think of how many absurd court cases have occurred in just the past few years because certain students came to school with outlandishly colored hair, electric blue, orange, or even bright green. More often than not, these students run afoul of the authorities. They are said to be a "distraction" to others and, therefore, a hindrance to the learning process. They are told to go home. During the Viet Nam war, it was the length of young men's hair that could get them into trouble. The so-called "long hairs" were identified as radicals who sought to challenge authority, and some of them actually did. In all of these cases it is clear that "the establishment," as Emerson famously called it, felt threatened by those who looked different, or were inclined to think or act differently.

Emerson was well aware of this tendency. He was himself the victim of bitter personal attacks on his "heretical" religious views following his ***Divinity School Address*** at Harvard in 1838. As noted earlier in Chapter One, in this address to the graduating class of young ministers he expressed sharp criticisms of the church that once nurtured him. Because of this he was viciously attacked in the press. Later in his career, he would be threatened and shouted down by angry mobs for expressing his uncompromising opposition to slavery. Conservatives always saw his Transcendental philosophy as a threat because it validated self-reliance and the moral authority of the individual. Emerson placed the individual conscience above the authority of both church and state. Because society tends to act like a "joint-stock company" where material profit often out-weighs moral integrity, any expression of non-conformity is likely to be met with intense hostility.

Society everywhere is in conspiracy against the manhood of every one of its members. Society is a joint-stock company, in which the members agree, for the better securing of his bread to each shareholder, to surrender the liberty and culture of the eater. The virtue in most request is conformity. Self-reliance is its aversion. It loves not realities and creators, but names and customs.

Whoso would be a man, must be a nonconformist. He who would gather immortal palms must not be hindered by the name of goodness, but must explore if

Self-Reliance

it be goodness. Nothing is at last sacred but the integrity of your own mind. Absolve you to yourself, and you shall have the suffrage [i.e. approval] of the world.

If we capitulate to society, if we allow ourselves to be bullied by the shallow people who seem to set the tenor of the time, then we will live in fear. Fear that we will not be accepted. Fear that we have the wrong look. Fear that we hold the wrong values. Fear that we will say the wrong thing. Fear that the thought police will pay us a midnight visit. Paranoia does, indeed, strike deep. But Emerson calls upon us to be brave and to stand our ground, over and above "the madding crowd."

If any man consider the present aspects of what is called by distinction society, he will see the need of these ethics [of self-determination]. The sinew and heart of man seem to be drawn out, and we are become timorous, desponding whimperers. We are afraid of truth, afraid of fortune, afraid of death, and afraid of each other. Our age yields no great and perfect persons. We want men and women who shall renovate life and our social state, but we see that most natures are insolvent, cannot satisfy their own wants, have an ambition out of all proportion to their practical force and do lean and beg day and night continually. Our housekeeping is mendicant [i.e. subservient to others], our arts, our occupations, our marriages, our religion we have not chosen, but society has chosen for us. We are parlor soldiers. We shun the rugged battle of fate, where strength is born.

✿✿✿✿✿✿✿✿✿

And truly it demands something godlike in him who has cast off the common motives of humanity and has ventured to trust himself for a taskmaster. High be his heart, faithful his will, clear his sight, that he may in good earnest be doctrine, society, law, to himself, that a simple purpose may be to him as strong as iron necessity is to others!

Self-Reliance

DEALING WITH CRITICISM

Often when you do something unique or exceptional because you're convinced that it's the right thing to do, some well-intended person will take you aside and warn you that acting on your personal intuitions can get you into trouble. The assumption is that the devil lurks in all of us, figuratively or literally. Therefore, how can you trust yourself when the "voice within" might be the devil's own? Also, if we insist on the notion that we all have a moral obligation to follow our inner voice (i.e. our conscience), critics will retort that we are running the risk of encouraging a hoard of Charles Manson-like murderers and psychopaths. Chaos would ensue. It would be the end of civilization as we know it.

The simple answer to this fear is, of course, that Charles Manson was a sick, demented man. To assume that human conduct must be subjected to strict authoritarian control because we're all Charles Mansons at heart is to assume that all of humanity is sick and demented (except, presumably, those who are in control of the rest of us). Clearly, such a proposition is an insult to humanity and the God that created us. Not surprisingly, being the rebel that he was, Emerson had an experience with a well-intended and "valued advisor" who felt compelled to warn him of his own "devil within."

I remember an answer which when quite young I was prompted to make to a valued adviser who was wont to importune me with the dear old doctrines of the church. On my saying, "What have I to do with the sacredness of traditions, if I live wholly from within?" my friend suggested,—"But these impulses may be from below, not from above." I replied, "They do not seem to me to be such; but if I am the Devil's child, I will live then from the Devil." No law can be sacred to me but that of my nature. Good and bad are but names very readily transferable to that or this; the only right

~ 85 ~

is what is after my constitution; the only wrong what is against it. A man is to carry himself in the presence of all opposition as if every thing were titular [i.e. in name only] and ephemeral [i.e. short-lived] but he. I am ashamed to think how easily we capitulate to badges and names, to large societies and dead institutions.

Emerson's position here is both courageous and necessary. If we are deterred by the criticism of others from acting on our own sense of what is right and wrong, then we cease, in effect, to be moral agents. We substitute someone else's values for our own out of fear and intimidation. We grant others moral authority over us. Sadly, history shows that the greatest injuries to the human family have been wrought by tyrants and dictators who managed to impose their wills upon entire societies by seducing or otherwise compelling others to put aside their own consciences in order to "follow the leader." Conversely, great revolutions have been wrought when individuals threw off the yoke of conformity and insisted on following their consciences. Most of us will never be called upon to mount the barricades in a social revolution, as some did not too long ago in the Civil Rights and Women's Movements in this country.

The great challenge for the majority of folks these days is the tendency to capitulate quietly to the fashion and the values of the so-called silent majority. We are advised to "go along" in order to "get along," but in doing so we lose all sense of who we are and what our individual lives should be about. Emerson insists that we must always do our own thing. Our primary obligation is to be who we are. This can, at times, be difficult and even painful, especially if we belong, as so many of us do, to civic organizations, churches, or political parties. Even one's own family can be a hindrance, at times, to the exercise of moral choice and individuality. All of these external influences tend to define us in a certain way, even if our personal beliefs run contrary to some generally accepted norm. To maintain our personal integrity while living in society can be a great challenge.

Self-Reliance

What I must do is all that concerns me, not what the people think. This rule, equally arduous in actual and in intellectual life, may serve for the whole distinction between greatness and meanness. It is the harder because you will always find those who think they know what is your duty better than you know it. It is easy in the world to live after the world's opinion; it is easy in solitude to live after our own; but the great man is he who in the midst of the crowd keeps with perfect sweetness the independence of solitude.

THE CONSEQUENCES OF CONFORMITY

The problem with conforming to any institution is that our personal identity, our authentic self, can become lost to the world. Our lives then become an exercise in hypocrisy as we silently assent to what we don't believe and accept that which we don't approve. We thus are led to present a false face to the world. One that pains us at times.

The objection to conforming to usages that have become dead to you is that it scatters your force. It loses your time and blurs the impression of your character. If you maintain a dead church, contribute to a dead Bible-society, vote with a great party either for the government or against it, spread your table like base housekeepers,—under all these screens I have difficulty to detect the precise man you are: and of course so much force is withdrawn from your proper life. But do your work, and I shall know you. Do your work, and you shall reinforce yourself. A man must consider what a blindman's-buff is this game of conformity. If I know your sect I anticipate your argument. I hear a preacher announce for his text and topic the expediency of one of the institutions of his church. Do I not know beforehand that not possibly can he say a new and spontaneous word? Do I not know that with all this ostentation of examining the grounds of the institution he will do no such thing? Do I not know that he is pledged to himself not to look but at one side, the permitted side, not as a man, but as a parish minister? He is a retained attorney, and these airs of the bench are the emptiest affectation. Well, most men have bound their eyes with one or another handkerchief, and attached themselves to some one of these communities of opinion. This conformity makes them not false in a few particulars, authors of a few lies, but false in all particulars. Their every truth is not quite true. Their two is not the real two, their four not the real four; so that every word they say chagrins us and we know not where to begin to set them right. Meantime nature is not slow to equip us in the prison-uniform of the party to which we adhere. We come to wear one cut of face and figure, and acquire by degrees the gentlest asinine expression. There is a mortifying experience in particular, which does not fail to wreak itself also in the general history; I mean "the foolish face of praise," the forced smile which we put on in company where we do not feel at ease, in answer to conversation which does not interest us. The muscles, not spontaneously moved but moved by a low usurping wilfulness, grow tight about the outline of the face, with the most disagreeable sensation.

If you insist on going it alone, maintaining the integrity of your own beliefs and opinions, there is always a price to be paid. The displeasure of those around us will soon become apparent. For those in public life, withstanding the rage of "the ignorant and the poor" and "the unintelligent brute force that lies at the bottom of society" can be a great personal challenge.

For nonconformity the world whips you with its displeasure. And therefore a man must know how to estimate a sour face. The by-standers look askance on him in the public street or in the friend's parlor. If this aversion had its origin in contempt and resistance like his own he might well go home with a sad countenance; but the sour faces of the multitude, like their sweet faces, have no deep cause, but are put on and off as the wind blows and a newspaper directs. Yet is the discontent of the multitude more formidable than that of the senate and the college. It is easy enough for a firm man who knows the world to brook the rage of the cultivated classes. Their rage is decorous and prudent, for they are timid, as being very vulnerable themselves. But when to their feminine rage the indignation of the people is added, when the ignorant and the poor are aroused, when the unintelligent brute force that lies at the bottom of society is made to growl and mow, it needs the habit of magnanimity and religion to treat it godlike as a trifle of no concernment.

Self-Reliance

AVOIDING A FOOLISH CONSISTENCY

One of the greatest hindrances to maintaining our personal integrity and authenticity is the demand of others that we be absolutely consistent in everything we think, say, and do. This is a patently absurd demand, and yet small-minded people make it all the time and think that it is perfectly reasonable. If a politician, for example, should have the audacity to change his or her mind on any issue, even over a broad period of time, he or she will immediately be branded as a "flip-flopper," a person who simply cannot be trusted. The idea here seems to be that upon reaching biological maturity, the human brain is expected to flat line. The gates must be closed, the doors shut, the windows barred, the lights extinguished. We are never from this point forward to think new thoughts, to have new experiences, or to achieve new insights. Every tomorrow is to be the same as today. Nothing is allowed to change. We are expected, henceforth, to repeat the thinking of the past, to *"drag about this corpse of [our] memory,"* no matter how unsuccessful, or irrelevant, or pernicious the old way of thinking has become. Emerson famously referred to this as a *"foolish consistency"* and he dismissed it outright.

> *The other terror that scares us from self-trust is our consistency; a reverence for our past act or word because the eyes of others have no other data for computing our orbit than our past acts, and we are loth to disappoint them.*

But we should have no fear of doing so. Our thoughts, like ourselves, should "live ever in a new day," unencumbered by the past.

> *But why should you keep your head over your shoulder? Why drag about this corpse of your memory, lest you contradict somewhat you have stated in this or that public place? Suppose you*

should contradict yourself; what then? It seems to be a rule of wisdom never to rely on your memory alone, scarcely even in acts of pure memory, but to bring the past for judgment into the thousand-eyed present, and live ever in a new day. In [my] metaphysics [I] have denied personality to the Deity, yet when the devout motions of the soul come, [I] yield to them heart and life, though they should clothe God with shape and color. Leave your theory, as Joseph his coat in the hand of the harlot, and flee.

A foolish consistency is the hobgoblin of little minds, adored by little statesmen and philosophers and divines. With consistency a great soul has simply nothing to do. He may as well concern himself with his shadow on the wall. Speak what you think now in hard words and tomorrow speak what to-morrow thinks in hard words again, though it contradict every thing you said to-day.— 'Ah, so you shall be sure to be misunderstood.'—Is it so bad then to be misunderstood? Pythagoras was misunderstood, and Socrates, and Jesus, and Luther, and Copernicus, and Galileo, and Newton, and every pure and wise spirit that ever took flesh. To be great is to be misunderstood.

This is not to say that Emerson had no regard for consistency. He most certainly did, just not the foolish kind. Instead, Emerson insists that we should be consistently true to ourselves, to the conscience and the vision within us, to those authentic thoughts and feelings that make us who we are. We must take a stand in the very center of our world. If we do this, our actions will speak for themselves.

Self-Reliance

> *There will be an agreement in whatever variety of actions, so they be each honest and natural in their hour. For of one will, the actions will be harmonious, however unlike they seem. These varieties are lost sight of at a little distance, at a little height of thought. One tendency unites them all. The voyage of the best ship is a zigzag line of a hundred tacks. See the line from a sufficient distance, and it straightens itself to the average tendency. Your genuine action will explain itself and will explain your other genuine actions. Your conformity explains nothing.*

I especially like Emerson's image of the ship here, and his concept of the "average tendency" of our lives. In his day, most ships were sailing ships. If you plotted the course of such a ship as it sailed, say, from Boston to London, it would look like a zigzag line. This is because a sailing ship has to adjust its course, to "tack," in response to prevailing winds and currents. So at certain times during the crossing a compass reading from this vessel might indicate that it was headed towards Africa or Iceland rather than England. Eventually, however, the ship's "average tendency" becomes apparent and it makes port, at last, in London. Emerson's point here is that as imperfect human beings we all make mistakes in life. We get off course a bit. This is either because there were things that we simply didn't know at the time we made our decision, or, for one reason or another we failed to use good judgment. But it is always possible to get back on track.

If our overriding intention is to do what is right, if our ultimate goal is to be honest with ourselves and just in our relations with others, then our "average tendency" will emerge as we move in that direction. We will get to where we want to go, defining ourselves in the process. The opposite is also true. If we are not honest with ourselves, if we compromise our integrity by capitulating to the false voices that surround us, if we lack the will to live our lives with integrity and courage, that too will become apparent. Life presents us with choices and our decisions will ultimately determine who we really are. Emerson reminds us that it is the Great Soul within us that informs our sense of truth. It is the source of our personal confidence that *"there is a great responsible Thinker and Actor"* at work whenever we speak what we truly believe.

> *I hope in these days we have heard the last of conformity and consistency. Let the words be gazetted and ridiculous henceforward. Instead of the gong for dinner, let us hear a whistle from the Spartan fife. Let us never bow and apologize more. A great man is coming to eat at my house. I do not wish to please him; I wish that he should wish to please me. I will stand here for humanity, and though I would make it kind, I would make it true. Let us affront and reprimand the smooth mediocrity and squalid contentment of the times, and hurl in the face of custom and trade and office, the fact which is the upshot of all history, that there is a great responsible Thinker and Actor working wherever a man works; that a true man belongs to no other time or place, but is the centre of things. Where he is, there is nature. He measures you and all men and all events. Ordinarily, every body in society reminds us of somewhat else, or of some other person. Character, reality, reminds you of nothing else; it takes place of the whole creation. The man must be so much that he must make all circumstances indifferent.*

Few of us ever achieve the highest level of self-confident and independent thought, but those who do have the privilege of leaving their mark on history.

Self-Reliance

Every true man is a cause, a country, and an age; requires infinite spaces and numbers and time fully to accomplish his design;—and posterity seem to follow his steps as a train of clients. A man Caesar is born, and for ages after we have a Roman Empire. Christ is born, and millions of minds so grow and cleave to his genius that he is confounded with [i.e. seen as the representation of] virtue and the possible of man. An institution is the lengthened shadow of one man; as, Monachism, of the Hermit Antony; the Reformation, of Luther; Quakerism, of Fox; Methodism, of Wesley; Abolition, of Clarkson. Scipio, Milton called "the height of Rome;" and all history resolves itself very easily into the biography of a few stout and earnest persons.

No matter the apparent distance between oneself and such historically memorable personages, the same spirit that dwelt in them dwells in us. Within all of us there beats the heart of a *"true prince"* or princess. We, too, are capable of manifesting the noblest of virtues in our lives.

Let a man then know his worth, and keep things under his feet. Let him not peep or steal, or skulk up and down with the air of a charity-boy, a bastard, or an interloper in the world which exists for him. But the man in the street, finding no worth in himself which corresponds to the force which built a tower or sculptured a marble god, feels poor when he looks on these. To him a palace, a statue, or a costly book have an alien and forbidding air, much like a gay equipage, and seem to say like that, "Who are you, Sir?" Yet they all are his, suitors for his notice, petitioners to his faculties that they will come out and take possession. The picture waits for my verdict; it is not to command me, but I am to settle its claims to praise. That popular fable of the sot who was picked up dead-drunk in the street, carried to the duke's house, washed and dressed and laid in the duke's bed, and, on his waking, treated with all obsequious ceremony like the duke, and assured that he had been insane, owes its popularity to the fact that it symbolizes so well the state of man, who is in the world a sort of sot, but now and then wakes up, exercises his reason and finds himself a true prince.

Our reading is mendicant and sycophantic [i.e. extremely deferential]. In history our imagination plays us false. Kingdom and lordship, power and estate, are a gaudier vocabulary than private John and Edward in a small house and common day's work; but the things of life are the same to both; the sum total of both is the same. Why all this deference to Alfred and Scanderbeg and Gustavus? Suppose they were virtuous; did they wear out virtue? As great a stake depends on your private act to-day as followed their public and renowned steps. When private men shall act with original views, the lustre will be transferred from the actions of kings to those of gentlemen.

The world has been instructed by its kings, who have so magnetized the eyes of nations. It has been taught by this colossal symbol the mutual reverence that is due from man to man. The joyful loyalty with which men have everywhere suffered [i.e. allowed] the king, the noble, or the great proprietor to walk among them by a law of his own, make his own scale of men and things and reverse theirs, pay for benefits not with money but with honor, and represent the law in his person, was the hieroglyphic by which they obscurely signified their consciousness of their own right and comeliness, the right of every man.

THE ULTIMATE SOURCE OF OUR SELF-TRUST

Where do our feelings and intuitions come from? Why can we trust them? The ultimate source, Emerson assures us, is the great Soul, the divinity, the "immense intelligence" that is the source of all life and all truth. The Founding Fathers were convinced that the truths they believed to be "self-evident" were trustworthy. They staked their lives on it. Emerson was equally confident that every truth revealed to the heart and confirmed by the mind of an honest person is also trustworthy. The reason is that the ultimate source of these truths is God within us. This is the compass that points us in the right direction in life.

The magnetism which all original action exerts is explained when we inquire the reason of self-trust. Who is the Trustee? What is the aboriginal Self, on which a universal reliance may be grounded? What is the nature and power of that science-baffling star, without parallax [i.e. distortion], without calculable elements, which shoots a ray of beauty even into trivial and impure actions, if the least mark of independence appear? The inquiry leads us to that source, at once the essence of genius, of virtue, and of life, which we call Spontaneity or Instinct. We denote this primary wisdom as Intuition, whilst all later teachings are tuitions. In that deep force, the last fact behind which analysis cannot go, all things find their common origin. For the sense of being which in calm hours rises, we know not how, in the soul, is not diverse from things, from space, from light, from time, from man, but one with them and proceeds obviously from the same source whence their life and being also proceed. We first share the life by which things exist and afterwards see them as

Self-Reliance

appearances in nature and forget that we have shared their cause. Here is the fountain of action and of thought. Here are the lungs of that inspiration which giveth man wisdom and which cannot be denied without impiety and atheism. We lie in the lap of immense intelligence, which makes us receivers of its truth and organs of its activity. When we discern justice, when we discern truth, we do nothing of ourselves, but allow a passage to its beams. If we ask whence this comes, if we seek to pry into the soul that causes, all philosophy is at fault. Its presence or its absence is all we can affirm. Every man discriminates between the voluntary acts of his mind and his involuntary perceptions, and knows that to his involuntary perceptions a perfect faith is due. He may err in the expression of them, but he knows that these things are so, like day and night, not to be disputed. My wilful actions and acquisitions are but roving;—the idlest reverie, the faintest native emotion, command my curiosity and respect. Thoughtless people contradict as readily the statement of perceptions as of opinions, or rather much more readily; for they do not distinguish between perception and notion. They fancy that I choose to see this or that thing. But perception is not whimsical, but fatal [i.e. dictated by fate]. If I see a trait, my children will see it after me, and in course of time all mankind,— although it may chance that no one has seen it before me. For my perception of it is as much a fact as the sun.

Emerson's Truth, Emerson's Wisdom

Any effort to capture in words the essence of this divine source of life and truth strains the power of language itself. At best, we can only hint at this ineffable dynamic of life.

> *And now at last the highest truth on this subject remains unsaid; probably cannot be said; for all that we say is the far-off remembering of the intuition. That thought by what I can now nearest approach to say it, is this. When good is near you, when you have life in yourself, it is not by any known or accustomed way; you shall not discern the footprints of any other; you shall not see the face of man; you shall not hear any name;—the way, the thought, the good, shall be wholly strange and new. It shall exclude example and experience. You take the way from man, not to man. All persons that ever existed are its forgotten ministers. Fear and hope are alike beneath it. There is somewhat low even in hope. In the hour of vision there is nothing that can be called gratitude, nor properly joy. The soul raised over passion beholds identity and eternal causation, perceives the self-existence of Truth and Right, and calms itself with knowing that all things go well. Vast spaces of nature, the Atlantic Ocean, the South Sea; long intervals of time, years, centuries, are of no account. This which I think and feel underlay every former state of life and circumstances, as it does underlie my present, and what is called life and what is called death.*

For Emerson, once we have truly opened ourselves to this vital force within, when our spirit becomes electric, kinetic, energized— then the true and spontaneous experience of life is ours. We flow constantly outward in a progressive, ongoing

Self-Reliance

unfolding of our lives. We do not concern ourselves with what others might think about us, or what was done in the past, or what is traditional or commonplace, or normally expected. If we are living in harmony with the spirit of life and love within us, we are complete. Once we have assumed our proper spiritual identity, we will naturally gravitate towards those who manifest this same original spirit. From units, we thus proceed to authentic (rather than synthetic) unity. We will live in the present tense, empowered by and obedient to the divine spirit that is the source of all meaning and all life.

Life only avails, not the having lived. Power ceases in the instant of repose; it resides in the moment of transition from a past to a new state, in the shooting of the gulf, in the darting to an aim. This one fact the world hates; that the soul becomes; for that forever degrades the past, turns all riches to poverty, all reputation to a shame, confounds the saint with the rogue, shoves Jesus and Judas equally aside. Why then do we prate of self-reliance? Inasmuch as the soul is present there will be power not confident [i.e. not merely trusting] but agent [i.e. active]. To talk of reliance is a poor external way of speaking. Speak rather of that which relies because it works and is. Who has more obedience than I masters me, though he should not raise his finger. Round him I must revolve by the gravitation of spirits. We fancy it rhetoric when we speak of eminent virtue. We do not yet see that virtue is Height, and that a man or a company of men, plastic [i.e. capable of being shared] and permeable to principles, by the law of nature must overpower and ride all cities, nations, kings, rich men, poets, who are not.

Emerson's Truth, Emerson's Wisdom

This is the ultimate fact which we so quickly reach on this, as on every topic, the resolution of all into the ever-blessed ONE. Self-existence is the attribute of the Supreme Cause, and it constitutes the measure of good by the degree in which it enters into all lower forms. All things real are so by so much virtue as they contain. Commerce, husbandry, hunting, whaling, war, eloquence, personal weight, are somewhat, and engage my respect as examples of its presence and impure action. I see the same law working in nature for conservation and growth. Power is, in nature, the essential measure of right. Nature suffers nothing to remain in her kingdoms which cannot help itself. The genesis and maturation of a planet, its poise and orbit, the bended tree recovering itself from the strong wind, the vital resources of every animal and vegetable, are demonstrations of the self-sufficing and therefore self-relying soul.

Self-Reliance

KNOWING DIVINITY FIRST-HAND

Emerson reminds us that we come to know the *"divine spirit"* by opening ourselves to its presence. It is not something that can be experienced second-hand from books and through churches and ministers. We can only know it first hand, through personal experience.

> *The relations of the soul to the divine spirit are so pure that it is profane to seek to interpose helps. It must be that when God speaketh he should communicate, not one thing, but all things; should fill the world with his voice; should scatter forth light, nature, time, souls, from the centre of the present thought; and new date and new create the whole. Whenever a mind is simple and receives a divine wisdom, old things pass away,—means, teachers, texts, temples fall; it lives now, and absorbs past and future into the present hour. All things are made sacred by relation to it,—one as much as another. All things are dissolved to their centre by their cause, and in the universal miracle petty and particular miracles disappear. If therefore a man claims to know and speak of God and carries you backward to the phraseology of some old mouldered nation in another country, in another world, believe him not. Is the acorn better than the oak which is its fullness and completion? Is the parent better than the child into whom he has cast his ripened being? Whence then this worship of the past? The centuries are conspirators against the sanity and authority of the soul. Time and space are but physiological colors which the eye makes, but the soul is light: where it is, is day; where it was, is night; and*

history is an impertinence and an injury if it be any thing more than a cheerful apologue or parable of my being and becoming.

Unfortunately, most of us have not opened ourselves to the power that is ours. As a result, we settle for a timid rather than a brave existence.

Man is timid and apologetic; he is no longer upright; he dares not say 'I think,' 'I am,' but quotes some saint or sage. He is ashamed before the blade of grass or the blowing rose. These roses under my window make no reference to former roses or to better ones; they are for what they are; they exist with God today. There is no time to them. There is simply the rose; it is perfect in every moment of its existence. Before a leaf-bud has burst, its whole life acts; in the fullblown flower there is no more; in the leafless root there is no less. Its nature is satisfied and it satisfies nature in all moments alike. But man postpones or remembers; he does not live in the present, but with reverted eye laments the past, or, heedless of the riches that surround him, stands on tiptoe to foresee the future. He cannot be happy and strong until he too lives with nature in the present, above time.

This should be plain enough. Yet see what strong intellects dare not yet hear God himself unless he speak the phraseology of I know not what David, or Jeremiah, or Paul. We shall not always set so great a price on a few texts, on a few lives. We are like children who repeat by rote the sentences of grandames and

Self-Reliance

tutors, and, as they grow older, of the men of talents and character they chance to see,—painfully recollecting the exact words they spoke; afterwards, when they come into the point of view which those had who uttered these sayings, they understand them and are willing to let the words go; for at any time they can use words as good when occasion comes. If we live truly, we shall see truly. It is as easy for the strong man to be strong, as it is for the weak to be weak. When we have new perception, we shall gladly disburden the memory of its hoarded treasures as old rubbish. When a man lives with God, his voice shall be as sweet as the murmur of the brook and the rustle of the corn.

✧✧✧✧✧✧✧✧✧

Thus all concentrates: let us not rove; let us sit at home with the cause. Let us stun and astonish the intruding rabble of men and books and institutions by a simple declaration of the divine fact. Bid the invaders take the shoes from off their feet, for God is here within. Let our simplicity judge them, and our docility to our own law demonstrate the poverty of nature and fortune beside our native riches.

Emerson's Truth, Emerson's Wisdom

STANDING UP TO THOSE WE LOVE

Sometimes the obligation to be true to ourselves puts us in opposition to those who are closest to us. Dealing with this situation requires a special kind of courage. There comes a time in our lives when we discover that we must become our own person. We must think our own thoughts and walk our own walk. Emerson is uncompromising in acknowledging the painfulness but also the necessity of making such a personal stand for self. He undoubtedly felt this very pain when he decided to leave the Unitarian ministry and thus separate himself from the traditions and values of family, friends, and forefathers. It was a brave, courageous, and difficult move and also a necessary one.

> *If we cannot at once rise to the sanctities of obedience and faith, let us at least resist our temptations; let us enter into the state of war and wake Thor and Woden, courage and constancy, in our Saxon breasts. This is to be done in our smooth times by speaking the truth. Check this lying hospitality and lying affection. Live no longer to the expectation of these deceived and deceiving people with whom we converse. Say to them, 'O father, O mother, O wife, O brother, O friend, I have lived with you after appearances hitherto. Henceforward I am the truth's. Be it known unto you that henceforward I obey no law less than the eternal law. I will have no covenants but proximities. I shall endeavor to nourish my parents, to support my family, to be the chaste husband of one wife,—but these relations I must fill after a new and unprecedented way. I appeal from your customs. I must be myself. I cannot break myself any longer for you, or you. If you can love me for what I am, we shall be the happier. If*

Self-Reliance

you cannot, I will still seek to deserve that you should. I will not hide my tastes or aversions. I will so trust that what is deep is holy, that I will do strongly before the sun and moon whatever inly rejoices me and the heart appoints. If you are noble, I will love you; if you are not, I will not hurt you and myself by hypocritical attentions. If you are true, but not in the same truth with me, cleave to your companions; I will seek my own. I do this not selfishly but humbly and truly. It is alike your interest, and mine, and all men's, however long we have dwelt in lies, to live in truth. Does this sound harsh to-day? You will soon love what is dictated by your nature as well as mine, and if we follow the truth it will bring us out safe at last.'—But so may you give these friends pain. Yes, but I cannot sell my liberty and my power, to save their sensibility. Besides, all persons have their moments of reason, when they look out into the region of absolute truth; then will they justify me and do the same thing.

If we are true to ourselves and live in accordance with the truths that are revealed to us, we shall eventually discover a tranquility, a peacefulness, a self-satisfaction that will transcend the petty concerns of everyday life. The politics of property, a world dominated by a concern for "things," will no longer burden our soul. We will lean to ignore those who "measure their esteem of each other by what each has, and not by what each is." One of the more obvious reasons for the gross materialism that infects American society today is that people are trying to make up for a lack of character with a superabundance of things.

In my own lifetime, I have witnessed a strange phenomenon where clothing labels have migrated from the inside of garments to the outside. Similarly, virtually all items of personal ware from sneakers to purses to sweatshirts are now "branded." Why is it important that people should know that my shoes are made by Nike, my shirt by Ralph Lauren, and my sunglasses by Versace? It is because, in addition to their reputation for quality, these products also sell at premium prices. And so, by wearing them we hope to make a statement to the world that we are worth something. Of course, from Emerson's perspective, personal worth is not a matter of what you have, but the values that inform your life. A truly self-reliant person is someone with integrity, someone who has been true to the divine voice within. For such a person, material things, beyond meeting one's basic needs, count for very little, as do alliances and associations, political parties, social cliques and all other things that exist outside of ourselves. The person who "stands alone" draws strength and confidence from the divinity within. Those who must lean on others, who find strength only in the validation that comes from others, will be forever weakened by this dependence.

And so the reliance on Property, including the reliance on governments which protect it, is the want of self-reliance. Men have looked away from themselves and at things so long that they have come to esteem the religious, learned and civil institutions as guards of property, and they deprecate assaults on these, because they feel them to be assaults on property. They measure their esteem of each other by what each has, and not by what each is. But a cultivated man becomes ashamed of his property, out of new respect for his nature. Especially he hates what he has if he see that it is accidental,—came to him by inheritance, or gift, or crime; then he feels that it is not having; it does not belong to him, has no root in him and merely lies there because no revolution or no robber takes it away. But that which a man is, does always by necessity acquire; and what the man acquires, is living property,

Self-Reliance

which does not wait the beck of rulers, or mobs, or revolutions, or fire, or storm, or bankruptcies, but perpetually renews itself wherever the man breathes. "Thy lot or portion of life," said the Caliph Ali, "is seeking after thee; therefore be at rest from seeking after it." Our dependence on these foreign goods leads us to our slavish respect for numbers. The political parties meet in numerous conventions; the greater the concourse and with each new uproar of announcement, The delegation from Essex! The Democrats from New Hampshire! The Whigs of Maine! the young patriot feels himself stronger than before by a new thousand of eyes and arms. In like manner the reformers summon conventions and vote and resolve in multitude. Not so, O friends! will the God deign to enter and inhabit you, but by a method precisely the reverse. It is only as a man puts off all foreign support and stands alone that I see him to be strong and to prevail. He is weaker by every recruit to his banner. Is not a man better than a town? Ask nothing of men, and, in the endless mutation, thou only firm column must presently appear the upholder of all that surrounds thee. He who knows that power is inborn, that he is weak because he has looked for good out of him and elsewhere, and, so perceiving, throws himself unhesitatingly on his thought, instantly rights himself, stands in the erect position, commands his limbs, works miracles; just as a man who stands on his feet is stronger than a man who stands on his head.

Emerson's Truth, Emerson's Wisdom

Emerson ends his meditation on self-reliance with a reflection on the true source of peace in life. He observes that some people believe that their lives will be improved by a chance occurrence, some force or power outside of themselves. They believe that if they could only win the lottery, then they would be happy, or if a lost friend returns, or if their stocks should rise, or their favorite team should win the championship this would fulfill them. Don't believe it, Emerson warns. Nothing outside of yourself can bring you true peace. "Cause and Effect" are the "Chancellors of God." We reap only what we sow, and there is no way to game the system. We will be nothing more and nothing less than what we are. Our destiny is not in the stars or in the lottery. It is in ourselves.

So use all that is called Fortune. Most men gamble with her, and gain all, and lose all, as her wheel rolls. But do thou leave as unlawful these winnings, and deal with Cause and Effect, the chancellors of God. In the Will work and acquire, and thou hast chained the wheel of Chance, and shall sit hereafter out of fear from her rotations. A political victory, a rise of rents, the recovery of your sick or the return of your absent friend, or some other favorable event raises your spirits, and you think good days are preparing for you. Do not believe it. Nothing can bring you peace but yourself. Nothing can bring you peace but the triumph of principles.

Emerson's final point about property is especially important today. This lesson came home to me in a particularly poignant way some time ago as my own mother lay dying. She had lived a long and fruitful life and now she was nearing the end of it. My sisters and I were keeping watch. As she looked around her hospital room with weary eyes, my mother said in a weak but assured voice, "I think that it's time for me to go home." In an effort to comfort her, one of my sisters responded, "Sure Ma, we'll take you home soon, but first you have to get a bit better." "No,"

Self-Reliance

my mother answered, "I don't mean that home. I mean my other home."

My sisters glanced at one another and then at me, and our hearts sank a bit. We understood. Soon my mother slipped into what seemed a deep sleep. The end was approaching. My brothers and sisters and I took turns keeping vigil at her bedside, each with our own special time alone with the mother who had given us life, and who was now taking leave of hers. When my turn came, I took the opportunity to tell my mother many things that had long been in my heart, but that I had never told her in words. We were a very loving family, but, like most New Englanders, rarely verbalized that love. But now I wanted to say what I felt. I didn't know how far she had already progressed on her journey "home," and I didn't know if she could hear me or not, but that didn't matter. I told her how much I loved her, how grateful I was to her for the care and love that she had given me and all of us. I told her that I knew how hard she and Dad had worked to raise the five of us, and what sacrifices they had made to provide a loving home for us all.

Most of all, I told her how grateful I was for her example. She taught us what it meant to be a good person. To have character. To stand for something. When I finished emptying my heart, I just sat there, holding her now frail hand, a hand that had been so strong for others. After a few moments, I felt a gentle pressure as her hand closed slightly on mine. Then her lips moved just a bit, as if she was trying to form a word. Gradually, in a voice that was weak but clear and determined, she said, "Money doesn't mean a thing." That was it. It was as if she was offering this final affirmation of a principle that had guided her life. It was a lesson that I had learned well from her example. And here it was again, in a nut shell. She had learned this lesson, undoubtedly, from her own difficult childhood.

My mother was born in 1915, one of twelve children in a family of poor Irish, who didn't, of course, think of themselves as poor. They all lived in a small house on the edge of town. Even for that time, it was an unusually Spartan home with no indoor plumbing, no central heat, and no electricity. Despite this, my mother remembered her childhood as a happy one. Somewhere along the way, her father, a day laborer, had acquired an old, used upright piano. Some of them learned to play this instrument "by ear" and with it they entertained themselves frequently. Holidays, especially, were occasions for family song fests. "Grandma Murphy" baked a week's supply of bread in the oven of a cast iron, wood-burning stove every Monday. On cold winter nights, she carefully wrapped irons, which had been heated on the stove, in towels and put them at the foot of her children's beds. Overcoats often served as extra blankets on these frigid nights (a practice that carried over to our own home). But still, my mother insists that her childhood was a happy one, and it was, apparently.

As a child, I never thought much about money. We never had any. My parents raised five children on my father's pay. He was a factory worker. As one of twelve children himself, he learned early on the value of hard work and the virtue of frugality. He was never stingy, but he never wasted anything either. He put his envelope in the basket at church every week, and never failed to scrape the oleomargarine off the foil wrappers before he threw them in the trash. We lived in a modest house in a modest neighborhood, with modest neighbors who all had kids. Parents drove around in used cars. Kids wore hand-me-down clothes and read recycled comic books that we traded endlessly among ourselves. Nobody I knew ever owned a new bicycle, but everyone had a bicycle. We played in the woods in the summer and went snow-sledding and ice-skating in the winter. Life was good.

My parents never read Emerson, but they lived Emersonian lives. They possessed faith in themselves and a strong commitment to character. It was more important to them to be good persons than to be rich people. I'm sure they never heard the term "Over-Soul," but their enduring lives provide many examples of love and quiet courage that reflect its ever-present influence. I would like to believe that at least some of it rubbed off on their children.

CHAPTER THREE: PERSONAL LOVE AND COSMIC LOVE

The Awakening of Spiritual Life; Cosmic Love and Personal Love; Marriage and Family; Transcendental Sex; Dealing with Bereavement and Loss; The Meaning of Suffering

EXPERIENCING LOVE AND LOSS

For Emerson, personal love and personal loss went hand-in-hand. His first experience with romantic love came as he was finishing his studies at Harvard's Divinity School in 1827. Before this he was inclined to disparage "passion," as did most of the scholars of his day. Rationalism was the hallmark of the Enlightenment, which dominated Western culture throughout the eighteenth century. Its influence continued to be felt well into the nineteenth. Young scholars in Emerson's day were routinely taught that "reason" was the only sure guide in life. Emotion, by contrast, was suspect because it often prompted spontaneous and irrational behavior. In an early journal entry, Waldo cautioned himself, *"Trust not the Passions; they are blind guides. They act, by the confessed experience of all the world, by the observation within reach of a child's attention, contrary to Reason."* He tried his best to live in accordance with this maxim during his college years.

As he neared the completion of his divinity studies, Emerson began to feel that something was missing in his life. He noted in his journal at the time, *"My days are made up of the irregular succession of a very few different tones of feeling."* But sometime later he added a notation to this page, an apparent afterthought that read, *"I ought to apprise the reader that I am a bachelor & to the best of my belief have never been in love."* It was around this time that Emerson met a beautiful young woman named Ellen Tucker. He was taken with her immediately. She was only sixteen but mature for her age. He was twenty-four. Within a year they became engaged. Around this time, the tone of Emerson's journal entries began to change noticeably. Following an outline of a sermon on *"The office of a Christian minister,"* he entered a simple and unexpected exclamation, *"Oh Ellen, I do dearly love you."* It was as if his heart had leaped up and overwhelmed his head, shattering, momentarily at least, the serious formality of his sermon.

Romance blossomed and the couple was married on September 30, 1829. By this time, Emerson had completed his theological studies, was ordained, and had assumed a prestigious appointment to Boston's Second Church. Waldo's romantic relationship with Ellen opened in him, for the first time in his life, a passionate pathway to the great Soul, the divinity within. It would prove to be a life-changing experience. This dynamic force would eventually become the mainstay of his spiritual life and the central element of his Transcendental faith. Love, he would come to understand, is the most powerful force on earth. But at this point, Emerson had taken only the first step on a very long and sometimes painful inward journey of discovery.

Even before their marriage, Ellen had suffered long bouts with a debilitating illness. It turned out to be the early stages of tuberculosis, the mysterious disease known at the time as "consumption." It was the plague of the nineteenth century. In an effort to ward off this grim harbinger of death, Ellen and Waldo gamely undertook the prescribed regimens of the day. These included sleeping in a cold bedroom and long and vigorous horseback rides in the chill winter air. The latter was presumably an aid to clearing Ellen's increasingly congested lungs. All of this, however, was of no avail. Despite these efforts, as well as their most ardent prayers, Ellen Tucker Emerson died on February 8, 1831, barely sixteen months from their wedding day. She was just nineteen.

Personal Love and Cosmic Love

Waldo was devastated. At the very moment when the fires of his heart had begun to burn with an emotional and spiritual intensity that he had never known before, the light of this new life was extinguished. His deep sorrow and personal anguish are reflected in the following journal entry.

> *Five days are wasted since Ellen went to heaven to see, to know, to worship, to love, to intercede. God be merciful to me a sinner & repair this miserable debility in which her death has left my soul. Two nights since, I have again heard her breathing, seen her dying. O willingly, my wife, I would lie down in your tomb. But I have no deserts like yours, no such purity, or singleness of heart. Pray for me Ellen & raise the friend you so truly loved, to be what you thought him . . . . Not for the world would I have left you here alone; stay by me & lead me upward. Reunite us, o thou Father of our Spirits.*

Not long after this, the young, heart-broken widower attempted to express his grief in verse.

> *Dost thou not hear me Ellen*
> *Is thy ear deaf to me*
> *Is thy radiant eye*
> *Dark that it cannot see*
>
> *In yonder ground thy limbs are laid*
> *Under the snow*
> *And earth has no spot so dear above*
> *As that below*
>
> *And there I know the heart is still*
> *And the eye is shut & the ear is dull*

But the spirit that dwelt in mine
The spirit wherein mine dwelt
The soul of Ellen the thought divine
From God, that came—for all that felt
Does it not know me now
Does it not share my thought
Is it prisoned from Waldo's prayer

Is its glowing love forgot

During this period of intense mourning Emerson turned to his Unitarian faith for comfort. He found that faith wanting. What he soon came to realize was that his religion was a hollow affair, a matter of the head mostly, and not the heart. As such, it was no faith at all. Years of studying theology at Harvard had filled his mind with a load of learned lumber, but his heart was empty. He became increasingly despondent. In his journal in April he wrote, "The days go by, griefs, & simpers, & sloth & disappointments. The dead do not return, & sometimes we are negligent of their image. Not of yours Ellen— I know too well who is gone from me."

At the same time, he became more and more dissatisfied with his church. His heart was torn by grief and he felt an excruciating sense of loss, but his formulaic religion could not bind this wound. In an increasingly somber mood, he began to refer in his journal to "the icehouse of Unitarianism." He also felt somewhat hypocritical in his ministerial role. How could he serve a church that he no longer believed in? How could he participate in rituals like the Communion Service if he felt them to be mere mechanical exercises? In his journal he confronted the issue squarely.

June 2, 1832. Cold cold.

Thermometer Says Temperate Yet
a week of moral excitement. It is
years & nations that guide my
pen. I have sometimes thought
that in order to be a good minister
it was necessary to leave the

ministry. The profession is antiquated. In an altered age we worship in the dead forms of our forefathers. Were not a Socratic paganism better than an effete superannuated [i.e. outmoded] Christianity? Does not every shade of thought have its own tone so that wooden voices denote wooden minds? Whatever there is of Authority in religion is that which the mind does not animate.

FINDING GOD AND LOVE IN THE WORLD

In the face of this looming emotional and spiritual crisis, Emerson withdrew to the one source of comfort that was still available to him, the natural world, the living God's creation. He retreated from Boston to the White Mountains in New Hampshire. There he found himself in contact with a living divinity, a stark contrast to the deadness of his church. Earlier in his journals he had observed, *"So love of nature. The soul & the body of things are harmonized, therefore, the deeper one knoweth the soul, the more intense is the love of outward nature in him."*

Through his passionate love for Ellen Tucker, Emerson had discovered the divine source of love itself. It ravished both his body and his soul. This combination of the sensual and the spiritual would be of enormous importance to his understanding of the interrelationship of personal and cosmic love. He would discover that one both reflects and leads to the other. The body is the conduit and the instrument of the soul. Nature is the embodiment of God. Later, he would write in his work **Nature** (1836), *"We are as much strangers in nature, as we are aliens from God."* In the mountains of New Hampshire, Emerson found himself face to face with this majestic *"First Cause."*

> *The good of going into the mountains is that life is reconsidered; it is far from the slavery of your own modes of living . . . . He who believes in the wood-loving muses must woo them here. And he who believes in the reality of his soul will therein find inspiration & muses & God & will come out here to undress himself of pedantry & judge righteous judgment & worship the First Cause*

This experience would help him to find a resolution to his crisis of faith. Shortly after, Emerson returned to Boston and promptly resigned his position at the Second Church. He put his furniture in storage and sailed for Europe. While there, he would continue

Personal Love and Cosmic Love

to draw closer to the divinity that he had come to discover in his own heart, in the common heart of humanity, and in all of creation. He found this spiritual dynamic expressed exquisitely in the magnificent cathedrals of Europe, especially St. Peter's in Rome. In his journal he wrote the following.

> *I love St. Peter's Church. It grieves me that after a few days I shall see it no more. It has a peculiar smell from the quantity of incense burned in it. The music that is heard in it is always good & the eye is always charmed. It is an ornament of the earth. It is not grand, it is so rich & pleasing; it should rather be called the sublime of the beautiful.*

Later he would discern this same sublime divinity in the cathedral-like woods near his home in Concord. Not long after he returned home he recorded the following in his journal. *"Fine walk this P.M. in the woods with C,"* he notes, *"beautiful Gothic arches yes & cathedral windows as of stained glass formed by the interlaced branches against the grey & gold of the western sky. We came to a little pond in the bosom of the hills, with echoing shores."*

By the time he returned to America in 1833, Emerson had pretty much worked out the general outline of his new, Transcendental faith, which he referred to in his journal as "this new thing." He soon launched himself on a new career as a public speaker. From the podium, in lecture after lecture, he proclaimed his new truth. He soon discovered that audiences would eagerly accept in a lecture on Monday sentiments that they would have roundly condemned as heresy if announced in any church the day before. Emerson was pleased with his initial success in covertly preaching a new faith. He came to consider the lecture platform "the new pulpit of the age."

COSMIC LOVE AND PERSONAL LOVE

While establishing himself in his new role as a secular preacher of Transcendental divinity, Emerson met and married Lydia Jackson in September, 1835. She was a year older than him (he was now thirty-two), and their brief courtship did not reflect the youthful passion of his first engagement. But he loved Lidian (as he would later call her) deeply. This mature love undoubtedly reflected his new understanding of the depth and meaning of personal, romantic love as a connecting link to a broader and all-encompassing cosmic love.

This is clearly suggested in the letter that Waldo sent to Lidian wherein he first proposed to her. "I obey my highest impulses," he explained, "in declaring to you the feeling of deep and tender respect with which you have inspired me. I am rejoiced in my Reason as well as in my Understanding by finding an earnest and noble mind whose presence quickens in mine all that is good and shames and repels from me my own weakness. Can I resist the impulse to beseech you to love me?" The terms he uses here, "Reason" and "Understanding," are key to Emerson's new Transcendental philosophy. He borrowed the terms from the German philosopher Immanuel Kant (1724-1804). "Reason" relates to intuition and feeling while "Understanding" refers to logic and what we normally call reason. What Emerson was telling Lidian, then, was that his love for her filled both his head and his heart, the ultimate Transcendental ideal.

In the course of his forty-seven year marriage to Lidian (or "Queenie," his pet name for her), the two would endure many hardships and trials. Just two years after they were married, Waldo became the subject of bitter public controversy and scorn because of his criticism of the educational establishment at Harvard College as well as his apparent betrayal of the Unitarian church (as expressed in a presentation at the Divinity School there which was discussed in Chapter One). During this turbulent and painful time, he turned to Lidian for emotional support. She did not fail him. In his journal at the time he recorded the following.

Personal Love and Cosmic Love

> **Blessed be the wife that in the talk tonight shared no vulgar [i.e. common] sentiment, but said, "In the gossip & excitement of the hour, be as one blind & deaf to it. Know it not. Do as if nothing had befallen."— And when it was said by [a] friend, "The end is not yet: wait till it is done"; she said "It is done in Eternity." Blessed be the wife!**

Throughout the many volumes of his personal journals, Emerson often alludes to what "Queenie" thought or said. It is clear that she was a mainstay of his life. Throughout their marriage, they found in one another a sustaining source of strength that was at once emotional and spiritual, personal and cosmic, reflective of this world and suggestive of the next. It was an ideal that Emerson expressed in his observation that a true marriage reached a level of spiritual harmony that pointed towards, and was a reflection of, the sublime. It far exceeds the mere infatuation that often signals the beginning of a relationship. This initial, impulsive love, as Emerson once noted, is temporary. It is in the enduring context of marriage, a relationship characterized by deep commitment, that personal love actually reaches its perfection.

> **Love is temporary & ends with marriage. Marriage is the perfection which love aimed at, ignorant of what it sought. Marriage is a good known only to the parties. A relation of perfect understanding, aid, contentment, possession of themselves & of the world.,— which dwarfs love to green fruit.**

TRANSCENDENT LOVE AND MARRIAGE

Emerson gives fullest expression of his views on marriage and love in an essay appropriately titled, *"Love."* Although Emerson's references throughout the work are to relationships between women and men (which was the public if not the private standard of his time), what he says of love between persons applies to all authentic relationships without regard to gender. His essay was published in his very first collection of essays in 1841. Obviously, the subject was important to him, even though he realized that some might consider it an unusual choice for a person known largely as an "intellectual." He states early on in the essay, *"I have been told that in some public discourses of mine my reverence for the intellect has made me unjustly cold to the personal relations."* As Emerson goes on to demonstrate, however, nothing could be further from the truth. Love, not intellect, he insists, is the life blood of our existence. All personal, social, and spiritual relationships rest on this foundation. Certainly it is his own experience that he describes in the following passage from the essay.

> *Every promise of the soul has innumerable fulfilments; each of its joys ripens into a new want. Nature, uncontainable, flowing, forelooking, in the first sentiment of kindness anticipates already a benevolence which shall lose all particular regards in its general light. The introduction to this felicity is in a private and tender relation of one to one, which is the enchantment of human life; which, like a certain divine rage and enthusiasm, seizes on man at one period and works a revolution in his mind and body; unites him to his race, pledges him to the domestic and civic relations, carries him with new sympathy into nature, enhances the power of the senses, opens the imagination, adds to his character heroic and sacred attributes,*

Personal Love and Cosmic Love

establishes marriage and gives permanence to human society.

Emerson's point here is that the experience of love leads to the expression of courage and virtue. The power of love prompts us to look beyond the self in caring for others. This caring eventually assumes *"heroic and sacred attributes."* Ego is diminished and love for others grows. What began as personal affection eventually expands to cosmic love. In the process, every individual becomes linked to the *"universal heart of all."* Emerson observes that, while youths may be skeptical of a mature man speaking thus of the power and passion of love, it is only in our maturity that we come to know love in *"a nobler"* form.

The natural association of the sentiment of love with the heyday of the blood seems to require that in order to portray it in vivid tints, which every youth and maid should confess to be true to their throbbing experience, one must not be too old. The delicious fancies of youth reject the least savor of a mature philosophy, as chilling with age and pedantry their purple bloom. And therefore I know I incur the imputation of unnecessary hardness and stoicism from those who compose the Court and Parliament of Love. But from these formidable censors I shall appeal to my seniors. For it is to be considered that this passion of which we speak, though it begin with the young, yet forsakes not the old, or rather suffers [i.e. allows] no one who is its servant to grow old, but makes the aged participators of it not less than the tender maiden, though in a different and nobler sort. For it is a fire that kindling its first embers in the narrow nook of a private bosom, caught from a wandering spark out of another private heart, glows and enlarges until it warms

> *and beams upon multitudes of men and women, upon the universal heart of all, and so lights up the whole world and all nature with its generous flames. It matters not therefore whether we attempt to describe the passion at twenty, thirty, or at eighty years. He who paints it at the first period will lose some of its later, he who paints it at the last, some of its earlier traits. Only it is to be hoped that by patience and the Muses' aid we may attain to that inward view of the law which shall describe a truth ever young and beautiful, so central that it shall commend itself to the eye at whatever angle beholden.*

Not surprisingly, in Emerson's time, as in our own, romantic love was a topic of endless interest. The number of songs, plays, stories, poems, novels (and now films and TV Soap Operas) that deal with the subject of romance are legion. This fact in itself is ample proof of the subject's enduring importance to the human species. The *"novels of passion"* in Emerson's day testified to the notion that we all *"take warmest interest in the development of the romance."* Even in societies torn by war, terror, and strife, weddings and wedding celebrations testify to the triumph of love over hate and life over death. As Emerson observes, "boy meets girl" (or person meets person) is a timeless and irresistible story, no matter how difficult the circumstances.

> *The strong bent of nature is seen in the proportion which this topic of personal relations usurps in the conversation of society. What do we wish to know of any worthy person so much as how he has sped in the history of this sentiment? What books in the circulating library circulate? How we glow over these novels of passion, when the story is told with any spark of truth and nature! And what fastens attention, in the*

intercourse of life, like any passage betraying affection between two parties? Perhaps we never saw them before and never shall meet them again. But we see them exchange a glance or betray a deep emotion, and we are no longer strangers. We understand them and take the warmest interest in the development of the romance. All mankind love a lover.

The beginnings of love serve to refine and improve character. Idle chatter is the natural prelude to the discovery of a "sincere and sweet mate," a truly significant other.

The earliest demonstrations of complacency and kindness are nature's most winning pictures. It is the dawn of civility and grace in the coarse and rustic. The rude village boy teases the girls about the school-house door;—but to-day he comes running into the entry and meets one fair child disposing her satchel; he holds her books to help her, and instantly it seems to him as if she removed herself from him infinitely, and was a sacred precinct. Among the throng of girls he runs rudely enough, but one alone distances him; and these two little neighbors, that were so close just now, have learned to respect each other's personality. Or who can avert his eyes from the engaging, half-artful, half-artless ways of school-girls who go into the country shops to buy a skein of silk or a sheet of paper, and talk half an hour about nothing with the broad-faced, good-natured shop-boy. In the village they are on a perfect equality, which love delights in, and without any coquetry the happy, affectionate nature of woman flows out in this pretty gossip. The girls may have little beauty, yet

> *plainly do they establish between them and the good boy the most agreeable, confiding relations; what with their fun and their earnest, about Edgar and Jonas and Almira, and who was invited to the party, and who danced at the dancing-school, and when the singing-school would begin, and other nothings concerning which the parties cooed. By and by that boy wants a wife, and very truly and heartily will he know where to find a sincere and sweet mate....*

As Emerson knew personally, the early experience of love is joyful and life-affirming. It brings to light, more than any other experience, the sublime beauty of life, which leads naturally to other important developments. Love is the source of all artistic feelings and all artistic expression. Indeed, all other experiences of life seem to pale by comparison to the experience of romantic love.

> *But be our experience in particulars what it may, no man ever forgot the visitations of that power to his heart and brain, which created all things anew; which was the dawn in him of music, poetry and art; which made the face of nature radiant with purple light, the morning and the night varied enchantments; when a single tone of one voice could make the heart bound, and the most trivial circumstance associated with one form is put in the amber of memory; when he became all eye when one was present, and all memory when one was gone; when the youth becomes a watcher of windows and studious of a glove, a veil, a ribbon, or the wheels of a carriage; when no place is too solitary and none too silent for him who has richer company and sweeter conversation in his new thoughts than*

any old friends, though best and purest, can give him; for the figures, the motions, the words of the beloved object are not, like other images, written in water, but, as Plutarch said, "enamelled in fire," and make the study of midnight:—

> *"Thou art not gone being gone,*
> *where'er thou art,*
> *Thou leav'st in him thy watchful eyes,*
> *in him thy loving heart."*

In the noon and the afternoon of life we still throb at the recollection of days when happiness was not happy enough, but must be drugged with the relish of pain and fear; for he touched the secret of the matter who said of love,—

> *"All other pleasures are not worth its pains:"*

and when the day was not long enough, but the night too must be consumed in keen recollections; when the head boiled all night on the pillow with the generous deed it resolved on; when the moonlight was a pleasing fever and the stars were letters and the flowers ciphers and the air was coined into song; when all business seemed an impertinence, and all the men and women running to and fro in the streets, mere pictures.

This personal experience of love, longing, and sacrifice enhances our sense of self and the essential dignity and value of life. It makes us more than what we were as it reveals the presence of a divine element in our being.

LOVE IS THE SOURCE OF HUMAN NOBILITY, VIRTUE, AND BEAUTY

Love elevates and ennobles even the most ordinary persons because it touches their souls. Through the experience of love, we are reborn as new and better persons, more sensitive, courageous, and virtuous. The power of love makes us capable of heroic acts of courage and self-sacrifice. We become aware of something within us that is greater than ourselves, that defines us as agents of a greater good. We become better than we have ever known ourselves to be.

> *The like force [of love] has the passion over all his nature. It expands the sentiment; it makes the clown [i.e. an uncultivated person] gentle and gives the coward heart. Into the most pitiful and abject it will infuse a heart and courage to defy the world, so only it have the countenance of the beloved object. In giving him to another it still more gives him to himself. He is a new man, with new perceptions, new and keener purposes, and a religious solemnity of character and aims. He does not longer appertain to his family and society; he is some[thing]; he is a person; he is a soul.*

The beauty that is revealed by love, especially by the love of one person for another, is a reflection of ideal beauty and virtue. Through a lover's eyes, the appearance of that special other, no matter how common or ordinary to the rest of the world, suggests "relations of transcendent delicacy and sweetness, . . . what roses and violets hint and foreshadow."

Like a tree in flower, so much soft, budding, informing loveliness is society for itself; and she teaches his eye why Beauty was pictured with Loves and Graces attending her steps. Her existence makes the world rich. Though she extrudes all other persons from his attention as cheap and unworthy, she indemnifies him by carrying out her own being into some[thing] impersonal, large, mundane, so that the maiden stands to him for a representative of all select [i.e. special] things and virtues. For that reason the lover never sees personal resemblances in his mistress to her kindred or to others. His friends find in her a likeness to her mother, or her sisters, or to persons not of her blood. The lover sees no resemblance except to summer evenings and diamond mornings, to rainbows and the song of birds.

The beauty of a lover hints at that divine power that is the source of all beauty, all love, and all life. Its voice speaks to us in whispers that are but the distant echoes of the infinite sublime. Emerson thus describes the mystery of love.

The ancients called beauty the flowering of virtue. Who can analyze the nameless charm which glances from one and another face and form? We are touched with emotions of tenderness and complacency, but we cannot find whereat this dainty emotion, this wandering gleam, points. It is destroyed for the imagination by any attempt to refer it to organization. Nor does it point to any relations of friendship or love known and described in society, but, as it seems to me, to a quite other and unattainable sphere, to relations of transcendent delicacy and sweetness, to what roses and violets hint and foreshow. We cannot approach beauty. Its nature is like opaline doves'-neck lustres, hovering and evanescent. Herein it resembles the most excellent things, which all have this rainbow character, defying all attempts at appropriation and use. What else did Jean Paul Richter signify, when he said to music, "Away! away! thou speakest to me of things which in all my endless life I have not found and shall not find." The same fluency may be observed in every work of the plastic arts. The statue is then beautiful when it begins to be incomprehensible, when it is passing out of criticism and can no longer be defined by compass and measuring-wand, but demands an active imagination to go with it and to say what it is in the act of doing. The god or hero of the sculptor is always represented in a transition from that which is representable to the senses, to that which is not. Then first it ceases to be a stone. The same remark holds of painting. And of poetry the success is not attained when it lulls and satisfies, but when it astonishes and fires us with new endeavors after the unattainable. Concerning it Landor inquires "whether it is not to be referred to some purer state of sensation and existence."

The love that we feel at the sight of our special loved one hints at and points towards an indescribable sublimity of which we are a part, but which we can never fully or completely possess. Our particular feeling is but a single ripple on the surface of infinity.

In like manner, personal beauty is then first charming and itself when it dissatisfies us with any end; when it becomes a story without an end; when it suggests gleams and visions and not earthly satisfactions; when it makes the beholder feel his unworthiness; when he cannot feel his right to it, though he were Caesar; he cannot feel more right to it than to the firmament and the splendors of a sunset.

LOVING ANOTHER AS A MEANS OF SELF RENEWAL

The beauty that is the object of love is not merely physical. To see it as such would lead to *"nothing but sorrow"* and disappointment. The beauty of true love is transcendent. It involves the union of body and soul. This union, in turn, leads to the formation of a new and better self for each. For Emerson the Transcendentalist, the never-ending improvement of human character though the practice of "self-culture" is naturally aided by a loving relationship with another. Through this unique intimacy, we help each other to improve because we *"are now able, without offense, to indicate blemishes and hindrances to each other, and to give each all help and comfort in curing the same."*

Because she enjoys a special position of trust, a wife (or any committed, significant other) can tell her husband things that he would never accept from anyone else. And he can do the same for her. The result is a better, more beautiful and loving character for both. This, in turn, allows each to be more discerning of the true and the good in society and in other human beings generally. The personal goodness we see in that special other and which that special other sees in us is a reflection of the great Soul, the Divinity that is the source of all life and goodness. It is through the love of another that we *"ascend to the highest beauty, to the love and knowledge of the Divinity."*

If however, from too much conversing with material objects, the soul was gross, and misplaced its satisfaction in the body, it reaped nothing but sorrow; body being unable to fulfil the promise which beauty holds out; but if, accepting the hint of these visions and suggestions which beauty makes to his mind, the soul passes through the body and falls to admire strokes of character, and the lovers contemplate one another in their discourses and their actions, then they pass to the true palace of beauty, more

Personal Love and Cosmic Love

> *and more inflame their love of it, and by this love extinguishing the base affection, as the sun puts out fire by shining on the hearth, they become pure and hallowed. By conversation with that which is in itself excellent, magnanimous, lowly, and just, the lover comes to a warmer love of these nobilities, and a quicker apprehension of them. Then he passes from loving them in one to loving them in all, and so is the one beautiful soul only the door through which he enters to the society of all true and pure souls. In the particular society of his mate he attains a clearer sight of any spot, any taint which her beauty has contracted from this world, and is able to point it out, and this with mutual joy that they are now able, without offence, to indicate blemishes and hindrances in each other, and give to each all help and comfort in curing the same. And beholding in many souls the traits of the divine beauty, and separating in each soul that which is divine from the taint which it has contracted in the world, the lover ascends to the highest beauty, to the love and knowledge of the Divinity, by steps on this ladder of created souls.*

The progress of love is a thing of beauty in itself. Love teaches us to care. It ennobles us. Eventually, we come to see others in somewhat the same light as those whom we hold closest to us. As we make our way on the journey of life, we accept responsibility for those closest to us, and from them to our extended family, and, finally, to the community at large. Our willingness to work hard, to sacrifice, and to act selflessly elevates us, and imbues us with strength and courage.

Ultimately, love is the glue that holds the family, society, and the universe itself together. The path, however, involves hardships. As a young couple sets out *"Danger, sorrow, and pain arrive to them, as to all."* Our personal imperfections are revealed along with our virtues. *"The angels that inhabit this temple of the body appear at the windows, and the gnomes and vices also."* But *"Love prays."* The true power of a loving relationship resides in the fact that the totality of its strength is always greater than the sum of its individual parts.

> *But this dream of love [between two people], though beautiful, is only one scene in our play. In the procession of the soul from within outward, it enlarges its circles ever, like the pebble thrown into the pond, or the light proceeding from an orb. The rays of the soul alight first on things nearest, on every utensil and toy, on nurses and domestics, on the house and yard and passengers, on the circle of household acquaintance, on politics and geography and history. But things are ever grouping themselves according to higher or more interior laws. Neighborhood, size, numbers, habits, persons, lose by degrees their power over us. Cause and effect, real affinities, the longing for harmony between the soul and the circumstance, the progressive, idealizing instinct, predominate later, and the step backward from the higher to the lower relations is impossible. Thus even love, which is the deification of persons, must become more impersonal every day. Of this at first it gives no hint. Little think the youth and maiden who are glancing at each other across crowded rooms with eyes so full of mutual intelligence, of the precious fruit long hereafter to proceed from this new, quite external stimulus.*

Personal Love and Cosmic Love

Every experience of personal, romantic love is reminiscent of Romeo and Juliet. That special someone becomes, for a time, the sole object of our being, the very center of our universe.

> *The work of vegetation begins first in the irritability [i.e. sensitivity] of the bark and leaf-buds. From exchanging glances, they advance to acts of courtesy, of gallantry, then to fiery passion, to plighting troth and marriage. Passion beholds its object as a perfect unit. The soul is wholly embodied, and the body is wholly ensouled:—*
>
> > *"Her pure and eloquent blood*
> > *Spoke in her cheeks, and so*
> > *distinctly wrought,*
> > *That one might almost say her*
> > *body thought. "*
>
> *Romeo, if dead, should be cut up into little stars to make the heavens fine. Life, with this pair, has no other aim, asks no more, than Juliet,—than Romeo. Night, day, studies, talents, kingdoms, religion, are all contained in this form full of soul, in this soul which is all form. The lovers delight in endearments, in avowals of love, in comparisons of their regards. When alone, they solace themselves with the remembered image of the other. Does that other see the same star, the same melting cloud, read the same book, feel the same emotion, that now delights me? They try and weigh their affection, and adding up costly advantages, friends, opportunities, properties, exult in discovering that willingly, joyfully, they would give all as a ransom for the beautiful, the beloved head, not one hair of which shall be harmed.*

But love cannot sustain this fever pitch. Eventually reality intrudes, our imperfections become apparent and adjustments must be made. But what remains at the end of this process is a greater appreciation for the "signs of loveliness, signs of virtue" that first attracted us. It is embraced now in a more mature way as a sign of the ultimate goodness and virtue that we seek to enact in our lives. We are now prepared to provide mutual support in reaching this loftier goal.

But the lot of humanity is on these children. Danger, sorrow and pain arrive to them as to all. Love prays. It makes covenants with Eternal Power in behalf of this dear mate. The union which is thus effected and which adds a new value to every atom in nature—for it transmutes every thread throughout the whole web of relation into a golden ray, and bathes the soul in a new and sweeter element—is yet a temporary state. Not always can flowers, pearls, poetry, protestations, nor even home in another heart, content the awful [i.e. filled with awe] soul that dwells in clay. It arouses itself at last from these endearments, as toys, and puts on the harness and aspires to vast and universal aims. The soul which is in the soul of each, craving a perfect beatitude, detects incongruities, defects and disproportion in the behavior of the other. Hence arise surprise, expostulation and pain. Yet that which drew them to each other was signs of loveliness, signs of virtue; and these virtues are there, however eclipsed. They appear and reappear and continue to attract; but the regard changes, quits the sign and attaches to the substance. This repairs the wounded affection. Meantime, as life wears on, it proves a game of permutation and combination of all possible positions of the parties, to

Personal Love and Cosmic Love

employ all the resources of each and acquaint each with the strength and weakness of the other. For it is the nature and end of this relation, that they should represent the human race to each other. All that is in the world, which is or ought to be known, is cunningly wrought into the texture of man, of woman:—

*"The person love does to us fit,
Like manna, has the taste of all in it."*

The world rolls; the circumstances vary every hour. The angels that inhabit this temple of the body appear at the windows, and the gnomes and vices also. By all the virtues they are united. If there be virtue, all the vices are known as such; they confess and flee. Their once flaming regard is sobered by time in either breast, and losing in violence what it gains in extent, it becomes a thorough good understanding. They resign each other without complaint to the good offices which man and woman are severally appointed to discharge in time, and exchange the passion which once could not lose sight of its object, for a cheerful disengaged furtherance, whether present or absent, of each other's designs. At last they discover that all which at first drew them together,—those once sacred features, that magical play of charms,— was deciduous, [i.e. for a season] had a prospective end, like the scaffolding by which the house was built; and the purification of the intellect [i.e. mind] and the heart from year to year is the real marriage, foreseen and prepared from the first, and wholly above their

consciousness. Looking at these aims with which two persons, a man and a woman, so variously and correlatively gifted, are shut up in one house to spend in the nuptial society forty or fifty years, I do not wonder at the emphasis with which the heart prophesies this crisis [i.e. significant event*] **from early infancy, at the profuse beauty with which the instincts deck the nuptial bower, and nature and intellect and art emulate each other in the gifts and the melody they bring to the epithalamium [**i.e. song in honor of a bride*].*

Personal Love and Cosmic Love

THE ULTIMATE OBJECT OF LOVE IS GOD

For Emerson, the ultimate end of love is a more complete communion with the "great Soul," the divinity that is the source of all life and all love. Through the course of marriage, as through the course of life, *"the progress of the soul"* emerges. At the end of our lives, lives that include sacrifice and love, joy and sorrow, procreation and death, we will finally lose our *"finite character and blend with God."* This is the ultimate consummation of a life well-lived, a life of personal love that was but *"training"* for that highest love.

Thus are we put in training for a love which knows not sex, nor person, nor partiality, but which seeks virtue and wisdom everywhere, to the end of increasing virtue and wisdom. We are by nature observers, and thereby learners. That is our permanent state. But we are often made to feel that our affections are but tents of a night. Though slowly and with pain, the objects of the affections change, as the objects of thought do. There are moments when the affections rule and absorb the man and make his happiness dependent on a person or persons. But in health the mind is presently seen again,—its overarching vault, bright with galaxies of immutable lights, and the warm loves and fears, that swept over us as clouds, must lose their finite character and blend with God, to attain their own perfection. But we need not fear that we can lose any thing by the progress of the soul. The soul may be trusted to the end. That which is so beautiful and attractive as these relations, must be succeeded and supplanted only by what is more beautiful, and so on for ever.

Emerson expresses his view of the integral and dynamic relationship between personal love and cosmic love in a poem appropriately titled *"Give All to Love."* In this poem, he speaks of the pervasive presence and power of love in our lives. He also describes the progress of love from individual romance to consummation in the eternal. As he makes clear in his essay, personal romantic love is a stepping stone to that all-encompassing, transcendent, cosmic love that is the very essence of life. Because of this, true love is always centrifugal and ascendant. It leads us onward and upward. Cupid is only a minor god who serves but to introduce his master. Hence, *"When half-gods go,/ The gods arrive."*

GIVE ALL TO LOVE

Give all to love;
Obey thy heart;
Friends, kindred, days,
Estate, good-fame,
Plans, credit and the Muse,—
Nothing refuse.
'T is a brave master;
Let it have scope:
Follow it utterly,
Hope beyond hope:
High and more high
It dives into noon,
With wing unspent,
Untold intent;
But it is a god,
Knows its own path
And the outlets of the sky.
It was never for the mean;
It requireth courage stout.
Souls above doubt,
Valor unbending,
It will reward,—
They shall return
More than they were,
And ever ascending.
Leave all for love;

Personal Love and Cosmic Love

Yet, hear me, yet,
One word more thy heart behoved,
One pulse more of firm endeavor,—
Keep thee to-day,
To-morrow, forever,
Free as an Arab
Of thy beloved.
Cling with life to the maid;
But when the surprise,
First vague shadow of surmise
Flits across her bosom young,
Of a joy apart from thee,
Free be she, fancy-free;
Nor thou detain her vesture's hem,
Nor the palest rose she flung
From her summer diadem.

Though thou loved her as thyself,
As a self of purer clay,
Though her parting dims the day,
Stealing grace from all alive;
Heartily know,
When half-gods go,
The gods arrive.

THE EMBODIMENT OF SPIRIT: TRANSCENDENTAL SEX

Although Victorian propriety and his own natural reticence deterred Emerson from speaking explicitly about human sexuality, the implications of his Transcendental philosophy in this regard are clear. He saw all of life as a dynamic combination of body and soul, flesh and spirit. For Emerson, *"The soul is wholly embodied, and the body is wholly ensouled."* The physical is infused with the spiritual. To be close to nature is to be close to God. The spirit abides in nature and in us. We sometimes loose sight of the fact that humanity itself is an essential element of the natural world. Communion with nature, therefore, includes communion with other human beings. Sexual intercourse is a particularly profound, and profoundly important, form of this communion. For Transcendentalists, sexuality possesses both a physical and a spiritual dimension.

Emerson was raised in the Christian religious tradition. The central sacramental ritual in this religion is the Communion Service or the Sacrament of the Eucharist. In this ritual, the body and blood of Christ are consumed by the communicant. In some Christian denominations, such as Roman Catholicism, this consummation is held to be literal, not merely symbolic. According to the principle of Transubstantiation, the bread and wine used in the service are miraculously and mysteriously transformed into the actual body and blood of Christ before they are consumed. The common principle in all versions of this tradition is the necessary union of the spirit and the flesh. Emerson eventually became dissatisfied with the Communion Service as practiced in the Unitarian church at the time. He felt that this once vital and meaningful ritual had become a mere routine, a mechanical exercise that had lost its spiritual charge.

As an alternative, he turned to nature and a spontaneous communion with the natural world where he found a continuous and ongoing miracle of spiritual renewal. By opening himself to this miracle, he became one with it. His individual ego was consumed by a ravishment of the soul as he became, in his own words, *"part or parcel of God."* This same consummation of spirit and overwhelming feeling of oneness and harmony are the

Personal Love and Cosmic Love

natural and ideal results of sexual union. While his Transcendental philosophy inevitably leads to the spiritualization of sexual union, Emerson himself only hints at it, as in his poem **"Eros—October."**

> *I cannot tell rude listeners*
> *Half the tell-tale South-wind said,—*
> *'T would bring the blushes of yon maples*
> *To a man and to a maid.*

There is, however, a marvelous example of the spiritual element in Transcendental sexuality and the sexual element in Transcendental spirituality in Walt Whitman's classic poem, "Song of Myself." Whitman was much admired by Emerson, who undoubtedly found in this self-proclaimed Bohemian a more robust and explicit articulation of his own Transcendental sensuality. He probably also sensed that Whitman possessed the kind of hermaphroditic personality that Transcendentalists considered ideal.

I believe in you my soul, the other I am must not abase
    itself to you,
And you must not be abased to the other.

Loafe with me on the grass, loose the stop from your
    throat,
Not words, not music or rhyme I want, not custom or
    lecture, not even the best,
Only the lull I like, the hum of your valved voice.

I mind how once we lay such a transparent summer
    morning,
How you settled your head athwart my hips and gently
    turn'd over upon me,
And parted the shirt from my bosom-bone, and plunged
    your tongue to my bare-stript heart,
And reach'd till you felt my beard, and reach'd till you
    held my feet.

Swiftly arose and spread around me the peace and
    knowledge that pass all the argument of the earth,

*And I know that the hand of God is the promise of my
own,
And I know that the spirit of God is the brother of my
own,
And that all the men ever born are also my brothers, and
the women my sisters and lovers,
And that a kelson of the creation is love, ...*

In this beautiful and poignant passage Whitman captures what Emerson acknowledged as the dramatic intermingling of the sensual and the spiritual in human experience. As the opening lines make clear, what follows is essentially a dialogue between body and soul. Each possesses the other, and the result of this is an overwhelming sense of oneness both with the Divine and with the entire human family. "All the men ever born are also my brothers, and the women my sisters and lovers." As noted earlier, this is precisely the kind of unifying, rapturous experience that Emerson described in his first major work, **Nature** (1836).

In his lifetime, Whitman was notorious for his frankness in acknowledging and celebrating the power of human sexuality. Because of this, contemporary literary critics and defenders of public morality reacted with a vengeance in condemning his "barbaric" and "obscene" verse. Other, more perceptive critics, however, noted that his poetry appeared to express, as one of them put it, a "mixture of Yankee transcendentalism and New York rowdyism." These latter critics were obviously responding to Whitman's unique blending of the spiritual and the sensual in his poems. Emerson was sensitive to this quality in Whitman, as was Thoreau. Early on, when he first became acquainted with Whitman's **Leaves of Grass** (1855), Emerson sent the then unknown poet a letter filled with praise, acknowledging him as one who is stands at "the threshold of a great career." Even later, when Whitman had become more or less notorious in polite circles, Emerson never backed off from his earlier estimate of his genius. He found in this Bohemian a Transcendental soul mate, a poet who expressed explicitly the full sensual and spiritual range of his own dynamic and transforming philosophy, especially the notion of sexual and spiritual harmony.

SEX AND THE HERMAPHRODITIC IDEAL

Like other Transcendentalists, Emerson believed that every individual possessed both male and female characteristics. Margaret Fuller expressed this concept succinctly in her revolutionary statement of Transcendental feminism, **Woman in the Nineteenth Century** (1845). There she observed that while "the especial genius of woman [is] . . . intuitive in function, spiritual in tendency," it is also true that "male and female represent two sides of the great radical dualism." As a result, "They are perpetually passing into one another. Fluid hardens to solid, solid rushes to fluid. There is no wholly masculine man, no purely feminine woman."

Emerson expressed the same notion in his journals. There he observed that "The finest people marry the two sexes in their own person. Hermaphrodite is then the symbol of the finished soul. It was agreed that in every act should appear the married pair: the two elements should mix in every act." It is because of this natural inclination that we seek in sexual relations that which completes us by correcting the imbalance of our natures and thus bringing about an ideal unity and perfect harmony. This is an ancient concept, as Emerson well knew. It is expressed beautifully, for example, in the **"The Ecstasy,"** by John Donne, one of Emerson's favorite seventeenth-century poets. Following a remarkable conversion, Donne also became one of the greatest preachers of his day. In the stanzas below, Donne describes a dialogue between lovers where the passionate speaker explains to his love that intercourse is a consummation devoutly to be wished because the spirit and the flesh naturally and mysteriously seek such a union.

But, O alas! so long, so far,
Our bodies why do we forbear?
They are ours, though not we ; we are
Th' intelligences, they the spheres.

We owe them thanks, because they thus
Did us, to us, at first convey,
Yielded their senses' force to us,
Nor are dross to us, but allay.

On man heaven's influence works not so,
But that it first imprints the air;
For soul into the soul may flow,
Though it to body first repair.

As our blood labours to beget
Spirits, as like souls as it can;
Because such fingers need to knit
That subtle knot, which makes us man;

So must pure lovers' souls descend
To affections, and to faculties,
Which sense may reach and apprehend,
Else a great prince in prison lies.

To our bodies turn we then, that so
Weak men on love reveal'd may look;
Love's mysteries in souls do grow,
But yet the body is his book.

Another famous seventeenth-century poet, and perhaps the one most admired by Emerson for his virtue as well as his art, was John Milton, the Puritan author of the epic **Paradise Lost** (1667). For Milton, as for Donne, and Emerson, and Whitman, sexuality and spirituality go hand-in-hand and lead the way to heaven. In *Book VIII* of the poem, the angel Raphael has been sent by God to a yet unfallen Paradise to speak with Adam about life and love. In what turns out to be a frank and candid discussion, Adam describes the delight he finds in his sexual relations with his newly-created Eve. He then asks Raphael how angels express love, and if there is sex in heaven. The angel, who blushes a "celestial rosy red" answers the question frankly. Angels, he reveals, not only have sex but their embrace is "total," an expression of the ultimate Emersonian ideal of harmony and oneness. Adam speaks first.

Personal Love and Cosmic Love

*To love, thou blamest me not; for Love, thou
    sayest,
Leads up to Heaven, is both the way and guide;
Bear with me then, if lawful what I ask:
Love not the heavenly Spirits, and how their
    love
Express they? by looks only? or do they mix
Irradiance, virtual or immediate touch?
To whom the Angel, with a smile that glowed
Celestial rosy red, Love's proper hue,
Answered. Let it suffice thee that thou knowest
Us happy, and without love no happiness.
Whatever pure thou in the body enjoyest,
(And pure thou wert created) we enjoy
In eminence; and obstacle find none
Of membrane, joint, or limb, exclusive bars;*

*Easier than air with air, if Spirits embrace,
Total they mix, union of pure with pure
Desiring, nor restrained conveyance need,
As flesh to mix with flesh, or soul with soul.*

    For Emerson and other Transcendentalists, sex is a sacrament through which human beings experience physical and spiritual fulfillment. Sexuality is not casual, is not a conquest or a competition. It is only through the honest giving of ourselves that we can receive that which completes us and makes us whole. As with all other aspects of human existence, sexuality is always a work in progress. Fulfillment is not instantaneous. Relationships deepen as trust grows. As we become ever more open and more vulnerable, we also become stronger and more confident. Eventually, and ideally, in those special moments of spiritual and physical coitus our ego dissolves in a sea of harmony and transcendent oneness. As Emerson notes in his essay **"Love,"** over time, through the growth of a loving relationship, partners are able to ennoble and complete one another, and in this ongoing process of refinement they reach higher and higher levels of oneness that, in turn, lead to a more perfect state of existence.

DEALING WITH DEATH AND DYING

Emerson understood that true love inevitably involves shared suffering and sacrifice. One of the greatest challenges faced by Lidian and Waldo was the death, at the tender age of five, of their first-born son. This tragic event came unexpectedly. One winter's day in January the young boy went out to enjoy a day of fun in the freshly-fallen snow. By the end of the day, he had developed a slight fever. The anxious parents put the boy to bed and hovered over him, doing what they could to comfort him, but the fever grew worse. Eventually it became clear that this was no mere mid-winter cold. The child had scarlet fever. In just three short days it claimed young Waldo's life. The event was devastating. Emerson had doted on this special child. His normally serious journals are dotted with references to his little boy's antics. In one such passage he observes,

> *Little Waldo cheers the whole house by his moving calls to the cat, to the birds, to the flies,— "Pussy cat come see Waddow! Liddel Birdy come see Waddo! Pies! pies! come see Waddo!"*

Lidian felt the same deep affection for her prodigy. "His mother shows us the two apples that his Grandfather gave him," Emerson writes, "which he brought home one in each hand & did not begin to eat till he nearly got home. 'See where the dear little Angel has gnawed them,' said Lidian. 'The are worth a barrel of apples that he has not touched.'" The death of young Waldo tested Emerson's faith as no event since Ellen's tragic passing eleven years earlier. At that time, he had only the comfort of "the icehouse Unitarianism," which proved to be cold comfort, indeed. Now he was a self-made Transcendentalist. Would his new faith carry him through this overwhelming tragedy?

Emerson's initial reaction to his son's death was stunned disbelief. He recorded Waldo's death in a brief entry on a single journal page dated 28 January, 1842. "*Yesterday night at 15 minutes after eight my little Waldo ended his life.*" This stark entry is followed by several blank pages, perhaps far more eloquent of his feelings than any words could possibly express at the time. Days later he wrote the following.

> *What he looked upon is better, what he looked not upon is insignificant. The morning of Friday I woke at 3 oclock, & every cock in every barnyard was shrilling with the most unnecessary noise. The sun went up the morning sky with all his light, but the landscape was dishonored by this loss. For this boy in whose remembrance I have both slept & awaked so oft, decorated for me the morning star, & the evening cloud, how much more all the particular of daily economy [i.e. everyday life]; for he had touched with his lively curiosity every trivial fact & circumstance in the household.*

He followed this with the observation that "Sorrow makes us all children again, destroys all differences of intellect. The wisest knows nothing." On the day of his son's death, Emerson wrote to his friend Margaret Fuller, "Shall I ever dare to love any thing again"?

Despite his deep and devastating sorrow, Emerson had to continue with the routine of life. His lecture engagements required him to travel to Providence, RI. From a distance, he tried to comfort his grieving wife.

> *And how art thou, Sad wifey? Have the clouds yet broken, & let in the sunlight? Alas! Alas! that one of your sorrows, that our one sorrow can never in this world depart from us! Well perhaps we shall never be frivolous again. . . . Meantime Ellen & Edith [his younger children] shall love you well, & fill all your time, and the remembrances of the Angel shall draw you to sublime thoughts.*

Emerson's Truth, Emerson's Wisdom

Five days later, Emerson wrote again to Lidian expressing his dismay that he had not heard from her in days. He questioned, "Well, is this to punish my philosophy? I must think then, must I? that it is mere idleness of mind that sets me to ask these gossiping questions?" Obviously, self-reliance has its limits, even for a philosopher of Emerson's stature. It is clear from his tone that he himself was deeply in need of the very comfort that he tried to offer. In speaking longingly of his lost child, he compared his forlorn feelings to those of his three-year-old daughter, who waited in vain for the return of her lost brother and playmate. "I look out the windows of the [train] cars for him," he says, "as Ellen does from the chamber window." Indeed, grief does make us all children again.

Emerson's acute sorrow over the loss of his son remained with him for some time. The image of the child, caught in the stillness of death, as he told Margaret Fuller two years later, *"often comes to me to tax the world with frivolity."* He tried to understand the meaning behind the loss of his precious son, but it remained largely an unsolved puzzle. He strove mightily to listen to the guiding voice within to find comfort and to comprehend the meaning of it all, *"but the inarticulateness of the Supreme Power,"* as he told Fuller, made it very difficult. The deadening numbness of the loss remained and depressed his spirit. As any other person might, Emerson wondered why, in a universe infused with the just and benevolent spirit of divine love, his beautiful and innocent child had been torn from him. Much, if not most, of Emerson's Transcendental philosophy was driven by the notion that we can trust our feelings as a means to discover truth. But his feelings now revealed only the devastation and pain of loss. How could this possibly be right? The answer would eventually emerge, but it would take time.

In his essay *"Experience,"* published two years after the event, Emerson gives expression to the dreamy melancholy and unreality of his loss.

> **Dream delivers us to dream, and there is no end to illusion. Life is a train of moods like a string of beads, and as we pass through them they prove to be many-**

Personal Love and Cosmic Love

colored lenses which paint the world their own hue, and each shows only what lies in its focus.

He once hoped that the suffering he endured would at least displace the haunting feeling that in life nothing is permanent or real, that all is but a dream. Ironically, his suffering only added to this disturbing and surreal effect. Clearly, this was Emerson's dark night of the soul.

There are moods in which we court suffering, in the hope that here at least we shall find reality, sharp peaks and edges of truth. But it turns out to be scene-painting and counterfeit. The only thing grief has taught me is to know how shallow it is. That, like all the rest, plays about the surface, and never introduces me into the reality, for contact with which we would even pay the costly price of sons and lovers. Was it Boscovich who found out that bodies never come in contact? Well, souls never touch their objects. An innavigable sea washes with silent waves between us and the things we aim at and converse with. Grief too will make us idealists. In the death of my son, now more than two years ago, I seem to have lost a beautiful estate,—no more. I cannot get it nearer to me. If to-morrow I should be informed of the bankruptcy of my principal debtors, the loss of my property would be a great inconvenience to me, perhaps, for many years; but it would leave me as it found me,—neither better nor worse. So is it with this calamity; it does not touch me; something which I fancied was a part of me, which could not be torn away without tearing me nor enlarged without enriching me, falls off from me and leaves no scar. It was caduceus [i.e. transitory]. I grieve that grief can teach me nothing, nor carry me one step into real nature. The Indian who was laid under a curse that the wind should not blow on him, nor water flow to him, nor fire burn him, is a type of us all. The dearest events are summer-rain, and we the Para [i.e. waterproof] coats that shed every drop. Nothing is left us now but death. We look to that with a grim satisfaction, saying, There at least is reality that will not dodge us.

For her part, Lidian continued to deal with bouts of depression that challenged both of them. In his journal, Waldo recorded her despairing words. *"Dear Husband,"* she said, *"I wish that I had never been born. I do not see how God can compensate me for the sorrow of existence."* Undoubtedly, it is feelings such as these that underlie Emerson's melancholic observation here that *"Every roof is agreeable to the eye until it is lifted; then we find tragedy and moaning women and hard-eyed husbands."*

Eventually, however, despite this heavy burden, Emerson began to feel the stirring of the great Soul within him. Not surprisingly, this occurred when he was in the woods, in the lap of nature. He had taken a manuscript there to review. The natural world had always been his cathedral of the spirit. While ensconced comfortably in the *"the armchair of the upturned root of a pine tree,"* as he reports in his journal, he *"felt for the first time since Waldo's death some efficient faith again in the repairs of the Universe, some independency of natural relations whilst spiritual affinities can be so perfect & compensating."* He also took comfort in the buoyant health and sprightliness of his two little daughters. In Edith, just six months old at the time of young Waldo's death, he witnessed a continuing affirmation of life and the spirit. *"The babe is not disconcerted,"* he observed. *"I delight in her eyes; they receive good humouredly everything that appears before them, but give way to nothing."*

Later, he records a similar reaction from Lidian.

Cheerfulness is so much the order of nature that the superabundant glee of a child lying on its back & not yet strong enough to get up or to sit up, yet cooing, warbling, laughing, screaming joy is an image of independence which makes power no part of independence. Queenie looks at Edie kicking up both feet into the air & thinks that Edie says "The world was made on purpose to carry round the little baby; and the world goes round the sun only to bring titty-time and creeping-on-the-floor-time to the Baby."

The innocence and sheer joyfulness of the infant reminded Emerson of the irrepressible power of divine love that informs our lives and insures that we can endure, no matter how great the loss or severe the challenge. The great Soul had spoken eloquently through the tiny and precious life of his infant daughter.

TRANSCENDENTAL FAITH AND THE TRIUMPH OF LIFE OVER DEATH

Emerson's long struggle in coming to grips with the death of his son, and the eventual triumph of his Transcendental faith, are movingly described, and re-enacted, in his poem, *"Threnody"* (which is Greek for elegy). There are two voices in dialogue in the poem. The first represents a grieving parent who has lost his son and cannot comprehend the cosmic justice of such a tragedy. The poem opens with a description of the abundant vitality that animates the natural world. However, the speaker is unable to appreciate the beauty of the landscape because he mourns for "The darling who shall not return." Following a moving description of the happy events and circumstances of the boy's living existence is the painfully blunt statement, *"But the deep-eyed boy is gone."*

THRENODY

*The South-wind brings
Life, sunshine and desire,
And on every mount and meadow
Breathes aromatic fire;
But over the dead he has no power,
The lost, the lost, he cannot restore;
And, looking over the hills, I mourn
The darling who shall not return.
I see my empty house,
I see my trees repair their boughs;
And he, the wondrous child,
Whose silver warble wild
Outvalued every pulsing sound
Within the air's cerulean round,—
The hyacinthine boy, for whom
Morn well might break and April bloom,
The gracious boy, who did adorn
The world whereinto he was born,
And by his countenance repay
The favor of the loving Day,—
Has disappeared from the Day's eye;
Far and wide she cannot find him;*

Personal Love and Cosmic Love

My hopes pursue, they cannot bind him.
Returned this day, the South-wind searches,
And finds young pines and budding birches;
But finds not the budding man;
Nature, who lost, cannot remake him;
Fate let him fall, Fate can't retake him;
Nature, Fate, men, him seek in vain.
And whither now, my truant wise and sweet,
O, whither tend thy feet?
I had the right, few days ago,
Thy steps to watch, thy place to know:
How have I forfeited the right?
Hast thou forgot me in a new delight?
I hearken for thy household cheer,
O eloquent child!
Whose voice, an equal messenger,
Conveyed thy meaning mild.
What though the pains and joys
Whereof it spoke were toys
Fitting his age and ken,
Yet fairest dames and bearded men,
Who heard the sweet request,
So gentle, wise and grave,
Bended with joy to his behest
And let the world's affairs go by,
A while to share his cordial game,
Or mend his wicker wagon-frame,
Still plotting how their hungry ear
That winsome voice again might hear;
For his lips could well pronounce
Words that were persuasions.
Gentlest guardians marked serene
His early hope, his liberal mien;
Took counsel from his guiding eyes
To make this wisdom earthly wise.
Ah, vainly do these eyes recall
The school-march, each day's festival,
When every morn my bosom glowed
To watch the convoy on the road;
The babe in willow wagon closed,
With rolling eyes and face composed;

With children forward and behind,
Like Cupids studiously inclined;
And he the chieftain paced beside,
The centre of the troop allied,
With sunny face of sweet repose,
To guard the babe from fancied foes.
The little captain innocent
Took the eye with him as he went;
Each village senior paused to scan
And speak the lovely caravan.
From the window I look out
To mark thy beautiful parade,
Stately marching in cap and coat
To some tune by fairies played;—
A music heard by thee alone
To works as noble led thee on.
Now Love and Pride, alas! in vain,
Up and down their glances strain.
The painted sled stands where it stood;
The kennel by the corded wood;
His gathered sticks to stanch the wall
Of the snow-tower, when snow should fall;
The ominous hole he dug in the sand,
And childhood's castles built or planned;
His daily haunts I well discern,—
The poultry-yard, the shed, the barn,—
And every inch of garden ground
Paced by the blessed feet around,
From the roadside to the brook
Whereinto he loved to look.
Step the meek fowls where erst they ranged;
The wintry garden lies unchanged;
The brook into the stream runs on;
But the deep-eyed boy is gone.

The sad fact of the child's loss colors the speaker's entire perception of nature, and he wonders aloud if *"Perchance not he but Nature ailed,/ The world and not the infant failed."* This sense of despair is pervasive as the trauma of the sorrowful event serves to bring *"the old order into doubt."*

Personal Love and Cosmic Love

On that shaded day,
Dark with more clouds than tempests are,
When thou didst yield thy innocent breath
In birdlike heavings unto death,
Night came, and Nature had not thee;
I said, 'We are mates in misery.'
The morrow dawned with needless glow;
Each snowbird chirped, each fowl must crow;
Each tramper started; but the feet
Of the most beautiful and sweet
Of human youth had left the hill
And garden,—they were bound and still.
There's not a sparrow or a wren,
There's not a blade of autumn grain,
Which the four seasons do not tend
And tides of life and increase lend;
And every chick of every bird,
And weed and rock-moss is preferred.
O ostrich-like forgetfulness!
O loss of larger in the less!
Was there no star that could be sent,
No watcher in the firmament,
No angel from the countless host
That loiters round the crystal coast,
Could stoop to heal that only child,
Nature's sweet marvel undefiled,
And keep the blossom of the earth,
Which all her harvests were not worth?
Not mine,—I never called thee mine,
But Nature's heir,—if I repine,
And seeing rashly torn and moved
Not what I made, but what I loved,
Grow early old with grief that thou
Must to the wastes of Nature go,—
'T is because a general hope
Was quenched, and all must doubt and grope.
For flattering planets seemed to say
This child should ills of ages stay,
By wondrous tongue, and guided pen,
Bring the flown Muses back to men.
Perchance not he but Nature ailed,

Emerson's Truth, Emerson's Wisdom

The world and not the infant failed.
It was not ripe yet to sustain
A genius of so fine a strain,
Who gazed upon the sun and moon
As if he came unto his own,
And, pregnant with his grander thought,
Brought the old order into doubt.
His beauty once their beauty tried;
They could not feed him, and he died,
And wandered backward as in scorn,
To wait an aeon to be born.
Ill day which made this beauty waste,
Plight broken, this high face defaced!
Some went and came about the dead;
And some in books of solace read;
Some to their friends the tidings say;
Some went to write, some went to pray;
One tarried here, there hurried one;
But their heart abode with none.
Covetous death bereaved us all,
To aggrandize one funeral.
The eager fate which carried thee
Took the largest part of me:
For this losing is true dying;
This is lordly man's down-lying,
This his slow but sure reclining,
Star by star his world resigning.
O child of paradise,
Boy who made dear his father's home,
In whose deep eyes
Men read the welfare of the times to come,
I am too much bereft.
The world dishonored thou hast left.
O truth's and nature's costly lie!
O trusted broken prophecy!
O richest fortune sourly crossed!
Born for the future, to the future lost!

At this point, the second voice in the poem, identified as the *"deep heart,"* speaks. He challenges the mourner to summon his faith and reminds him of the truth that is lodged deep within

Personal Love and Cosmic Love

his own heart. It is this voice that reaffirms the existence of a vital spirit that animates all reality, a power of eternal becoming that denies the momentary fact of death since death is not an end, but merely *"Pours finite into infinite."* It is only our conscious minds that perceive reality as static and fixed. In this limited dimension, death seems final, absolute, and tragic. It is exactly such short-sighted vision that this voice warns against when asking, *"Wilt thou freeze love's tidal flow,/ Whose streams through Nature circling go?"*

There is a dynamic unity in life that must be acknowledged, *"And many-seeming life is one,—/ Wilt thou transfix and make it none?"* The grieving parent is here reminded that heaven itself was not made *"stark and cold,"* a fixed and static entity, but rather it is *"a nest of bending reeds,/ Flowing grass and scented weeds."* The association of "heaven" with images drawn from nature affirms Emerson's continuing association of nature with the living spirit of divinity. Ultimately, the deep heart shows the mourning father that his son's existence must be comprehended in the context of a transpersonal, universal, and cyclic process of eternal being and becoming. Thus, while *"House and tenant go to ground,"* they are, *"Lost in God,"* but ultimately *"in Godhead found."* As the poem shows, Emerson finally came to see that little Waldo was not lost to him forever. He was simply now more fully a part of a sacred, cosmic and eternal life.

> **The deep Heart answered, 'Weepest thou?**
> **Worthier cause for passion wild**
> **If I had not taken the child.**
> **And deemest thou as those who pore,**
> **With aged eyes, short way before,—**
> **Think'st Beauty vanished from the coast**
> **Of matter, and thy darling lost?**
> **Taught he not thee—the man of eld,**
> **Whose eyes within his eyes beheld**
> **Heaven's numerous hierarchy span**
> **The mystic gulf from God to man?**
> **To be alone wilt thou begin**
> **When worlds of lovers hem thee in?**
> **To-morrow, when the masks shall fall**

Emerson's Truth, Emerson's Wisdom

That dizen Nature's carnival,
The pure shall see by their own will,
Which overflowing Love shall fill,
'T is not within the force of fate
The fate-conjoined to separate.
But thou, my votary, weepest thou?
I gave thee sight—where is it now?
I taught thy heart beyond the reach
Of ritual, bible, or of speech;
Wrote in thy mind's transparent table,
As far as the incommunicable;
Taught thee each private sign to raise
Lit by the supersolar blaze.
Past utterance, and past belief,
And past the blasphemy of grief,
The mysteries of Nature's heart;
And though no Muse can these impart,
Throb thine with Nature's throbbing breast,
And all is clear from east to west.
'I came to thee as to a friend;
Dearest, to thee I did not send
Tutors, but a joyful eye,
Innocence that matched the sky,
Lovely locks, a form of wonder,
Laughter rich as woodland thunder,
That thou might'st entertain apart
The richest flowering of all art:
And, as the great all-loving Day
Through smallest chambers takes its way,
That thou might'st break thy daily bread
With prophet, savior and head;
That thou might'st cherish for thine own
The riches of sweet Mary's Son,
Boy-Rabbi, Israel's paragon.
And thoughtest thou such guest
Would in thy hall take up his rest?
Would rushing life forget her laws,
Fate's glowing revolution pause?
High omens ask diviner guess;
Not to be conned to tediousness
And know my higher gifts unbind

Personal Love and Cosmic Love

The zone that girds the incarnate mind.
When the scanty shores are full
With Thought's perilous, whirling pool;
When frail Nature can no more,
Then the Spirit strikes the hour:
My servant Death, with solving rite,
Pours finite into infinite.
Wilt thou freeze love's tidal flow,
Whose streams through Nature circling go?
Nail the wild star to its track
On the half-climbed zodiac?
Light is light which radiates,
Blood is blood which circulates,
Life is life which generates,
And many-seeming life is one,—
Wilt thou transfix and make it none?
Its onward force too starkly pent
In figure, bone and lineament?
Wilt thou, uncalled, interrogate,
Talker! the unreplying Fate?
Nor see the genius of the whole
Ascendant in the private soul,
Beckon it when to go and come,
Self-announced its hour of doom?
Fair the soul's recess and shrine,
Magic-built to last a season;
Masterpiece of love benign,
Fairer that expansive reason
Whose omen 't is, and sign.
Wilt thou not ope thy heart to know
What rainbows teach, and sunsets show?
Verdict which accumulates
From lengthening scroll of human fates,
Voice of earth to earth returned,
Prayers of saints that inly burned,—
Saying, What is excellent,
As God lives, is permanent;
Hearts are dust, hearts' loves remain;
Heart's love will meet thee again.
Revere the Maker; fetch thine eye
Up to his style, and manners of the sky.

Emerson's Truth, Emerson's Wisdom

Not of adamant and gold
Built he heaven stark and cold;
No, but a nest of bending reeds,
Flowering grass and scented weeds;
Or like a traveller's fleeing tent,
Or bow above the tempest bent;
Built of tears and sacred flames,
And virtue reaching to its aims;
Built of furtherance and pursuing,
Not of spent deeds, but of doing.
Silent rushes the swift Lord
Through ruined systems still restored,
Broadsowing, bleak and void to bless,
Plants with worlds the wilderness;
Waters with tears of ancient sorrow
Apples of Eden ripe to-morrow.
House and tenant go to ground,
Lost in God, in Godhead found.'

Personal Love and Cosmic Love

TRANSCENDENCE AND THE PAIN OF LOSS: THE VALUE AND MEANING OF SUFFERING

Most of us have at one time or another felt the pain of unanticipated loss such as Emerson experienced with the sudden and unexpected death of his son. These losses often strike like a hammer blow and leave us, for a time at least, benumbed. Emily Dickinson, a person who read and admired Emerson, captured this experience exquisitely in a poem that she never titled.

> *After great pain a formal feeling comes—*
> *The nerves sit ceremonious like tombs;*
> *The stiff Heart questions—was it He that bore?*
> *And yesterday—or centuries before?*
>
> *The feet, mechanical, go round*
> *A wooden way*
> *Of ground, or air, or ought,*
> *Regardless grown,*
> *A quartz contentment, like a stone.*
>
> *This is the hour of lead*
> *Remembered if outlived,*
> *As freezing persons recollect the snow—*
> *First chill, then stupor, then the letting go.*

Dickinson describes the devastating effects of loss while offering no promise of recovery from it. Emerson's Transcendental faith ultimately apprised him of the illusion of death, and it enabled him to overcome the emotional and spiritual devastation that the death of his son initially caused. Little Waldo was not lost, after all. He is still part of the "great Soul" from whence his being was derived. It is an intuition of a truth that Emerson had experienced some years before, when contemplating the inevitability of his own passing. In his journal, in 1837, he recorded the following.

> *"I said when I awoke, After some more sleepings & wakings I shall lie on this mattrass sick; then dead; and through my gay entry they will carry these bones.*

Where shall I be then? I lifted up my head and beheld the spotless light of the morning beaming up from the dark hills into the wide Universe."

The question had obviously answered itself. As his Transcendental friend William Ellery Channing once expressed it, "If my bark sinks, 't is to another sea." Death is an illusion. Emerson expressed this truth in what many see as one of his most mystical poems.

BRAHMA

IF the red slayer think he slays,
Or if the slain think he is slain,
They know not well the subtle ways
I keep, and pass, and turn again.
Far or forgot to me is near;
Shadow and sunlight are the same;
The vanished gods to me appear;
And one to me are shame and fame.
They reckon ill who leave me out;
When me they fly, I am the wings;
I am the doubter and the doubt,
And I the hymn the Brahmin sings.
The strong gods pine for my abode,
And pine in vain the sacred Seven;
But thou, meek lover of the good!
Find me, and turn thy back on heaven.

As Emerson knew, Brahma is the Hindu creator God and the ultimate source of all being. Once one is in alignment with this divine source of life, any discussion of the location of the spirit is irrelevant. We don't "go to heaven" when we die because we don't die, and "heaven" as a destination is a false distinction. Heaven is here and now, everywhere and forever. Heaven is oneness with the divine of which we are all part and parcel, and the divine is ubiquitous in time and space, that is to say, the divine is eternal. Emerson made this point emphatically in his essay **"Circles"** when affirming Saint Augustine's description of God as *"a circle whose centre was everywhere and its circumference nowhere."*

Overall, the question of human suffering and the inevitability of physical death have challenged theologians and philosophers throughout recorded time. Obviously, it was not an easy issue for Emerson to deal with personally, even fortified as he was by his Transcendental faith. Judging from my own life, with the aid of Emerson's insights, it is clear to me that suffering has a definite and valuable role to play. Suffering serves to intensify and purify the experience of life. It provides both the occasion and the spiritual energy that is required to discern, among the diffuse and scattered particles of our existence, the hard, gem-like essence of our true being.

The experience of tragedy serves to clarify our vision. It enables us to distinguish immediately what is important and meaningful from what is frivolous and insignificant. In the purifying crucible of pain, we are able to meld the qualities of courage, fortitude, and endurance that are the very essence of character. Virtue, love, commitment, and sacrifice are but hollow words in the absence of pain and suffering. The reality of our ideal selves can only emerge when we confront, with dignity, grace, and courage "the thousand natural shocks that flesh is heir to."

Correspondingly, the pure, loving heart of humanity is only revealed when we extend both our sympathy and our support to those whose suffering is especially acute. There is also nobility and great meaning in our willingness to endure suffering and pain as the cost of helping others in need. Sometimes we do this by speaking out against injustice, cruelty, and selfishness, even if it means risking our own comfort, in order to defend those who are defenseless. It is all of this, and more, that makes life worth living and prepares us for dying. As we face that final transition we will be fortified by the suffering we have endured, the good that we have done, the love that we have given to others and, lastly, by the love that those others have given to us.

CHAPTER FOUR: SOCIETY AND SELF

*Vocation and Life Changes; Friendship;
Social Engagement;
The Responsibilities of Citizenship;
Transcendental Politics*

Although it may not always seem that way, our world actually abounds with unarticulated but nevertheless real friendship that is based on universal love. The old saying that "A stranger is only a friend that you haven't met yet," is essentially true. Emerson believed that the "great Soul," of which we are all a part, unites us in important and fundamental ways. One of the reasons for this is so that we might be useful to one another. In his *"American Scholar"* address, Emerson expresses the notion explicitly.

> *It is one of those fables which out of an unknown antiquity convey an unlooked-for wisdom, that the gods, in the beginning, divided Man into men, that he might be more helpful to himself; just as the hand was divided into fingers, the better to answer its end.*

He then indicates that this ideal has somehow been lost. Alienation now characterizes the human condition.

> *But, unfortunately, this original unit, this fountain of power, has been so distributed to multitudes, has been so minutely subdivided and peddled out, that it is spilled into drops, and cannot be gathered. The state of society is one in which the members have suffered amputation from the trunk, and strut about so many*

> *walking monsters,—a good finger, a neck, a stomach, an elbow, but never a man.*
>
> *Man is thus metamorphosed into a thing, into many things. The planter, who is Man sent out into the field to gather food, is seldom cheered by any idea of the true dignity of his ministry. He sees his bushel and his cart, and nothing beyond, and sinks into the farmer, instead of Man on the farm. The tradesman scarcely ever gives an ideal worth to his work, but is ridden by the routine of his craft, and the soul is subject to dollars. The priest becomes a form; the attorney a statute-book; the mechanic a machine; the sailor a rope of the ship.*

Despite such apparent alienation and fragmentation, Emerson proclaims his belief in the essential unity of the human family. The *"old fable,"* mentioned above, *"covers a doctrine ever new and sublime,"* which holds that,

> *there is One Man,—present to all particular men only partially, or through one faculty; and . . . you must take the whole society to find the whole man. Man is not a farmer, or a professor, or an engineer, but he is all. Man is priest, and scholar, and statesman, and producer, and soldier. In the divided or social state these functions are parcelled out to individuals, each of whom aims to do his stint of the joint work, whilst each other performs his. . . . The individual, to possess himself, must sometimes return from his own labor to embrace all the other laborers.*

Living in a society that prides itself on its commitment to "rugged individualism," most of us don't think much about how truly dependent we are on one another. But this dependence connects us in a very real, albeit complex, way. The poet John Donne wrote that "No man is an island," and it is truer today than ever. When we flip the light switch, we expect the lights to go on. When we turn on the faucet, we expect water to come out. When we set out on our way to work, we travel over roads and bridges to get to our destination. Perhaps we stop at a fast food restaurant or a coffee shop for breakfast or just a "cup of joe." All of these very mundane functions depend very much on an incredibly complex network of human beings, working together, in order to make them happen.

The homes we live in, the clothes we wear, the food we eat, and the cars we drive are all provided to us by the efforts of an amazing number of hardworking human beings somewhere on the globe. Other examples abound, from the protection provided by police and fire personnel, to the first responders who care for us when there is an accident or other emergency, to the doctors and nurses who address our ills, to the pharmacist who prepares our medications, to the teachers who provide us with the keys to a vast treasure of learning and knowledge.

There are also more mundane but still very necessary functionaries, like the mechanic who repairs our car or the sanitation worker who takes away our rubbish. How could we ever get along without such people, and a myriad more like them? Even though we don't often think about our dependence on others and their dependence on us, in truth, we need one another. And this need makes us connected, part of a complex but still unified whole. Emerson saw such connectivity not so much as the product of need, but as the product of love. It was designed by the great Soul to be that way. We are all part of the human family, and this connection is a source of warmth and comfort in an otherwise cold and often threatening world. Emerson describes this loving unity in his essay *"Friendship."*

> *We have a great deal more kindness than is ever spoken. Maugre [i.e. despite] all the selfishness that chills like east winds the world, the whole human family is bathed with an element of love like a fine ether.*

> *How many persons we meet in houses, whom we scarcely speak to, whom yet we honor, and who honor us! How many we see in the street, or sit with in church, whom, though silently, we warmly rejoice to be with! Read the language of these wandering eye-beams. The heart knoweth.*
>
> *The effect of the indulgence of this human affection is a certain cordial exhilaration. In poetry and in common speech the emotions of benevolence and complacency which are felt towards others are likened to the material effects of fire; so swift, or much more swift, more active, more cheering, are these fine inward irradiations. From the highest degree of passionate love to the lowest degree of good-will, they make the sweetness of life.*

Ah, yes, *"the sweetness of life."* We all cherish the kind of general warmth that Emerson describes here, the simple joy of interacting with other human beings. Our days seem to go much better when they include such simple expressions as "How ya doing," or "Beautiful day, isn't it?," or "Have a good one" exchanged with people who cross our paths. A warm "Thank you," or "Have a nice day" from the young person across the counter at the coffee shop or "Thanks" from the person you held the door for (I hold the door for everyone, by the way) makes our days cheerier than they otherwise would be.

Conversely, that sullen look, blank stare, or the mute non-response to our own "Hello," "Hi," or "Good Morning" can be a real downer. Worse yet are those people who chatter mindlessly into a cell phone while rudely ignoring the flesh and blood humanity that stands before them. Perhaps not surprisingly, these folks often appear to be involved in an unhappy conversation. "Cheer up," I want to say. "I'm here, and God is in his heaven and all is right with the world." Life is too short not to

Society and Self

be happy, or at least not gloomy. There will be moments when real sadness is unavoidable. Let's not go out of our way to create it for no good reason. I think Emerson is right that the cordial interactions between people provide *the "sweetness of life."* Why be sour when *"cordial exhilaration"* is the alternative?

Emerson's Truth, Emerson's Wisdom

FINDING OUR VOCATION IN LIFE

Each of us contributes to the sweetness of life by doing what we were born to do. In doing that special something we serve the human family, both those near to us and those at a distance. In his essay, *"Spiritual Laws,"* Emerson speaks of vocations, a term that comes from the Latin word, "vocare," to call. Thus, the great Soul "calls us" to do our part. Responding to this call, we discover and develop our innate talents. Denying the call only brings frustration and disappointment.

Each man has his own vocation. The talent is the call. There is one direction in which all space is open to him. He has faculties silently inviting him thither to endless exertion. He is like a ship in a river; he runs against obstructions on every side but one, on that side all obstruction is taken away and he sweeps serenely over a deepening channel into an infinite sea. This talent and this call depend on his organization, or the mode in which the general soul incarnates itself in him.

He inclines to do something which is easy to him and good when it is done, but which no other man can do. He has no rival. For the more truly he consults his own powers, the more difference will his work exhibit from the work of any other. His ambition is exactly pro-portioned to his powers. The height of the pinnacle is determined by the breadth of the base. Every man has this call of the power to do some[thing] unique, and no man has any other call. The pretence that he has another call, a summons by name and personal election and outward "signs that mark him extraordinary and not in the roll of common men," is fanaticism, and

Society and Self

betrays obtuseness to perceive that there is one mind in all the individuals, and no respect of persons therein.

By doing his work he makes the need felt which he can supply, and creates the taste by which he is enjoyed. By doing his own work he unfolds himself. It is the vice of our public speaking that it has not abandonment. Somewhere, not only every orator but every man should let out all the length of all the reins; should find or make a frank and hearty expression of what force and meaning is in him. The common experience is that the man fits himself as well as he can to the customary details of that work or trade he falls into, and tends it as a dog turns a spit. Then is he a part of the machine he moves; the man is lost. Until he can manage to communicate himself to others in his full stature and proportion, he does not yet find his vocation. He must find in that an outlet for his character, so that he may justify his work to their eyes. If the labor is mean [i.e. menial], let him by his thinking and character make it liberal.

For most of us, our calling will lead to a role that appears common and ordinary. But Emerson reminds us that what we personally bring to that common role is unique to ourselves and, therefore, special. We must always remember that *"any thing man can do may be divinely done."*

Whatever he knows and thinks, whatever in his apprehension is worth doing, that let him communicate, or men will never know and honor him aright. Foolish, whenever you take the meanness and formality of that thing you do, instead of converting it into the obedient spiracle [i.e. outlet] of your character and aims. We like only such actions as have already long had the praise of men, and do not perceive that any thing man can do may be divinely done. We think greatness entailed or organized in some places or duties, in certain offices or occasions, and do not see that Paganini can extract rapture from a catgut, and Eulenstein from a jews-harp, and a nimble-fingered lad out of shreds of paper with his scissors, and Landseer out of swine, and the hero out of the pitiful habitation and company in which he was hidden. What we call obscure condition or vulgar society is that condition and society whose poetry is not yet written, but which you shall presently make as enviable and renowned as any. In our estimates let us take a lesson from kings. The parts of hospitality, the connection of families, the impressiveness of death, and a thousand other things, royalty makes its own estimate of, and a royal mind will. To make habitually a new estimate,—that is elevation.

Our special path, our vocation, will emerge as we consider those things that interest us and attract us, without our being able to say why. The reason some people are interested in software engineering, chemical reactions, or cell structures, while others are interested in caring for the elderly, injured, or infirm, and yet still others have an interest in poetry or politics, is because they were born to do something in that special area. We have all occasionally wondered how someone could possibly enjoy doing this, that, or another thing (even to the point of claiming that it's "the best job in the world") when we find it to be positively repugnant. What we don't realize is that they probably feel the same way about what we do. We are all born to do something that is special to us. That's our gift. What attracts us in life inevitably relates to that gift, even if we don't fully understand

Society and Self

it at the time. As Emerson assures us, *"the soul's emphasis is always right."*

> *What a man does, that he has. What has he to do with hope or fear? In himself is his might. Let him regard no good as solid but that which is in his nature and which must grow out of him as long as he exists. The goods of fortune may come and go like summer leaves; let him scatter them on every wind as the momentary signs of his infinite productiveness.*
>
> *He may have his own. A man's genius, the quality that differences him from every other, the susceptibility to one class of influences, the selection of what is fit for him, the rejection of what is unfit, determines for him the character of the universe. A man is a method, a progressive arrangement; a selecting principle, gathering his like to him wherever he goes. He takes only his own out of the multiplicity that sweeps and circles round him. He is like one of those booms which are set out from the shore on rivers to catch drift-wood, or like the loadstone [i.e. magnet] amongst splinters of steel. Those facts, words, persons, which dwell in his memory without his being able to say why, remain because they have a relation to him not less real for being as yet unapprehended. They are symbols of value to him as they can interpret parts of his consciousness which he would vainly seek words for in the conventional images of books and other minds. What attracts my attention shall have it, as I will go to the man who knocks at my door, whilst a thousand*

> *persons as worthy go by it, to whom I give no regard. It is enough that these particulars speak to me. A few anecdotes, a few traits of character, manners, face, a few incidents, have an emphasis in your memory out of all proportion to their apparent significance if you measure them by the ordinary standards. They relate to your gift. Let them have their weight, and do not reject them and cast about for illustration and facts more usual in literature. What your heart thinks great, is great. The soul's emphasis is always right.*

This notion of vocation applies to all of us, no matter how high or low our position might be on the social scale. The work we are called to do as individuals is God's work. All work has dignity when it is done in the name of God as a service to humanity, no matter how lowly.

> *Let a man believe in God, and not in names and places and persons. Let the great soul incarnated in some woman's form, poor and sad and single, in some Dolly or Joan, go out to service and sweep chambers and scour floors, and its effulgent [i.e. brilliant] day-beams cannot be muffled or hid, but to sweep and scour will instantly appear supreme and beautiful actions, the top and radiance of human life, and all people will get mops and brooms; until, lo! suddenly the great soul has enshrined itself in some other form and done some other deed, and that is now the flower and head of all living nature.*

Not surprisingly, given its importance to him personally, Emerson also discusses the notion of vocation in his essay **"Self-Reliance."** His point here is that it is only by being our own true,

Society and Self

unique selves that we can best serve our society and thus be fulfilled. Each one of us has a special gift and we have an obligation to make use of it.

> *Insist on yourself; never imitate. Your own gift you can present every moment with the cumulative force of a whole life's cultivation; but of the adopted talent of another you have only an extemporaneous half possession. That which each can do best, none but his Maker can teach him. No man yet knows what it is, nor can, till that person has exhibited it. Where is the master who could have taught Shakspeare? Where is the master who could have instructed Franklin, or Washington, or Bacon, or Newton? Every great man is a unique. The Scipionism of Scipio is precisely that part he could not borrow. Shakspeare will never be made by the study of Shakspeare. Do that which is assigned you, and you cannot hope too much or dare too much. There is at this moment for you an utterance brave and grand as that of the colossal chisel of Phidias, or trowel of the Egyptians, or the pen of Moses or Dante, but different from all these. Not possibly will the soul, all rich, all eloquent, with thousand-cloven tongue, deign to repeat itself; but if you can hear what these patriarchs say, surely you can reply to them in the same pitch of voice; for the ear and the tongue are two organs of one nature. Abide in the simple and noble regions of thy life, obey thy heart, and thou shalt reproduce the Foreworld [i.e. the first world] again.*

RESISTING THE DEMANDS OF OTHERS

Sometimes it is hard to obey your own heart. Emerson himself had a very difficult vocational choice to make at a critical point in his life. At the time of his first wife's death, he held a very prestigious position in Boston's Second Church, and his future in the ministry was predictable and bright. He came from a long line of New England divines. His father had been a notable figure in the Unitarian church, in which Waldo now served, before his untimely demise. Virtually all of Emerson's male ancestors had distinguished themselves as preachers. By following in their footsteps, he appeared to be fulfilling his proper role, his destiny even. The only problem was that he didn't feel that way.

Resigning his position and abandoning the church that had once nourished and supported him was a remarkable act of personal heroism. Emerson felt that he could never accomplish his true purpose in life if he remained where he was, no matter how comfortable and proper that position appeared to be to others. What exactly he would do after leaving the church, he wasn't quite sure. He just knew that he could no longer honestly play the role of devout minister. It was a real challenge to do what he did, but, as he asserts in *"Self-Reliance," "God will not have his work done by cowards."* And so, being true to himself and the great Soul within, he left the church of his fathers and the comfort of the life he had known.

Most of us will never have to face that kind of challenge. However, for some it can be very difficult to determine what path in life to follow. It can be even more difficult to actually follow that path, once having discovered it. Often enough the reason for this is that we are too readily influenced by the opinions of others. Also, it may appear that the career that we are called to is not considered "high status" by contemporary standards. Those standards, however, are all too predictable. In America today a "good job" is usually defined simply as one that pays a lot of money. A poor job is one that doesn't. The irony here is that those jobs that truly serve the most immediate and critical needs of humanity, that bring a high level of personal fulfillment, such as teacher, health care worker, emergency responder, social worker,

Society and Self

law enforcement officer, laborer, etc. are not, strictly speaking, high paying. And yet they are absolutely essential.

Great-hearted people are called to these jobs every day, but the voice of the world often intimidates and unnerves those who are thus chosen. We are afraid of being seen as underachievers who have settled for less. We are reluctant to listen to our own inner voice, which prompts us to follow the path that promises to be most fulfilling, simply because other voices are so loud. Sometimes these are the very "trusted advisors" to whom we have turned in the past for advice and guidance. Sometimes, they are parents. Sometimes they are friends. Sometimes even spouses. As difficult as it may be, we have to hold these well-intended folks at arms length in making our final decisions. We should not discount their advice entirely, of course, but they must be given to understand that the final decision is ours and ours alone to make.

As a young man, when I was searching for my own path in life, I had a general notion of what I wanted to do. In high school I realized that I liked to read and write. And I also liked to talk to others about what I had found in my reading. I was interested in searching out and discovering facts, opinions, and insights of all sorts. Virtually every form of learning attracted me, especially if the subject was what might be called "the human condition." When I explained all of this to a counselor at my school, she said "If you want to make a living reading and writing, and you enjoy explaining things to others, then you should be a teacher. For this, you will have to go to college. Once there, if you want to study just about everything (which I did), you should major in English. You'll be reading all the time." This made sense to me.

Because neither of my parents had gone to college, they did not attempt to influence my choice in the matter of majors. My mother, especially, was just happy to see her youngest son on his way to a college degree, any college degree. As an undergraduate, I found that I enjoyed the study of literature immensely, and I was successful at it. I wanted more of it, and so I decided to go on to graduate school. Not knowing quite what that would require of me, and not being completely confident that

I had the "right stuff," I enrolled initially in the Master's Degree program. I found that graduate studies also agreed with me, and that I could be a successful graduate student. Also, after one year I was granted a Teaching Assistantship. My experience in the classroom confirmed what I had always suspected, that I loved teaching. It was a perfect fit.

After completing my master's degree, the next step would be the doctorate. At the time (early seventies) jobs in higher education were very hard to find. To continue on the long road to a Ph.D. in English was a bit dicey since there was no guarantee that a job would be waiting at the end of that road. Also, I married in the first year of grad school and started a family. With a wife and child to think about, I had "given hostages to fortune," as Francis Bacon once put it. This made career decisions all the more perilous. Nevertheless, after completing my master's degree "with distinction," I knew that I had to go on. It was my calling, my vocation. But this was not a popular decision at home. A Ph.D. brought no certainty of a job, and if a job did materialize, it would most likely be out of state and far away.

To make matters even more difficult, at this same time I was offered a permanent teaching position at the local high school. To some, this would have seemed like a godsend. It was a steady job teaching, and I would never have to leave home. I could spend the rest of my life in a comfortable position in a familiar setting, raise a family, and retire at fifty-five after thirty years of teaching. Like Emerson's position at the Second Church, it seemed to be perfect, to everyone but me. It was difficult to say "No," but I knew in my heart that teaching high school was not my true calling. And so, difficult as it was to decline such a tempting offer, I felt it was what I had to do. I was reminded of Emerson's brave and challenging words in *"Self-Reliance."*

> *Say to them, 'O father, O mother, O wife, O brother, O friend, I have lived with you after appearances hitherto. Henceforward I am the truth's. Be it known unto you that henceforward I obey no law less than the eternal law. I will have no covenants but proximities. I shall*

Society and Self

endeavor to nourish my parents, to support my family, to be the chaste husband of one wife,—but these relations I must fill after a new and unprecedented way. I appeal from your customs. I must be myself. I cannot break myself any longer for you, or you. If you can love me for what I am, we shall be the happier.

And so I went on. I ended up writing my dissertation (on Emerson and the power of love), completed my Ph.D., and, against all odds at the time, was hired to teach (at a modest salary) at a university in another state. At last, I felt that I found my proper place, and I have never doubted the correctness of the decision that brought me here. I know that I am exactly where I should be. After thirty-five years of teaching, I still love it and look forward to the beginning of each new semester with the enthusiasm of a dimple-cheeked freshman. The bottom line, trite as it may sound, is that you have to be true to your true self. You have to be the person that you were born to be. There are simply no alternatives. And, as far as making money is concerned, I would say, don't worry about it. All the money in the world will not make you happy if you are not doing what you were born to do, if you have not fulfilled your obligation to be yourself.

As a college teacher, I have often advised students, both formally and informally. Some have been especially memorable. One of these was a young woman of exceptional ability. She clearly loved the study of literature, had a lively and creative mind, and was energetic and outgoing. She wanted to be an English teacher. I thought it was a great choice. Early in her senior year, she came to see me. She told me that she wasn't going into teaching after all. Her father, as it turns out, was himself a high school English teacher. He was nearing the end of his long career, had seen many negative changes in the profession from the time he had started, and was generally depressed. He had all the symptoms of late career burn-out. He couldn't wait to retire. Fine, it was clearly time for him to pack it in. The sad part, however, is that he turned his daughter away from a teaching career by exposing her to his own negativity. "Teaching is a terrible job," he told her. The pay was poor, the work was hard, the students were disrespectful. "Get a better job," he told her, "a better paying job. Go to law school; become a lawyer."

And so, although somewhat reluctant, she applied to law school and was accepted. I wasn't surprised. She did very well in law school. Also, not a surprise. After all, she was an exceptional and gifted student. After finishing law school, she took a position in a District Attorney's office, specializing in child welfare cases because, as she later told me, she liked to work with children. Unfortunately, she found this work disappointing. The legal system, she discovered, moves at glacial speed and matters of critical human need are often subject to the dictates of case law and precedent. It was clearly not her calling, but it did pay reasonably well. I assume her father was happy. She was not.

The last I heard from her was when she wrote to me to request a letter of recommendation. She was applying to teach a course on "Literature and the Law" at a local community college. "God bless her," my mother would say, "What's born in the bone comes out in the flesh," eventually. Emerson's wisdom and insight still obtain today. You should do what you are born to do, even if your father, or your mother, or your spouse, or your friends, or the people down the street disagree. They have their lives. You have yours. Perhaps the greatest wisdom I have ever learned on this matter comes from a fortune cookie. It read simply, "If you are happy, you are successful." Enough said.

Society and Self

THE VALUE OF FRIENDSHIP

In his essay *"Friendship,"* Emerson suggests that friendship, somewhat like marriage, is ideally a social relationship that helps us to grow, and to become better persons. A true friend, like an *"accurate mate,"* is a gift from God. As with everything else in his life, Emerson set a very high standard for friendship. Indeed, he observes in his essay that true friendship, *"like the immortality of the soul, is too good to be believed."* It is one of God's most precious gifts.

> *I awoke this morning with devout thanksgiving for my friends, the old and the new. Shall I not call God the Beautiful, who daily showeth himself so to me in his gifts? I chide society, I embrace solitude, and yet I am not so ungrateful as not to see the wise, the lovely and the noble-minded, as from time to time they pass my gate. Who hears me, who understands me, becomes mine,—a possession for all time. Nor is Nature so poor but she gives me this joy several times, and thus we weave social threads of our own, a new web of relations; and, as many thoughts in succession substantiate themselves, we shall by and by stand in a new world of our own creation, and no longer strangers and pilgrims in a traditionary globe. My friends have come to me unsought. The great God gave them to me. By oldest right, by the divine affinity of virtue with itself, I find them, or rather not I, but the Deity in me and in them derides and cancels the thick walls of individual character, relation, age, sex, circumstance, at which he usually connives, and now makes many one. High thanks I owe you, excellent lovers, who carry out the world for me to new and noble depths, and enlarge the meaning of*

> *all my thoughts. These are new poetry of the first Bard,—poetry without stop,— hymn, ode and epic, poetry still flowing, Apollo and the Muses chanting still. Will these too separate themselves from me again, or some of them? I know not, but I fear it not; for my relation to them is so pure that we hold by simple affinity, and the Genius of my life being thus social, the same affinity will exert its energy on whomsoever is as noble as these men and women, wherever I may be.*

We expect, and even demand, truth and sincerity from true and sturdy friends. This is a tall order, and it requires candor and courage to accomplish.

> *I do not wish to treat friendships daintily, but with roughest courage. When they are real, they are not glass threads or frostwork, but the solidest thing we know. For now, after so many ages of experience, what do we know of nature or of ourselves? Not one step has man taken toward the solution of the problem of his destiny. In one condemnation of folly stand the whole universe of men. But the sweet sincerity of joy and peace which I draw from this alliance with my brother's soul is the nut itself where-of all nature and all thought is but the husk and shell. Happy is the house that shelters a friend!*

There are two things that we expect from a friend, truth and sincerity. We can be nakedly honest with a friend.

> *There are two elements that go to the composition of friendship, each so sovereign that I can detect no superiority in either, no reason why either should be*

first named. One is truth. A friend is a person with whom I may be sincere. Before him I may think aloud. I am arrived at last in the presence of a man so real and equal that I may drop even those undermost garments of dissimulation, courtesy, and second thought, which men never put off, and may deal with him with the simplicity and wholeness with which one chemical atom meets another. Sincerity is the luxury allowed, like diadems and authority, only to the highest rank; that being permitted to speak truth, as having none above it to court or conform unto. Every man alone is sincere. At the entrance of a second person, hypocrisy begins. We parry and fend the approach of our fellow-man by compliments, by gossip, by amusements, by affairs. We cover up our thought from him under a hundred folds.

A true friend is close enough to be, in a sense, a part of me, a partial reflection of what and who I am.

But a friend is a sane man who exercises not my ingenuity, but me. My friend gives me entertainment without requiring any stipulation on my part. A friend therefore is a sort of paradox in nature. I who alone am, I who see nothing in nature whose existence I can affirm with equal evidence to my own, behold now the semblance of my being, in all its height, variety and curiosity, reiterated in a foreign form; so that a friend may well be reckoned the masterpiece of nature.

In addition to truthfulness and sincerity, we expect our friends to be sensitive and sympathetic. We expect "aid and comfort" from them when we are in need.

The other element of friendship is tenderness. We are holden to men by every sort of tie, by blood, by pride, by fear, by hope, by lucre, by lust, by hate, by admiration, by every circumstance and badge and trifle,—but we can scarce believe that so much character can subsist in another as to draw us by love. Can another be so blessed and we so pure that we can offer him tenderness? When a man becomes dear to me I have touched the goal of fortune.

✿✿✿✿✿✿✿✿✿

The end of friendship is a commerce [i.e. an exchange between persons] the most strict and homely that can be joined; more strict than any of which we have experience. It is for aid and comfort through all the relations and passages of life and death. It is fit for serene days and graceful gifts and country rambles, but also for rough roads and hard fare, shipwreck, poverty and persecution. It keeps company with the sallies of the wit and the trances of religion. We are to dignify to each other the daily needs and offices of man's life, and embellish it by courage, wisdom and unity. It should never fall into something usual and settled, but should be alert and inventive and add rhyme and reason to what was drudgery.

And, of course, true friendship brings with it a certain intimacy that limits its range to a special circle of persons. Because of its

Society and Self

special nature, the most sincere and intimate conversation between friends is possible only on a one-on-one basis.

Friendship may be said to require natures so rare and costly, each so well tempered and so happily adapted, and withal so circumstanced (for even in that particular, a poet says, love demands that the parties be altogether paired), that its satisfaction can very seldom be assured. It cannot subsist in its perfection, say some of those who are learned in this warm lore of the heart, betwixt more than two. I am not quite so strict in my terms, perhaps because I have never known so high a fellowship as others. I please my imagination more with a circle of god-like men and women variously related to each other and between whom subsists a lofty intelligence. But I find this law of one to one peremptory for conversation, which is the practice and consummation of friendship. Do not mix waters too much. The best mix as ill as good and bad. You shall have very useful and cheering discourse at several times with two several men, but let all three of you come together and you shall not have one new and hearty word. Two may talk and one may hear, but three cannot take part in a conversation of the most sincere and searching sort. In good company there is never such discourse between two, across the table, as takes place when you leave them alone. In good company the individuals merge their egotism into a social soul exactly co-extensive with the several consciousnesses there present. No partialities of friend to friend, no fondnesses of brother to sister, of wife to husband, are there pertinent, but quite

> *otherwise. Only he may then speak who can sail on the common thought of the party, and not poorly limited to his own. Now this convention, which good sense demands, destroys the high freedom of great conversation, which requires an absolute running of two souls into one.*

Ideally, friends should be different from us, but not too different.

> *Friendship requires that rare mean betwixt likeness and unlikeness that piques each with the presence of power and of consent in the other party. Let me be alone to the end of the world, rather than that my friend should overstep, by a word or a look, his real sympathy. I am equally balked by antagonism and by compliance. Let him not cease an instant to be himself. The only joy I have in his being mine, is that the not mine is mine. I hate, where I looked for a manly furtherance or at least a manly resistance, to find a mush of concession. Better be a nettle in the side of your friend than his echo. The condition which high friendship demands is ability to do without it. That high office requires great and sublime parts. There must be very two, before there can be very one. Let it be an alliance of two large, formidable natures, mutually beheld, mutually feared, before yet they recognize the deep identity which, beneath these disparities, unites them.*

There is also a truly transcendent quality to personal friendship so that it does not require constant proximity in order to endure.

Society and Self

Let us buy our entrance to this guild by a long probation. Why should we desecrate noble and beautiful souls by intruding on them? Why insist on rash personal relations with your friend? Why go to his house, or know his mother and brother and sisters? Why be visited by him at your own? Are these things material to our covenant? Leave this touching and clawing. Let him be to me a spirit. A message, a thought, a sincerity, a glance from him, I want, but not news, nor pottage [i.e. food]. I can get politics and chat and neighborly conveniences from cheaper companions. Should not the society of my friend be to me poetic, pure, universal and great as nature itself?

Friendship cannot be forced. It must come naturally or not at all. Friendship is a state of being. Thus, *"the only way to have a friend is to be one."*

What is so great as friendship, let us carry with what grandeur of spirit we can. Let us be silent,—so we may hear the whisper of the gods. Let us not interfere. Who set you to cast about what you should say to the select souls, or how to say any thing to such? No matter how ingenious, no matter how graceful and bland. There are innumerable degrees of folly and wisdom, and for you to say aught is to be frivolous. Wait, and thy heart shall speak. Wait until the necessary and everlasting overpowers you, until day and night avail themselves of your lips. The only reward of virtue is virtue; the only way to have a friend is to be one. You shall not come nearer a man by getting into his house. If unlike, his soul only flees the faster from you, and you shall never catch a true glance of his eye. We see the noble afar off and they repel us; why should we intrude? Late,— very late,—we perceive that no arrangements, no introductions, no consuetudes [i.e. customs] or habits of society would be of any avail to establish us in such relations with them as we desire,—but solely the uprise of nature in us to the same degree it is in them; then shall we meet as water with water; and if we should not meet them then, we shall not want them, for we are already they. In the last analysis, love is only the reflection of a man's own worthiness from other men. Men have sometimes exchanged names with their friends, as if they would signify that in their friend each loved his own soul.

True friends are rare. At times it seems that such ideal persons only exist in "dreams and fables." But such friendships are possible after all. They call out the best in us, and they are well worth the wait.

The higher the style we demand of friendship, of course the less easy to establish it with flesh and blood. We walk alone in the world. Friends such as we desire are dreams and fables. But a sublime hope cheers ever the faithful heart, that elsewhere, in other regions of the universal power, souls are now acting, enduring and daring, which can love us and which we can love. We may congratulate ourselves that the period of nonage, of follies, of blunders and of shame, is passed in solitude, and when we are finished men we shall grasp heroic hands in heroic hands. Only be admonished by what you already see, not

> to strike leagues of friendship with cheap persons, where no friendship can be. Our impatience betrays us into rash and foolish alliances which no god attends. By persisting in your path, though you forfeit the little you gain the great. You demonstrate yourself, so as to put yourself out of the reach of false relations, and you draw to you the first-born of the world,—those rare pilgrims whereof only one or two wander in nature at once, and before whom the vulgar great show as spectres and shadows merely.

Finally, true friends provide a comforting presence in our lives without dominating them. Through knowing them, we further our own self-knowledge, but this does not mean that their particular idea become ours. And so *"I shall receive from them not what they have but what they are."*

> *I do then with my friends as I do with my books. I would have them where I can find them, but I seldom use them. We must have society on our own terms, and admit or exclude it on the slightest cause. I cannot afford to speak much with my friend. If he is great he makes me so great that I cannot descend to converse. In the great days, presentiments [i.e. signs] hover before me in the firmament. I ought then to dedicate myself to them. I go in that I may seize them, I go out that I may seize them. I fear only that I may lose them receding into the sky in which now they are only a patch of brighter light. Then, though I prize my friends, I cannot afford to talk with them and study their visions, lest I lose my own. It would indeed give me a certain household joy to quit this lofty seeking, this spiritual astronomy or search of stars, and come*

down to warm sympathies with you; but then I know well I shall mourn always the vanishing of my mighty gods. It is true, next week I shall have languid moods, when I can well afford to occupy myself with foreign objects; then I shall regret the lost literature of your mind, and wish you were by my side again. But if you come, perhaps you will fill my mind only with new visions; not with yourself but with your lustres, and I shall not be able any more than now to converse with you. So I will owe to my friends this evanescent intercourse. I will receive from them not what they have but what they are. They shall give me that which properly they cannot give, but which emanates from them. But they shall not hold me by any relations less subtle and pure. We will meet as though we met not, and part as though we parted not.

Society and Self

TRANSCENDENTAL POLITICS

In addition to personal friendship, Emerson understood the importance of those specific responsibilities we share with one another as citizens. These, he believed, are of critical importance in a democracy where, ideally, the collective will of the people carries enormous weight. His thoughts on politics and the relationship of the individual to the state are nowhere more clearly and powerfully expressed than in the speeches that he gave in his personal crusade against the most heinous moral abomination of his time, American slavery.

Emerson did not hold professional politicians in high regard. Politics in his day was a very rough and tumble affair that often served to bring out the worst in people. In the 1850s, the nation was sharply divided on the issue of slavery. Slaves were first brought to America in 1619 by Dutch traders. Eventually, the institution became firmly entrenched, especially in the South. It was an important main stay of the American economy. The Founding Fathers acknowledged this fact by making a special allowance for the "peculiar institution" in the U. S. Constitution, a document that sought to codify the rights of mankind in America. In a nation that was presumably dedicated to the proposition that "all men are created equal" black slaves were relegated to the status of property.

Even in the beginning, there were those who objected to this inhumane and hypocritical compromise, but to little avail. By the 1830s, however, a grass roots abolition movement began to emerge and take hold. Throughout the 1840s, thanks to the leadership of committed reformers like William Lloyd Garrison, Wendell Phillips, Lydia Maria Child, and African-American abolitionists like Frederick Douglass and Sojourner Truth, the issue had become a matter of national debate. Emerson began speaking out forcefully on the slavery issue in 1844. By 1850, slavery had become so divisive an issue that a series of laws were passed to reduce tensions between slave and free states. Collectively, these laws became known as the "Compromise of 1850." The most controversial of them was the Fugitive Slave Law. This law required the return of fugitive slaves to their "owners," even if they had managed to find refuge in a free state.

Furthermore, the law made it a crime punishable by a heavy fine and imprisonment, to provide any form of aid to a fugitive slave. Most distressingly, the law also allowed slave catchers from the South to pursue their prey into the free states, where, previously, fugitives had been protected by "Personal Liberty Laws," which granted them freedom.

The passage of the Fugitive Slave Law came as a tremendous shock to Emerson and other abolitionists. One of the key figures in assuring its passage was Senator Daniel Webster of Massachusetts. Webster rose in the Senate on 7 March 1850 to announce his support for the measure, and the other legislation comprising the Great Compromise. This was, he contended, out of regard for preserving the Union, a Union that had been threatened by the growing agitation over the slavery issue. Emerson was an early admirer of the eloquence of Massachusetts Senator Daniel Webster, who was perhaps the greatest orator of his day. But he was appalled and disgusted when Webster, at the height of his career, unexpectedly threw his support behind the Fugitive Slave Law. Some say Webster made the move because he had presidential ambitions that could not succeed without support from the South.

To Emerson, Webster's treachery stood as an example of how blind ambition could trump morality and justice in an American society that was now dominated by conservative, materialistic concerns. He had warned in *"Self-Reliance"* of the dangers of valuing private property above moral principle. Abominations like the Fugitive Slave Law were the inevitable result. Most citizens then, as now, were naturally inclined to follow the law of the land, no matter what it might require of them. Even today, to be "law-abiding" is considered the hallmark of good citizenship. Emerson knew, however, that not all laws are good. We are able to make a distinction between those that are and those that are not by trusting ourselves to the influence of the "moral sentiment," which is the voice of the great Soul within us. As noted earlier, the core of Transcendentalism is a belief in the divinity, unity, and equality of humankind.

This unity derives from the fact that all human beings participate in a universal, spiritual dynamic that Emerson called,

Society and Self

"the Over-Soul" or "the great Soul," or simply "God." He believed that *all* people share in this divinity. In his essay, *"Circles,"* as noted earlier, he appropriates St. Augustine's description of God as *"a circle whose centre was everywhere, and its circumference nowhere."* Because divinity is all encompassing, all of humanity is necessarily included in this divine circle and, therefore, all of humanity shares in the divinity that is the ultimate source of human dignity and self-worth. This fundamental belief lies at the center of Emerson's concept of liberal, democratic equality. It also informs his opposition to slavery and all other forms of social injustice. As he notes in an early journal entry, *"Democracy/Freedom has its root in the Sacred truth that every man hath in him the divine Reason."* This is *"the equality & the only equality of all men, [and] because every man hath in him some[thing] really divine therefore is slavery the unpardonable outrage it is."*

Obviously, Emerson, and other citizens of conscience, did not have to study law books to know that it was fundamentally wrong to buy and sell human beings like cattle. We know such things intuitively, just as Americans of good conscience in the following century knew that racism and segregation were wrong, as was the political disenfranchisement and unequal treatment of women. These things were at one time perfectly legal, but they were never perfectly moral.

Emerson, like Lincoln, believed that democracy was truly "government of the people, by the people, for the people." To believe in democracy is to believe in the essential goodness of humankind. This essential goodness assures that we can be trusted with our freedom to do the right thing and to pass just laws that acknowledge the fundamental dignity, freedom, and equality of all people. We are guided in this effort by "self-evident" truths. In order for such a system of government to work, however, *all* citizens must accept the obligations of active citizenship. It is only through our collective wisdom that the best policies can be discerned and acted upon. The "great Soul" speaks through all of us, individually. From these units, we forge a dynamic unity. Together, we are far wiser than any one of us could be individually.

Emerson's Truth, Emerson's Wisdom

Emerson realized from the start that American democrcy was a major step forward in the progress of humankind, a progress that he believed was inevitable and ongoing. In a true democracy, every citizen has a voice and is morally obligated to use that voice. We educate one another in the marketplace of ideas. Then, after all have been heard, we make a choice as to the kind of laws and policies we wish to have. Democracy is founded on the notion that nothing is fixed and forever, and that the social state is always and necessarily a work in progress. *"A congress,"* said Emerson, *"is a standing insurrection."* At least it should be. Ideally, a democracy is in a constant state of revolution and evolution where beliefs and assumptions are constantly being tested. That which was once helpful but is now a hindrance to progress is discarded, to be replaced by new ideas that reflect the needs of the time. Constant, progressive change was another universal law that Emerson learned from nature. All things grow, and as they grow they change. The same applies to the body politic. Sometimes the change is slow, at other times it is dramatic and revolutionary (like the election of Barack Obama as our first president of African descent). Emerson describes this revolutionary ideal in his ***"American Scholar"*** address.

If there is any period one would desire to be born in, is it not the age of Revolution; when the old and the new stand side by side and admit of being compared; when the energies of all men are searched by fear and by hope; when the historic glories of the old can be compensated by the rich possibilities of the new era? This time, like all times, is a very good one, if we but know what to do with it.

Transcendentalists like Emerson realized that a law made yesterday may require changing today. At one time in our recent history, for example, in many places in America, society was legally segregated according to race. Most accepted this arrangement because it was sanctioned by time and, therefore, appeared to be permanent and even for some, God-given. It had become an integral part of the status quo. Any effort to change

Society and Self

this pernicious system was seen as a threat to the American way of life and was bitterly opposed. Emerson reminds us, however, that the permanence of any social or political arrangement is only an illusion. We have an ongoing obligation to challenge old assumptions and, when necessary for the greater good, to change things. Progress demands that we acknowledge that everything can be changed for the better, if we have the will and the moral courage to do it. He begins his essay *"Politics"* with this point.

> *In dealing with the State we ought to remember that its institutions are not aboriginal [i.e. from the beginning of time], though they existed before we were born; that they are not superior to the citizen; that every one of them was once the act of a single man; every law and usage was a man's expedient to meet a particular case; that they all are imitable [i.e. capable of being imitated], all alterable; we may make as good, we may make better. Society is an illusion to the young citizen. It lies before him in rigid repose, with certain names, men and institutions rooted like oak-trees to the centre, round which all arrange themselves the best they can. But the old statesman knows that society is fluid; there are no such roots and centres, but any particle may suddenly become the centre of the movement and compel the system to gyrate round it.*

THE POLITICS OF HUMAN NATURE

Emerson maintains that, despite its susceptibility to change, *"politics rest on necessary foundations, and cannot be treated with levity."* The basic foundation for all politics rests in human nature. Everybody is a combination of both conservative and liberal impulses. We simply shade off as individuals to one side or the other, right or left. While his own politics was, with some exceptions, consistently on the liberal side, Emerson had great respect for authentic conservatism (as opposed to a sham conservatism that is merely self-interest wearing the disguise of an ideology). He explains the need for both polarities in his essay *"The Conservative."*

The two parties which divide the state, the party of Conservatism and that of Innovation, are very old, and have disputed the possession of the world ever since it was made. This quarrel is the subject of civil history. The conservative party established the reverend hierarchies and monarchies of the most ancient world. The battle of patrician and plebeian, of parent state and colony, of old usage and accommodation to new facts, of the rich and the poor, reappears in all countries and times. The war rages not only in battle-fields, in national councils and ecclesiastical synods, but agitates every man's bosom with opposing advantages every hour. On rolls the old world meantime, and now one, now the other gets the day, and still the fight renews itself as if for the first time, under new names and hot personalities.

Such an irreconcilable antagonism of course must have a correspondent depth of seat in the human constitution. It is the opposition of Past and Future, of

Society and Self

Memory and Hope, of the Understanding [i.e. logic] and the Reason [i.e. intuition, feeling]. It is the primal antagonism, the appearance in trifles of the two poles of nature.

Each side in this polarity has its strengths and its weaknesses. It is easy to see today's political divide accurately captured in Emerson's description of the clash between *"conservatism"* and *"innovation."*

> *There is always a certain meanness in the argument of conservatism, joined with a certain superiority in its fact. It affirms because it holds. Its fingers clutch the fact, and it will not open its eyes to see a better fact. The castle which conservatism is set to defend is the actual state of things, good and bad. The project of innovation is the best possible state of things. Of course conservatism always has the worst of the argument, is always apologizing, pleading a necessity, pleading that to change would be to deteriorate: it must saddle itself with the mountainous load of the violence and vice of society, must deny the possibility of good, deny ideas, and suspect and stone the prophet; whilst innovation is always in the right, triumphant, attacking, and sure of final success. Conservatism stands on man's confessed limitations, reform on his indisputable infinitude; conservatism on circumstance, liberalism on power; one goes to make an adroit member of the social frame, the other to postpone all things to the man himself; conservatism is debonair and social, reform is individual and imperious. We are reformers in spring and summer, in*

autumn and winter we stand by the old; reformers in the morning, conservers at night. Reform is affirmative, conservatism negative; conservatism goes for comfort, reform for truth. Conservatism is more candid to behold another's worth; reform more disposed to maintain and increase its own. Conservatism makes no poetry, breathes no prayer, has no invention; it is all memory. Reform has no gratitude, no prudence, no husbandry. It makes a great difference to your figure and to your thought whether your foot is advancing or receding. Conservatism never puts the foot forward; in the hour when it does that, it is not establishment, but reform. Conservatism tends to universal seeming and treachery, believes in a negative fate; believes that men's temper governs them; that for me it avails not to trust in principles, they will fail me, I must bend a little; it distrusts nature; it thinks there is a general law without a particular application,—law for all that does not include any one. Reform in its antagonism inclines to asinine resistance, to kick with hoofs; it runs to egotism and bloated self-conceit; it runs to a bodiless pretension, to unnatural refining and elevation which ends in hypocrisy and sensual reaction.

Despite their mutual antagonism, conservatism and liberalism are both essential to the success of the social state.

And so, whilst we do not go beyond general statements, it may be safely affirmed of these two meta-physical antagonists, that each is a good half, but an impossible whole. Each exposes the

Society and Self

abuses of the other, but in a true society, in a true man, both must combine. Nature does not give the crown of its approbation, namely beauty, to any action or emblem or actor but to one which combines both these elements; not to the rock which resists the waves from age to age, nor to the wave which lashes incessantly the rock, but the superior beauty is with the oak which stands with its hundred arms against the storms of a century, and grows every year like a sapling; or the river which ever flowing, yet is found in the same bed from age to age; or, greatest of all, the man who has subsisted for years amid the changes of nature, yet has distanced himself, so that when you remember what he was, and see what he is, you say, What strides! what a disparity is here!

As with all other fundamental truths, Emerson finds in nature a true expression of his political philosophy. Here present and past, new life and old life, spontaneous growth and enduring stability, combine in the dynamic cycle of life.

Throughout nature the past combines in every creature with the present. Each of the convolutions of the sea-shell, each node and spine marks one year of the fish's life; what was the mouth of the shell for one season, with the addition of new matter by the growth of the animal, becoming an ornamental node. The leaves and a shell of soft wood are all that the vegetation of this summer has made; but the solid columnar stem, which lifts that bank of foliage into the air, to draw the eye and to cool us with its shade, is the gift and legacy of dead and buried years.

In nature, each of these elements being always present, each theory has a natural support. As we take our stand on Necessity, or on Ethics, shall we go for the conservative, or for the reformer. If we read the world historically, we shall say, Of all the ages, the present hour and circumstance is the cumulative result; this is the best throw of the dice of the nature that has yet been, or that is yet possible. If we see it from the side of Will, or the Moral Sentiment, we shall accuse the Past and the Present, and require the impossible of the Future.

REFORMING THE STATUS QUO

Progress requires change. Conservatism provides the launching point for innovation. It is the shore from which the reformer shoves off, the parental home he eventually leaves, the institution that he reforms.

Moreover, so deep is the foundation of the existing social system, that it leaves no one out of it. We may be partial, but Fate is not. All men have their root in it. You who quarrel with the arrangements of society, and are willing to embroil all, and risk the indisputable good that exists, for the chance of better, live, move, and have your being in this, and your deeds contradict your words every day. For as you cannot jump from the ground without using the resistance of the ground, nor put out the boat to sea without shoving from the shore, nor attain liberty without rejecting obligation, so you are under the necessity of using the Actual order of things, in order to disuse it; to live by it, whilst you wish to take away its life. The past has baked your loaf, and in the strength of its bread you would break up the oven. But you are betrayed by your own nature. You also are conservatives. However men please to style themselves, I see no other than a conservative party. You are not only identical with us in your needs, but also in your methods and aims. You quarrel with my conservatism, but it is to build up one of your own; it will have a new beginning, but the same course and end, the same trials, the same passions; among the lovers of the new I observe that there is a jealousy of the newest, and that the seceder from the seceder is as damnable as the pope himself.

The obligation of the good citizen is to listen to the voice of the great Soul within, and to translate the dictates of that voice into political and social actions that move the society towards the good. This action will always be opposed by the establishment, by conservatism, because it requires change, and conservatives by nature don't like change. The political "hero," however, while acknowledging the legitimate claims of the past, will also insist on the need for progress, even in the face of opposition.

It will never make any difference to a hero what the laws are. His greatness will shine and accomplish itself unto the end, whether they second him or not. If he have earned his bread by drudgery, and in the narrow and crooked ways which were all an evil law had left him, he will make it at least honorable by his expenditure. Of the past he will take no heed; for its wrongs he will not hold himself responsible: he will say, All the meanness of my progenitors shall not bereave me of the power to make this hour and company fair and fortunate. Whatsoever streams of power and commodity flow to me, shall of me acquire healing virtue, and become fountains of safety. Cannot I too descend a Redeemer into nature? Whosoever hereafter shall name my name, shall not record a malefactor but a benefactor in the earth. If there be power in good intention, in fidelity, and in toil, the north wind shall be purer, the stars in heaven shall glow with a kindlier beam, that I have lived. I am primarily engaged to myself to be a public servant of all the gods, to demonstrate to all men that there is intelligence and good will at the heart of things, and ever higher and yet higher leadings. These are my engagements; how can your law further or hinder me in what I shall do to men? On the other hand, these dispositions establish their relations to me. Wherever there is worth, I shall be greeted. Wherever there are men, are the objects of my study and love. Sooner or later all men will be my friends, and will testify in all methods the energy of their regard. I cannot thank your law for my protection. I protect it. It is not in its power to protect me. It is my business to make myself revered. I depend on my honor, my labor, and my dispositions for my place in the affections of mankind, and not on any conventions or parchments of yours.

THE OBLIGATIONS OF CITIZENSHIP

Emerson took politics very seriously. He always voted, and encouraged others to do the same. He had a boundless faith in American democracy, which was founded on the self-evident truth that "all men are created equal." Ideally, the freedom afforded within a democracy allows all citizens to listen to the voice that is within them, and to engage in open debate regarding the present state of the society and its future. What this required, of course, is that citizens express their beliefs in a self-reliant manner. The worse thing that can happen in a democracy is that citizens simply go along with the majority, even if they feel it is wrong, simply because it was the path of least resistance. Go along to get along. Don't rock the boat. Also, in a society that prides itself on a free market and rugged individualism, there is a constant danger that material self-interest might override morality and social justice.

It was just such a situation that allowed slavery to flourish in America for so long. The government was dominated by a minority of forceful characters who represented the interests of slave owners. People who knew better were cowed into submission. The passage of the Fugitive Slave Law in 1850 was a typical result. Emerson felt, in the light of this travesty, that a strong response was necessary. He openly declared his intention to defy the law, and encouraged others to do the same. Being as good as his word, he continued to assist the escape of runaway slaves who passed through Concord on their way north to Canada and freedom. If caught in this act of civil disobedience, he would have been subject to a heavy fine as well as imprisonment. But he accepted the risk, declaring of this loathsome law, "I will not obey it, by God."

Emerson was a morally tough guy. He was by all accounts as gentle as a lamb in his personal relationships, but he was fierce in defending principles that he felt were necessary to maintain a sense of dignity in life. As he reminds us in *"Self-Reliance," "God will not have his work made manifest by cowards."* Our commitment to principles reflects our essential character. These values express who we are. A commitment to truth and justice becomes a source of power in our lives. Others sense it immediately. Emerson makes this clear in the following passages from his essay *"Character"* where he speaks of personal strength. At any particular point in time, society depends on individuals who, because of their exceptional strength of character, emerge as leaders. They speak for what is right and just. They are *"the consciences of the society."* The importance of such exceptional people is apparent in the modern period in the lives and accomplishments of such figures as Mahatma Gandhi, Martin Luther King, Jr., and Nelson Mandela, to name but a few. All of them possessed the power of character.

This is a natural power, like light and heat, and all nature coöperates with it. The reason why we feel one man's presence and do not feel another's is as simple as gravity. Truth is the summit of being; justice is the application of it to affairs. All individual natures stand in a scale, according to the purity of this element in them. The will of the pure runs down from them into other natures, as water runs down from a higher into a lower vessel. This natural force is no more to be withstood than any other natural force. We can drive a stone upward for a moment into the air, but it is yet true that all stones will forever fall; and whatever instances can be quoted of unpunished theft, or of a lie which somebody credited, justice must prevail, and it is the privilege of truth to make itself believed. Character is this moral order seen through the medium of an individual nature. An individual is an encloser. Time and space, liberty and necessity, truth and thought, are left at large no longer. Now, the universe is a close or pound. All things exist in the man tinged with the manners of his soul. With what quality is in him he infuses all nature that he can reach; nor does he tend to lose himself in vastness, but, at how long a curve soever, all his regards return into his own good at last. He animates all he can, and he sees only what he animates. He encloses the world, as the patriot does his country, as a material basis for his character, and a theatre for action. A healthy soul stands united with the Just and the True, as the magnet arranges itself with the pole; so that he stands to all beholders like a transparent object betwixt them and the sun, and whoso journeys towards the sun, journeys towards that person. He is thus the medium of the highest influence to all who are not on the same level. Thus men of character are the conscience of the society to which they belong.

If you are fully committed to the truth that is spoken from your heart, you must be prepared to fight for it because *"There is nothing real or useful that is not a seat of war."* Morality is always a contest.

The face which character wears to me is self-sufficingness. I revere the person who is riches; so that I cannot think of him as alone, or poor, or exiled, or unhappy, or a client, but as perpetual patron, benefactor and beatified man. Character is centrality, the impossibility of being displaced or overset. A man should give us a sense of mass. Society is frivolous, and shreds its day into scraps, its conversation into ceremonies and escapes. But if I go to see an ingenious man I shall think myself poorly entertained if he give me nimble pieces of benevolence and etiquette; rather he shall stand stoutly in his place and let me apprehend, if it were only his resistance;

know that I have encountered a new and positive quality;—great refreshment for both of us. It is much that he does not accept the conventional opinions and practices. That nonconformity will remain a goad and remembrancer, and every inquirer will have to dispose of him, in the first place. There is nothing real or useful that is not a seat of war. Our houses ring with laughter and personal and critical gossip, but it helps little. But the uncivil, unavailable man, who is a problem and a threat to society, whom it cannot let pass in silence but must either worship or hate,—and to whom all parties feel related, both the leaders of opinion and the obscure and eccentric,—he helps; he puts America and Europe in the wrong, and destroys the scepticism which says, 'Man is a doll, let us eat and drink, 't is the best we can do,' by illuminating the untried and unknown. Acquiescence in the establishment and appeal to the public, indicate infirm faith, heads which are not clear, and which must see a house built before they can comprehend the plan of it. The wise man not only leaves out of his thought the many, but leaves out the few. Fountains, the self-moved, the absorbed, the commander because he is commanded, the assured, the primary,—they are good; for these announce the instant presence of supreme power.

Emerson leaned on this "supreme power" when he involved himself directly in the campaign of a Free Soil candidate for Congress from his district. This was in the spring of 1851, following the passage of the Fugitive Slave Law. Emerson felt compelled to challenge the status quo directly in the political arena. It was not a pleasant ride. As a stump speaker for his friend, John Gorham Palfrey, he was frequently subjected to verbal abuse from rowdies in the audience, as well as bitter personal attacks in the press. But he persisted nonetheless. In his *"Address to the Citizens of Concord on the Fugitive Slave Law"*(1851), Emerson provides an excellent example of how Transcendental principles can be deployed in a highly-charged, political context.

His specific subject here is the infamous Fugitive Slave Law, but the principles invoked are universal. They could just as easily be applied to combat any unjust law today. We have had many throughout our history, such as laws mandating racial segregation and forbidding interracial marriage, laws denying women equal rights, Presidential Executive Orders mandating the internment of 120,000 Japanese-American citizens at the outset of World War II, and more recently, Presidential Executive Orders sanctioning the torture of suspected terrorists and the suspension of habeas corpus. There is also the Patriot Act that, in the form in which it was originally passed in 2001, provided for the virtual suspension of a variety of Constitutional rights, including the right to privacy. In all of these cases, fundamental and universal principles of human freedom and dignity were trampled upon. In his address, Emerson fulfills his dual role of citizen and public intellectual by arguing for a *"Higher Law"* that opposes such abuses and in doing so stands as the basis for all human rights.

Society and Self

EMERSON'S CAMPAIGN FOR SOCIAL JUSTICE

Emerson began his crusade against the Fugitive Slave Law in his home town of Concord, Massachusetts. He delivered his address to his fellow citizens at their request on the third of May, 1851. In this emotionally charged speech, Emerson presents Senator Daniel Webster of Massachusetts as an example of a talented politician who put his personal ambitions ahead of moral principle and the general good of the nation. It wasn't the first time (and, as our own recent experience shows, it wouldn't be the last time) that personal ambition triumphed over principle in American politics. Emerson saw the corrosive effects of pro-slavery politics as an indication of what can happen when good people stand silent as the basic moral principles that are the foundation of a just society are overridden by fear, greed, and self-interest.

At the outset of the address, Emerson expresses the deep pain he felt in realizing that the nation was now prepared to acquiesce to the immoral demands of a corrupt regime centered in the nation's capital. Just recently, a young fugitive named Thomas Sims had bravely risked his life to escape from the hell of slavery. He made it all the way to Boston, the self-proclaimed cradle of American democracy, only to find on arriving that the good citizens of that city were ready to act as his master's minions. After all, they said, it was the law. For Emerson, such actions poison the air with the stench of moral corruption and point to worse times ahead. The cancer of slavery was spreading throughout the American body politic. *"There is infamy in the air,"* Emerson declared.

Fellow Citizens: I accepted your invitation to speak to you on the great question of these days, with very little consideration of what I might have to offer: for there seems to be no option. The last year has forced us all into politics, and made it a paramount duty to seek what it is often a duty to shun. We do not breathe well. There is infamy in the air. I have a new experience. I wake in the morning with a painful sensation, which I carry about all day, and which, when traced home, is the odious remembrance of that ignominy which has fallen on Massachusetts, which robs the landscape of beauty, and takes the sunshine out of every hour. I have lived all my life in this state, and never had any experience of personal inconvenience from the laws, until now. They never came near me to any discomfort before. I find the like sensibility in my neighbors; and in that class who take no interest in the ordinary questions of party politics. There are men who are as sure indexes of the equity of legislation and of the same state of public feeling, as the barometer is of the weight of the air, and it is a bad sign when these are discontented, for though they snuff oppression and dishonor at a distance, it is because they are more impressionable: the whole population will in a short time be as painfully affected.

Every hour brings us from distant quarters of the Union the expression of mortification at the late events in Massachusetts, and at the behavior of Boston. The tameness was indeed shocking. Boston, of whose fame for spirit and character we have all been so proud; Boston, whose citizens, intelligent people in England told me they could always distinguish by their culture among Americans; the Boston of the American Revolution, which figures so proudly in John Adam's Diary, which the whole country has been reading; Boston, spoiled by prosperity, must bow its ancient honor in the dust, and make us irretrievably ashamed. In Boston, we have said with such lofty confidence, no fugitive slave can be arrested, and now, we must transfer our vaunt to the country, and say, with a little less confidence, no fugitive man can be arrested here; at least we can brag thus until to-morrow, when the farmers also may be corrupted.

The arrest of Thomas Sims followed on a similar instance where a fugitive slave named Shadrach, who had been living in Boston for a time, was seized by authorities. Fortunately, in that instance vigilant abolitionists, both black and white, managed to free him by force and send him on his way to Canada. Conservative Bostonians, including businessmen, lawyers, clergymen, and other prominent members of the establishment, were outraged by this act of lawlessness. Emerson applauded it.

The tameness is indeed complete. The only haste in Boston, after the rescue of Shadrach, last February, was, who should first put his name on the list of volunteers in aid of the marshal. I met the smoothest of Episcopal Clergymen the other day, and allusion being made to Mr. Webster's treachery, he blandly replied, "Why, do you know I think that the great action of his life." It looked as if in the city and the suburbs all were involved in one hot haste of terror,—presidents of colleges, and professors, saints, and brokers, insurers, lawyers, importers, manufacturers: not an unpleasing sentiment, not a liberal recollection, not so much as a snatch of an old song for freedom, dares intrude on their passive obedience.

Most of the newspapers of the day (the nation's primary medium of communication) simply ratified the feelings of the conservative establishment they served. The situation puts one in mind of the period immediately following 9-11 when the media of this country remained largely silent as the administration subverted basic Constitutional rights and principles in the name of defense. The subsequent rush to war in Iraq was not met with vigilant scrutiny by either the press or the Congress. Such scrutiny, it was feared, would be seen as "unpatriotic" under the circumstances. Even large communications companies agreed to violate the right to privacy in compliance with administration requests. Principle bowed to power and fear.

> *The panic has paralyzed the journals, with the fewest exceptions, so that one cannot open a newspaper without being disgusted by new records of shame. I cannot read longer even the local good news. When I look down the columns at the titles of paragraphs, "Education in Massachusetts," "Board of Trade," "Art Union," "Revival of Religion," what bitter mockeries! The very convenience of property, the house and land we occupy, have lost their best value, and a man looks gloomily at his children, and thinks, "What have I done that you should begin life in dishonor?" Every liberal study is discredited,— literature and science appear effeminate, and the hiding of the head. The college, the churches, the schools, the very shops and factories are discredited; real estate, every kind of wealth, every branch of industry, every avenue to power, suffers injury, and the value of life is reduced. Just now a friend came into my house and said, "If this law shall be repealed I shall be glad that I have lived; if not I shall be sorry that I was born." What kind of law is that which extorts language like this from the heart of a free and civilized people?*

Society and Self

This disgraceful event served to show that the vaunted commitment of the citizens of the state of Massachusetts to the principles of freedom and human dignity, principles that they celebrated every Fourth of July, was but a hollow show. Most citizens, it seems, are not inclined to practice what they preach when there is a cost attached to it. Their heads are filled with platitudes, but their hearts are empty. Many are intimated by the authority of the state, even though the state is presumably their servant. Others are more interested in protecting the material status quo and their warm suppers. They will not put these at risk by standing up for principle. Even the courts, the last refuge of justice and morality, have sacrificed principle to accommodate *"the political breath of the hour."* The Constitutional *"protection of liberty" is subverted by a "bad act of Congress."* In the contest for power, petty politics trumps principle.

One intellectual benefit we owe to the late disgraces. The crisis had the illuminating power of a sheet of lightning at midnight. It showed truth. It ended a good deal of nonsense we had been wont to hear and to repeat, on the 19th of April, the 17th of June, the 4th of July. It showed the slightness and unreliableness of our social fabric, it showed what stuff reputations are made of, what straws we dignify by office and title, and how competent we are to give counsel and help in a day of trial. It showed the shallowness of leaders; the divergence of parties from their alleged grounds; showed that men would not stick to what they had said, that the resolutions of public bodies, or the pledges never so often given and put on record of public men, will not bind them. The fact comes out more plainly that you cannot rely on any man for the defence of truth, who is not constitutionally or by blood and temperament on that side. A man of a greedy and unscrupulous selfishness may

> *maintain morals when they are in fashion: but he will not stick. However close Mr. Wolf's nails have been pared, however neatly he has been shaved, and tailored, and set up on end, and taught to say, "Virtue and Religion," he cannot be relied on at a pinch: he will say, morality means pricking a vein. The popular assumption that all men loved freedom, and believed in the Christian religion, was found hollow American brag; only persons who were known and tried benefactors are found standing for freedom: the sentimentalists went downstream. I question the value of our civilization, when I see that the public mind had never less hold of the strongest of all truths. The sense of injustice is blunted,—a sure sign of the shallowness of our intellect. I cannot accept the railroad and telegraph in exchange for reason and charity. It is not skill in iron locomotives that makes so fine civility, as the jealousy of liberty. I cannot think the most judicious tubing a compensation for metaphysical debility. What is the use of admirable law-forms, and political forms, if a hurricane of party feeling and a combination of monied interests can beat them to the ground? What is the use of courts, if judges only quote authorities, and no judge exerts original jurisdiction, or recurs to first principles?*

Emerson was especially concerned that even the judiciary seemed willing to ignore fundamental principles while capitulating to political pressures. The entire legal establishment is compromised by the passage of laws that offend our moral sentiments, our natural sense of what is right and wrong.

Society and Self

What is the use of a Federal Bench, if its opinions are the political breath of the hour? And what is the use of constitutions, if all the guaranties provided by the jealousy of ages for the protection of liberty are made of no effect, when a bad act of Congress finds a willing commissioner? The levity of the public mind has been shown in the past year by the most extravagant actions. Who could have believed it, if foretold that a hundred guns would be fired in Boston on the passage of the Fugitive Slave Bill? Nothing proves the want of all thought, the absence of standard in men's minds, more than the dominion of party. Here are humane people who have tears for misery, an open purse for want; who should have been the defenders of the poor man, are found his embittered enemies, rejoicing in his rendition,— merely from party ties. I thought none, that was not ready to go on all fours, would back this law. And yet here are upright men, compotes mentis, husbands, fathers, trustees, friends, open, generous, brave, who can see nothing in this claim for bare humanity, and the health and honor of their native State, but canting fanaticism, sedition and "one idea." Because of this preoccupied mind, the whole wealth and power of Boston—two hundred thousand souls, and one hundred and eighty millions of money— are thrown into the scale of crime: and the poor black boy, whom the fame of Boston had reached in the recesses of a vile swamp, or in the alleys of Savannah, on arriving here finds all this force employed to catch him. The famous town of Boston is his master's hound. The

> *learning of the universities, the culture of elegant society, the acumen of lawyers, the majesty of the Bench, the eloquence of the Christian pulpit, the stoutness of Democracy, the respectability of the Whig party are all combined to kidnap him.*

The moral laws of the universe, however, cannot be suspended by legislation passed in Washington, D.C., nor by corrupt rulings from the highest courts. Misery and disaster will follow where justice is denied. Throughout history, Emerson argues, the greatest jurists have recognized that a higher, moral law always trumps civil law when that civil law degrades and denies our natural instinct for justice. Average citizens know the difference between right and wrong because the great Soul within them illuminates it like a lightening flash. A society that attempts to enact injustice as law will suffer the consequences. "Natural retribution" will inevitably follow. In the light of Emerson's observations, it is difficult not to see the recent economic crisis that shook American society as the inevitable result of the erosion of moral, ethical, and legal standards in the nation's financial community. In the decade leading up to the crash, greed and corruption displaced common decency as well as common sense. The inevitable result was catastrophe.

> *The crisis is interesting as it shows the self-protecting nature of the world and of the Divine laws. It is the law of the world,—as much immorality as there is, so much misery. The greatest prosperity will in vain resist the greatest calamity. You borrow the succour of the devil and he must have his fee. He was never known to abate a penny of his rents. In every nation all the immorality that exists breeds plagues. But of the corrupt society that exists we have never been able to combine any pure prosperity. There is always something in the very advantages of a condition which hurts it. Africa has its malformation; England has its*

Society and Self

Ireland; Germany its hatred of classes; France its love of gunpowder; Italy its Pope; and America, the most prosperous country in the Universe, has the greatest calamity in the Universe, negro slavery.

Let me remind you a little in detail how the natural retribution acts in reference to the statute which Congress passed a year ago. For these few months have shown very conspicuously its nature and impracticability.

Emerson reminds his audience that the Fugitive Slave Law, like all immoral laws and practices, is opposed by all the powers of the universe, whose universal laws are inscribed in the hearts of humanity. One of them is the "inalienable" right to life and liberty. Hence, the Fugitive Slave Law, Emerson insists, is "contravened" in a number of ways.

It is contravened:

1. By the sentiment of duty. An immoral law makes it a man's duty to break it, at every hazard. For virtue is the very self of every man. It is therefore a principle of law that an immoral contract is void, and that an immoral statute is void. For, as laws do not make right, and are simply declaratory of a right which already existed, it is not to be presumed that they can so stultify themselves as to command injustice.

It is remarkable how rare in the history of tyrants is an immoral law. Some color, some indirection was always used. If you take up the volumes of the "Universal History," you will find it difficult searching. The precedents are few. It is not easy to parallel the wickedness of this American law. And that is the head and body of this discontent, that the law is immoral.

Here is a statute which enacts the crime of kidnapping,—a crime on one footing with arson and murder. A man's right to liberty is as inalienable as his right to life.

Pains seem to have been taken to give us in this statute a wrong pure from any mixture of right. If our resistance to this law is not right, there is no right. This is not meddling with other people's affairs: this is hindering other people from meddling with us. This is not going crusading into Virginia and Georgia after slaves, who, it is alleged, are very comfortable where they are:—that amiable argument falls to the ground: but this is befriending in our own State, on our own farms, a man who has taken the risk of being shot, or burned alive, or cast into the sea, or starved to death, or suffocated in a wooden box, to get away from his driver: and this man who has run the gauntlet of a thousand miles for his freedom, the statute says, you men of Massachusetts shall hunt, and catch, and send back again to the dog-hutch he fled from.

Emerson contends that it is *"the primal sense of duty"* to do what is right that elevates humanity above the beasts of the field. As with all other Transcendental truths, we are born with this *"primal sense."* Its promptings come through natural feeling and intuition. No one, Emerson contends, needs to be taught that returning a human being to the horrors of slavery is fundamentally wrong. Those who protested the injustice of racial bigotry and segregation during the Civil Rights Movement in the

Society and Self

1950s and 60s undoubtedly were acting in response to this same intuitive sense of justice. They were firm in their belief that others would eventually open themselves to this redeeming power. More recently, one might argue that no one needs to be taught that it's wrong to torture people, for whatever reason. Laws designed to prevent such things, like the Geneva Convention, are a codification of what all decent people naturally feel in their hearts. As Emerson notes above, just laws *"are simply declaratory of a right which already existed."* It therefore follows that all sincere people are the *"natural enemies"* of immoral laws.

It is contrary to the primal sentiment of duty, and therefore all men that are born are, in proportion to their power of thought and their moral sensibility, found to be the natural enemies of this law. The resistance of all moral beings is secured to it. I had thought, I confess, what must come at last would come at first, a banding of all men against the authority of this statute. I thought it a point on which all sane men were agreed, that the law must respect the public morality. I thought that all men of all conditions had been made sharers of a certain experience, that in certain rare and retired moments they had been made to see how man is man, or what makes the essence of rational beings, namely, that whilst animals have to do with eating the fruits of the ground, men have to do with rectitude, with benefit, with truth, with something which is, independent of appearances: and that this tie makes the substantiality of life, this, and not their ploughing, or sailing, their trade or the breeding of families. I thought that every time a man goes back to his own thoughts, these angels receive him, talk with him, and that, in the best hours, he is uplifted in virtue of this essence, into a peace and into a power which the material world cannot give: that these moments counterbalance the years of drudgery, and that this owning of a law, be it called morals, religion, or godhead, or what you will, constituted the explanation of life, the excuse and indemnity for the errors and calamities which sadden it. In long years consumed in trifles, they remember these moments, and are consoled. I thought it was this fair mystery, whose foundations are hidden in eternity, which made the basis of human society, and of law; and that to pretend anything else, as that the acquisition of property was the end of living, was to confound all distinctions, to make the world a greasy hotel, and, instead of noble motives and inspirations, and a heaven of companions and angels around and before us, to leave us in a grimacing menagerie of monkeys and idiots. All arts, customs, societies, books, and laws, are good as they foster and concur with this spiritual element: all men are beloved as they raise us to it; hateful as they deny or resist it. The laws especially draw their obligation only from their concurrence with it.

Opposition to immoral law is ultimately based on an intuitive perception of a *"Higher Law"* that countermands it. Emerson notes that this concept is also, by tradition, an important element in the history of jurisprudence, despite the fact that its abstract nature often renders it a subject of ridicule to conservative minds. As Emerson notes, the greatest legal minds over the centuries have consistently and emphatically affirmed this principle.

I am surprised that lawyers can be so blind as to suffer the principles of Law to be discredited. A few months ago, in my dismay at hearing that the Higher Law was reckoned a good joke in the courts, I took pains to look into a few lawbooks. I had often heard that the Bible constituted a part of every technical law library, and that it was a principle in law that immoral laws are void.

I found, accordingly, that the great jurists, Cicero, Grotius, Coke, Blackstone, Burlamaqui, Montesquieu, Vattel, Burke, Mack-intosh, Jefferson, do all affirm this. I have no intention to recite these passages I had marked:—such citation indeed seems to be something cowardly (for no reasonable person needs a quotation from Black-stone to convince him that white cannot be legislated to be black), and shall content myself with reading a single passage. Blackstone admits the sovereignty "antecedent to any positive precept, of the law of Nature," among whose principles are, "that we should live on, should hurt nobody, and should render unto every one his due," etc. "No human laws are of any validity, if contrary to this." "Nay, if any human law should allow or enjoin us to commit a crime" (his instance is murder), "we are bound to transgress that human law; or else we must offend both the natural and divine." Lord Coke held that where an Act of Parliament is against common right and reason, the common law shall control it, and adjudge it to be void. Chief Justice Hobart, Chief Justice Holt, and Chief Justice Mansfield held the same.

> *Lord Mansfield, in the case of the slave Somerset, wherein the dicta of Lords Talbot and Hardwicke had been cited, to the effect of carrying back the slave to the West Indies, said, "I care not for the supposed dicta of judges, however eminent, if they be contrary to all principle." Even the Canon Law says (in malis promissis non expedit servare fidem), "Neither allegiance nor oath can bind to obey that which is wrong."*

Emerson also makes it clear that no sovereign (or President) can justifiably command others to violate "the laws of God." Neither enslavement nor torture could possibly be construed as moral and, therefore, no citizens or civil servants can be compelled to obey.

> *No engagement (to a sovereign) can oblige or even authorize a man to violate the laws of Nature. All authors who have any conscience or modesty agree that a person ought not to obey such commands as are evidently contrary to the laws of God. Those governors of places who bravely refused to execute the barbarous orders of Charles IX. for the famous "Massacre of St. Bartholomew," have been universally praised; and the court did not dare to punish them, at least openly. "Sire," said the brave Orte, governor of Bayonne, in his letter, "I have communicated your majesty's command to your faithful inhabitants and warriors in the garrison, and I have found there only good citizens, and brave soldiers; not one hangman: therefore, both they and I must humbly entreat your majesty to be pleased to employ your arms and lives in things that are possible, however*

hazardous they may be, and we will exert ourselves to the last drop of our blood."

Emerson's point here is that these laws of the heart, dictated by the great Soul within us, are so compelling that no argument from an external authority can prevail against them. Even Webster with his incredible oratorical skills and encyclopedic knowledge of Constitutional law (he was known as the "Defender of the Constitution") cannot make what is unjust just, cannot make what is wrong right. Similarly, a memo from the Justice Department arguing for the legality of torture, like Webster's arguments supporting the Fugitive Slave Law, amount to little more than pissing against a granite wall. Every decent person knows intuitively that they're wrong.

The practitioners should guard this dogma well [of natural law], as the palladium [i.e. standard] of the profession, as their anchor in the respect of mankind. Against a principle like this, all the arguments of Mr. Webster are the spray of a child's squirt against a granite wall.

As a Transcendentalist, Emerson insists that it is the "moral sentiment" that provides the strongest and most compelling argument against the infamy of the Fugitive Slave Law. It is a law that every good and decent citizen will break at the first opportunity.

[This heinous act] is contravened by all the sentiments. How can a law be enforced that fines pity, and imprisons charity? As long as men have bowels, they will disobey. You know that the Act of Congress of September 18, 1850, is a law which every one of you will break on the earliest occasion. There is not a manly Whig, or a manly Democrat, of whom, if a slave were hidden in one of our houses from the hounds, we should not ask with confidence to lend his wagon in aid of his

escape, and he would lend it. The man would be too strong for the partisan.

Given this spontaneous opposition, as natural as the force of gravity, Emerson finds it especially absurd to hear some argue that it is the agitation of the abolitionists that has necessitated this law. This is similar to those who held civil rights demonstrators responsible for the violence that resulted when their protest marches were met by angry and violent mobs of bigots.

And here I may say that it is absurd, what I often hear, to accuse the friends of freedom in the North with being the occasion of the new stringency of the Southern slave-laws. If you starve or beat the orphan, in my presence, and I accuse your cruelty, can I help it? In the words of Electra in the Greek tragedy, "'T is you that say it, not I. You do the deeds, and your ungodly deeds find me the words." Will you blame the ball for rebounding from the floor, blame the air for rushing in where a vacuum is made or the boiler for exploding under pressure of steam? These facts are after laws of the world, and so is it law, that, when justice is violated, anger begins. The very defence which the God of Nature has provided for the innocent against cruelty is the sentiment of indignation and pity in the bosom of the beholder. Mr. Webster tells the President that "he has been in the North, and he has found no man, whose opinion is of any weight, who is opposed to the law." Oh, Mr. President, trust not the information! The gravid old Universe goes spawning on; the womb conceives and the breasts give suck to thousands and millions of hairy babes formed not in the image of your statute, but in the

> *image of the Universe; too many to be bought off; too many than they can be rich, and therefore peaceable; and necessitated to express first or last every feeling of the heart. You can keep no secret, for whatever is true some of them will unreasonably [i.e. naturally] say. You can commit no crime, for they are created in their sentiments conscious of and hostile to it; and unless you can suppress the newspaper, pass a law against bookshops, gag the English tongue in America, all short of this is futile. This dreadful English Speech is saturated with songs, proverbs and speeches that flatly contradict and defy every line of Mr. Mason's statute. Nay, unless you can draw a sponge over those seditious Ten Commandments which are the root of our European and American civilization; and over that eleventh commandment, "Do unto others as you would have them do to you," your labor is vain.*

Because all just laws are but codifications of the innate moral sentiments of humankind, many such laws contradict the Fugitive Slave Law. One of these is an Act of Congress ending the slave trade in 1807. Just as the Geneva Convention contradicts Presidential Executive Orders allowing torture, legislation forbidding trade in slaves not only contradicts but renders absurd the provisions of the Fugitive Slave Law.

> *[The Fugitive Slave Law] is contravened by the written laws themselves, because the sentiments, of course, write the statutes. Laws are merely declaratory of the natural sentiments of mankind, and the language of all permanent laws will be in contradiction to any immoral enactment. And thus it happens here: Statute fights*

against Statute. By the law of Congress March 2, 1807, it is piracy and murder, punishable with death, to enslave a man on the coast of Africa. By law of Congress September, 1850, it is a high crime and misdemeanor, punishable with fine and imprisonment, to resist the reënslaving a man on the coast of America. Off soundings, it is piracy and murder to enslave him. On soundings, it is fine and prison not to reënslave. What kind of legislation is this? What kind of constitution which covers it? And yet the crime which the second law ordains is greater than the crime which the first law forbids under penalty of the gibbet. For it is a greater crime to reënslave a man who has shown himself fit for freedom, than to enslave him at first, when it might be pretended to be a mitigation of his lot as a captive in war.

The Fugitive Slave Law provided a fee to specially appointed Federal Commissioners for every accused fugitive they returned to slavery. This amounted to a bribe, a necessary incentive to facilitate the administration of an evil law. Where justice is truly served, it is always its own reward.

[The Fugitive Slave Law] is contravened by the mischiefs it operates. A wicked law cannot be executed by good men, and must be by bad. Flagitious [i.e. wicked] men must be employed, and every act of theirs is a stab at the public peace. It cannot be executed at such a cost, and so it brings a bribe in its hand. This law comes with infamy in it, and out of it. It offers a bribe in its own clauses for the consummation of the crime. To serve it, low and mean people are found by the groping of the government. No

> *government ever found it hard to pick up tools for base actions. If you cannot find them in the huts of the poor, you shall find them in the palaces of the rich. Vanity can buy some, ambition others, and money others. The first execution of the law, as was inevitable, was a little hesitating; the second was easier; and the glib officials became, in a few weeks, quite practised and handy at stealing men. But worse, not the officials alone are bribed, but the whole community is solicited. The scowl of the community is attempted to be averted by the mischievous whisper, "Tariff and Southern market, if you will be quiet: no tariff and loss of Southern market, if you dare to murmur." I wonder that our acute people who have learned that the cheapest police is dear schools, should not find out that an immoral law costs more than the loss of the custom [i.e. commerce] of a Southern city.*

The Fugitive Slave Law is a "legal crime" that came about largely because the monied interests of both the North and the South were more concerned with protecting their wealth and comfort than in doing what was right. Property, economic security, and self-interest ruled the day. Those who did not cooperate were branded as malcontents.

> *The humiliating scandal of great men warping right into wrong was followed up very fast by the cities. New York advertised in Southern markets that it would go for slavery, and posted the names of merchants who would not. Boston, alarmed, entered into the same design. Philadelphia, more fortunate, had no conscience at all, and, in this auction of the rights of mankind, rescinded all*

> *its legislation against slavery. And the Boston "Advertiser," and the "Courier," in these weeks, urge the same course on the people of Massachusetts. Nothing remains in this race of roguery but to coax Connecticut or Maine to outbid us all by adopting slavery into its constitution.*

The compromise with slavery, like the conflicted effort of Congress in our own time to legitimize torture and other violations of human rights, *"contaminates"* our democracy and deprives our nation of its position of moral leadership in the world. The Commissioners who remanded fugitive slaves, like the Senators and Representatives who pushed for the hasty passage of the Patriot Act and tolerated abominations like torture and the gulag called Guantanamo, became complicit in the corruption of the system they served. *"Public opinion"* itself was warped by fear, conservative talk-show misinformation, and bigotry.

> *Great is the mischief of a legal crime. Every person who touches this business is contaminated. There has not been in our lifetime another moment when public men were personally lowered by their political action. But here are gentlemen whose believed probity was the confidence and fortification of multitudes, who, by fear of public opinion, or through the dangerous ascendency of Southern manners, have been drawn into the support of this foul business. We poor men in the country who might once have thought it an honor to shake hands with them, or to dine at their boards, would now shrink from their touch, nor could they enter our humblest doors. You have a law which no man can obey, or abet the obeying, without loss of self-respect and forfeiture of the name of gentleman. What shall we say of the functionary by whom the*

recent rendition was made? If he has rightly defined his powers, and has no authority to try the case, but only to prove the prisoner's identity, and remand him, what office is this for a reputable citizen to hold? No man of honor can sit on that bench. It is the extension of the planter's whipping-post; and its incumbents must rank with a class from which the turnkey, the hangman and the informer are taken, necessary functionaries, it may be, in a state, but to whom the dislike and the ban of society universally attaches.

The passage of the Fugitive Slave Law caused a huge backlash in the free states as Vigilance Committees were formed to protect fugitives. There were many violent clashes and stormy protests that rocked the government to its foundations and, ultimately, set the stage for the Civil War. Such spontaneous resistance by otherwise peace-loving citizens, Emerson argues, is yet another sign of the wrongness of the law. As he noted earlier, *"When justice is violated, anger begins."* The only good thing about the law is that it inspired the *"advocates of freedom"* to speak out in protest. Here, I am reminded of the Civil Rights Movement of the 1950s and 1960s of which we might say with Emerson, it *"was one of the best compensations for this calamity"* of racial bigotry and oppression. It was heroic.

These resistances appear in the history of the statute, in the retributions which speak so loud in every part of this business, that I think a tragic poet will know how to make it a lesson for all ages. Mr. Webster's measure was, he told us, final. It was a pacification, it was a suppression, a measure of conciliation and adjustment. These were his words at different times: "there was to be no parleying more;" it was "irrepealable." Does it look final now? His final settlement has dislocated the foundations. The state-house shakes likes a tent. His pacification has brought all the honesty in every house, all scrupulous and good-hearted men, all women, and all children, to accuse the law. It has brought United States swords into the streets, and chains round the court-house. "A measure of pacification and union." What is its effect? To make one sole subject for conversation and painful thought throughout the continent, namely, slavery. There is not a man of thought or of feeling but is concentrating his mind on it. There is not a clerk but recites its statistics; not a politician but is watching its in-calculable energy in the elections; not a jurist but is hunting up precedents; not a moralist but is prying into its quality; not an economist but is computing its profit and loss: Mr. Webster can judge whether this sort of solar microscope brought to bear on his law is likely to make opposition less. The only benefit that has accrued from the law is its service to education. It has been like a university to the entire people. It has turned every dinner-table into a debating-club, and made every citizen a student of natural law. When a moral quality comes into politics, when a right is invaded, the discussion draws on deeper sources: general principles are laid bare, which cast light on the whole frame of society. And it is cheering to behold what champions the emergency called to this poor black boy; what subtlety, what logic, what learning, what exposure of the mischief of the law; and, above all, with what earnestness and dignity the advocates of freedom were

Society and Self

inspired. It was one of the best compensations of this calamity.

But the conservative, moneyed interests of the North continued to insist on the enforcement of the law in order to placate Southern slave owners who were, in effect, their business partners. Their chief spokesperson in Emerson's view, was Daniel Webster, a man who should have known better. Emerson believed that Webster's desire for personal power and self-aggrandizement had displaced his moral sense and with it a proper concern for the welfare of the nation. Indeed, Webster stands as a good example of the immense harm that can be done when a national crisis, like that which followed the terrorist attack on September 11, 2001, is exploited to further the agenda of a narrow clique of politically ambitious people.

Emerson was convinced, however, that such evil machinations would bring retribution sooner or later. Even Presidents who were once popular will suffer infamy as the consequences of their immoral and unethical actions eventually come home to roost. Despite his earlier opposition to the expansion of slavery, as well as his moral condemnation of the institution, Webster, the man who would be President, was now *"irresistibly taking the bit in his mouth and the collar on his neck, and harnessing himself to the chariot of the planters."* It was not the first or the last time in American politics that the "straight talk express" would run off the tracks. People who should know better often become slaves to their own ambition. Presidential campaigns frequently present the sad spectacle of Senators and others in high places embracing policies that directly contradict the principled positions they once took because it is politically expedient to do so.

But the Nemesis [Greek Goddess of justice] works underneath again. It is a power that makes noonday dark, and draws us on to our undoing; and its dismal way is to pillory the offender in the moment of his triumph. The hands that put the chain on the slave are in that moment manacled. Who has seen

> anything like that which is now done? The words of John Randolph, wiser than he knew, have been ringing ominously in all echoes for thirty years, words spoken in the heat of the Missouri debate. "We do not govern the people of the North by our black slaves, but by their own white slaves. We know what we are doing. We have conquered you once, and we can and will conquer you again. Ay, we will drive you to the wall, and when we have you there once more, we will keep you there and nail you down like base money." These words resounding ever since from California to Oregon, from Cape Florida to Cape Cod, come down now like the cry of Fate, in the moment when they are fulfilled. By white slaves, by a white slave, are we beaten. Who looked for such ghastly fulfilment, or to see what we see? Hills and Halletts, servile editors by the hundred, we could have spared. But him, our best and proudest, the first man of the North, in the very moment of mounting the throne, irresistibly taking the bit in his mouth and the collar on his neck, and harnessing himself to the chariot of the planters.

The consequences of this perfidy are unavoidable. They plague not only the politician but also the party he or she represents. Such moral compromises inevitably end in infamy and disgrace.

> The fairest American fame ends in this filthy law. Mr. Webster cannot choose but regret his law. He must learn that those who make fame accuse him with one voice; that those who have no points to carry that are not identical with public morals and generous civilization, that the obscure and private who have no

voice and care for none, so long as things go well, but who feel the disgrace of the new legislation creeping like miasma into their homes, and blotting the daylight,—those to whom his name was once dear and honored, as the manly statesman to whom the choicest gifts of Nature had been accorded, disown him: that he who was their pride in the woods and mountains of New England is now their mortification,—they have torn down his picture from the wall, they have thrust his speeches into the chimney. No roars of New York mobs can drown this voice in Mr. Webster's ear. It will outwhisper all the salvos of the "Union Committees'" cannon. But I have said too much on this painful topic. I will not pursue that bitter history.

The irony is, that Webster could have used his influence at this moment of national crisis to show true leadership and to stand upon the finest principles of American democracy. It was one of *"those critical moments when his leadership would have turned the scale."* But he chose to serve himself rather than the nation and humanity. It is difficult not to be reminded here of the opportunity afforded this nation following the attacks on 9-11. With the good will and sympathy of the whole world behind us, the United States could have struck a blow for truth, justice, and rational restraint that would have been a model for all aspiring democracies as well as a bulwark against a tide of terrorism.

Instead, the tragedy was used to enhance the standing of a would-be "war president" and a clique, whose agenda included an unprovoked attack on a non-threatening, sovereign nation. The results have been catastrophic for all involved. Emerson's disappointment with Webster's actions were amplified by the fact that he possessed an incredible talent for public discourse. He could have been a powerful force on the side of justice. Regrettably, his actions at this critical juncture, like all immoral actions, put him on the wrong side of history.

But passing from the ethical to the political view, I wish to place this statute, and we must use the introducer and substantial author of the bill as an illustration of the history. I have as much charity for Mr. Webster, I think, as any one has. I need not say how much I have enjoyed his fame. Who has not helped to praise him? Simply he was the one eminent American of our time, whom we could produce as a finished work of Nature. We delighted in his form and face, in his voice, in his eloquence, in his power of labor, in his concentration, in his large understanding, in his daylight statement, simple force; the facts lay like the strata of a cloud, or like the layers of the crust of the globe. He saw things as they were, and he stated them so. He has been by his clear perceptions and statements in all these years the best head in Congress, and the champion of the interests of the Northern seaboard: but as the activity and growth of slavery began to be offensively felt by his constituents, the senator became less sensitive to these evils. They were not for him to deal with: he was the commercial representative. He indulged occasionally in excellent expression of the known feeling of the New England people: but, when expected and when pledged, he omitted to speak, and he omitted to throw himself into the movement in those critical moments when his leadership would have turned the scale. At last, at a fatal hour, this sluggishness accumulated to downright counter-action, and, very unexpectedly to the whole Union, on the 7th March, 1850, in opposition to his education, association, and to all his own most explicit language for thirty years, he crossed the line, and became the head of the slavery party in this country.

The crisis moment served only to elicit and energize Webster's worst qualities. Rather than acting as a man of principle and morality, a man who stood for the ideal, his vision was blinded by a concern *"for the animal good, that is, for property."* He was, in short, a narrow conservative who chose to re-live yesterday rather than create a better tomorrow. Like the politicians who supported segregation for so many years, the immorality of slavery was acceptable to Webster because it was agreed to in the past. Although he had the means and the opportunity to do great good, he chose not to play the role of reformer, visionary, or even a man of conscience. He *had "no moral sentiment,"* only a *"hole in the head"* where his conscience should have been. There was nothing in his nature that was revolutionary, morally progressive, or forward looking. He was a man without hope.

Mr. Webster perhaps is only following the laws of his blood and constitution. I suppose his pledges were not quite natural to him. Mr. Webster is a man who lives by his memory, a man of the past, not a man of faith or of hope. He obeys his powerful animal nature;—and his finely developed understanding only works truly and with all its force, when it stands for animal good; that is, for property. He believes, in so many words, that government exists for the protection of property. He looks at the Union as an estate, a large farm, and is excellent in the completeness of his defence of it so far. He adheres to the letter. Happily he was born late,—after the independence had been declared, the Union agreed to, and the constitution settled. What he finds already written, he will defend. Lucky that so much had got well written when he came. For he has no faith in the power of self-government; none whatever in extemporizing [i.e. improvising] a government. Not the smallest municipal provision, if it were new, would receive his sanction. In Massachusetts, in 1776, he would, beyond all question, have been a refugee. He praises Adams and Jefferson, but it is a past Adams and Jefferson that his mind can entertain. A present Adams and Jefferson he would denounce. So with the eulogies of liberty in his writings,— they are sentimentalism and youthful rhetoric. He can celebrate it, but it means as much from him as from Metternich or Talleyrand. This is all inevitable from his constitution. All the drops of his blood have eyes that look downward. It is neither praise nor blame to say that he has no moral perception, no moral sentiment, but in that region—to use the phrase of the phrenologists—a hole in the head. The scraps of morality to be gleaned from his speeches are reflections of the mind of others; he says what he hears said, but often makes signal blunders in their use. In Mr. Webster's imagination the American Union was a huge Prince Rupert's drop, which, if so much as the smallest end be shivered off, the whole will snap into atoms. Now the fact is quite different from this. The people are loyal, law-loving, law-abiding. They prefer order, and have no taste for misrule and uproar.

Some people in Emerson's time feared that agitation of the slavery question threatened the existence of the Union. More recently, there are some who believe that those who condemn torture, illegal detainment without trial, government eavesdropping on citizens and other such abuses are undermining the security of "the homeland." Emerson's point here is that the Union is not worth preserving, nor the homeland worth protecting, if the principles that make it worthy of preservation and protection are compromised in the process. The Union can only endure if it stands firmly on universal principles of justice. If the original structure is weakened by moral compromise, then the Union will not endure because *"as soon as the constitution ordains an immoral law, it ordains disunion."* Corrupt governments and corrupt policies are always doomed to failure.

The destiny of this country is great and liberal, and is to be greatly administered. It is to be administered according to what is, and is to be, and not according to what is dead and gone. The union of this people is a real thing, an alliance of men of one flock, one language, one religion, one system of manners and ideas. I hold it to be a real and not a statute union. The people cleave to the Union, because they see their advantage in it, the added power of each.

I suppose the Union can be left to take care of itself. As much real union as there is, the statutes will be sure to express; as much disunion as there is, no statute can long conceal. Under the Union I suppose the fact to be that there are really two nations, the North and the South. It is not slavery that severs them, it is climate and temperament. The South does not like the North, slavery or no slavery, and never did. The North likes the South well enough, for it knows its own advantages. I am willing to leave them to the facts. If they continue to have a binding interest, they will be pretty sure to find it out: if not, they will consult their peace in parting. But one thing appears certain to me, that, as soon as the constitution ordains an immoral law, it ordains disunion. The law is suicidal, and cannot be obeyed. The Union is at an end as soon as an immoral law is enacted. And he who writes a crime into the statute-book digs under the foundations of the Capitol to plant there a powder-magazine, and lays a train [i.e. a fuse].

American democracy will remain safe and secure not by passing laws and tolerating practices that undermine the very principles upon which the nation was founded. Our true strength lies in our stalwart defense of the basic rights of freedom, equality, and social justice. Emerson assures his fellow citizens that the evil of slavery can be conquered through peaceful means, if people of good will cooperate with the power of the Over-Soul that operates in all of us. In light of the nation's growing wealth and prosperity, the slaves' freedom could be granted with compensation to the planters.

Until this happens, opposition to this injustice will be ongoing and irreversible. Nothing satisfies at last but justice, and so abominations like the Fugitive Slave Law *"must be made inoperative. It must be abrogated and wiped out of the statute-book; but whilst it stands there, it must be disobeyed."* The obligation of good citizens and true patriots is not to blindly follow the laws of the land when these laws insult justice and morality. Protest and dissent should rule the day until justice is done. For Emerson, democracy demands proactive citizenship. When we quietly tolerate what we know to be wrong, we become complicit in the evil.

The immense power of rectitude is apt to be forgotten in politics. But they who have brought the great wrong on the country have not forgotten it. They avail themselves of the known probity and honor of Massachusetts, to endorse the statute. The ancient maxim still holds that never was any injustice effected except by the help of justice. The great game of the government has been to win the sanction of Massachusetts to the crime. Hitherto they have succeeded only so far as to win Boston to a certain extent. The behavior of Boston was the reverse of what it should have been: it was supple and officious, and it put itself into the base attitude of pander to the crime. It should have placed obstruction at every step. Let the attitude of the states be firm. Let us respect the Union to all honest ends. But also respect an older and wider union, the law of Nature and rectitude. Massachusetts is as strong as the Universe, when it does that. We will never intermeddle with your slavery,—but you can in no wise be suffered to bring it to Cape Cod and Berkshire. This law must be made inoperative. It must be abrogated and wiped out of the statute-book; but whilst it stands there, it must be disobeyed. We must make a small state great, by making every man in it true. It was the praise of Athens, "She could not lead countless armies into the field, but she knew how with a little band to defeat those who could." Every Roman reckoned himself at least a match for a Province. Every Dorian did. Every Englishman in Australia, in South Africa, in India, or in whatever barbarous country their forts and factories have been set up,— represents London, represents the art, power and law of Europe. Every man educated at the Northern school carries the like advantages into the South. For it is confounding distinctions to speak of the geographic sections of this country as of equal civilization. Every nation and every man bows, in spite of himself, to a higher *mental and moral existence; and the sting of the late disgraces is that this royal position of Massachusetts was foully lost, that the well-known sentiment of her people was not expressed. Let us correct this error. In this one fastness let truth be spoken and right done. Here let there be no confusion in our ideas. Let us not lie, not steal, nor help to steal, and let us not call stealing by any fine name, such as "Union" or "Patriotism." Let us know that not by the public, but by ourselves, our safety must be bought.*

Emerson realized early on that in a democracy, *"What great masses of men wish done, will be done."* A democracy is the ideal form of government for a Transcendentalist because in a democracy the spirit of the Over-Soul, which is present in the heart of every citizen, can express itself most readily. Because the Over-Soul, the great Soul, is the source of all divine goodness and light, and because we all share equally in this universal divinity, its ultimate political expression is actualized in the form of laws that assure equality, freedom, and social justice. In order for this to happen, however, it is necessary for those who possess the gift of expression, to come forward and give voice to the good. Emerson understood this. He believed that truth is universal. It is manifested in everything from the laws of physics and mathematics, to the instincts of animals, to the moral sentiments that enable us to distinguish right from wrong.

A recent article in *National Geographic* magazine (July, 2007) suggests that Emerson's notions of Transcendental politics and self-reliance are, in some ways, confirmed by evidence from the natural world. The author, Peter Miller, begins with the observation that insects often appear to be brilliant. "How else," he says, "could ants organize highways, build elaborate nests, stage epic raids, and do all of the other things ants do?" This phenomenon is all the more puzzling when close observation reveals that in a typical ant colony "no one's in charge. No generals command ant warriors. No managers boss ant workers. The queen plays no role except to lay eggs." And yet many complex functions are nevertheless executed to perfection. As it turns out, the brilliance of ants, and other such insects, is collective. Each member of the colony has an individual role to play, and by playing it a large, complex task is accomplished.

Scientists call this "Swarm Theory" (which is the title of the article). According to Miller, it consists of "simple creatures following simple rules, each one acting on local information. No ant sees the big picture. No ant tells any other ant what to do." This kind of collective intelligence has been observed in many other insect and animal groups, including honey bees, locusts, caribou, and schools of fish. In each instance, the safety and well being of the larger community depends on individual members playing their proper roles. Impressed by the elegant simplicity of this programmed organization, computer scientists have created "mathematical procedures for solving particularly complex human problems, such as routing trucks, scheduling airlines, or guiding military robots." (Emerson would undoubtedly be pleased to see how, once again, the natural laws of the universe were being appropriated for the potential benefit of mankind.)

The principle in evidence here that is most relevant to our discussion of Transcendental politics is the notion of collective wisdom serving the collective good. Miller quotes Thomas Malone of MIT's new (and appropriately named) Center for Collective Intelligence on this very topic. "No single person," says Malone, "knows everything that's needed to deal with problems we face as a society, such as health care or climate change, but collectively we know far more than we've been able to tap so far." This leads Miller to a conclusion that could serve as a gloss on Emerson's *"Self-Reliance"* and his concept of how units lead to unity. It also helps to explain his Transcendental theory of politics. "Crowds tend to be wise," Miller states, "only if individual members act responsibly and make their own decisions. A group won't be smart if its members imitate one another, slavishly follow fads, or wait for someone to tell them what to do. When a group is being intelligent, whether it's made up of ants or attorneys, it relies on its members to do their own part. For those of us who sometimes wonder if it's really worth recycling that extra bottle to lighten our impact on the planet, the bottom line is that our actions matter, even if we don't see how."

Emerson's Truth, Emerson's Wisdom

Recent history has revealed to us the harm and injury that can occur when democracy in America is subverted by a small clique of determined individuals. When collective wisdom is displaced by the notions of a select few, when ideological purity is substituted for truth, talent, and ability, when the will of the people is manipulated by deceit and falsehoods in order to serve a pre-determined end, then arrogance and stupidity, not wisdom, will rule. We are presently witnessing the disastrous aftermath of several such moments. In his appropriately titled essay *"Civilization,"* Emerson reminds us that politics, like all other worthwhile human endeavors, must always be informed by the highest principles. When this happens, all good things are possible.

And as our handiworks borrow the elements, so all our social and political action leans on principles. To accomplish anything excellent the will must work for catholic and universal ends. A puny creature, walled in on every side, as Daniel wrote,—

"Unless above himself he can Erect himself, how poor a thing is man!"

but when his will leans on a principle, when he is the vehicle of ideas, he borrows their omnipotence. Gibraltar may be strong, but ideas are impregnable, and bestow on the hero their invincibility. "It was a great instruction," said a saint in Cromwell's war, "that the best courages are but beams of the Almighty." Hitch your wagon to a star. Let us not fag [i.e. work hard] in paltry works which serve our pot and bag alone. Let us not lie and steal. No god will help. We shall find all their teams going the other way,—Charles's Wain, Great Bear, Orion, Leo, Hercules: every god will leave us. Work rather for those interests which the divinities honor and promote, —justice, love, freedom, knowledge, utility.

If we can thus ride in Olympian chariots by putting our works in the path of the celestial circuits, we can harness also evil agents, the powers of darkness, and force them to serve against their will the ends of wisdom and virtue.

Participation in the political process is the heart of American democracy. Emerson understood this. He repeated his **"Fugitive Slave Law"** many times as he stumped the Middlesex District in Massachusetts in support of John Gorham Palfrey's Congressional campaign. He knew that this kind of commitment was necessary if democracy was to work. Later he would remark that it is *"delicious to act with great masses to great aims."* In all of his political speeches, Emerson reminded his audiences that freedom was an essential American value and the cornerstone of democracy. Therefore, *"No citizen will go wrong who on every question leans to the side of general liberty."* In these days when fear of terrorism recently resulted in the compromising of essential freedoms and the erosion of fundamental principles of human decency, it is a lesson that we should all bear in mind. Liberty is the offspring of love. Repression is the offspring of fear.

Tensions between the free states and slave states increased dramatically throughout the decade of the 1850s. Emerson continued to speak and to act. He constantly reminded his audiences that they had to embrace in their own lives the values that are proclaimed in the nation's foundational documents, else those values would remain just words. Times required people of character to join what he now saw clearly as a contest between good and evil. In his second **"Fugitive Slave Law Address"** (7 March 1854) he struck a militant note: *"To make good the cause of Freedom,"* he told his listeners, *"you must draw off from all these foolish trusts on others. You must* be citadels and warriors, yourselves Declarations of Independence, the charter, the battle, and the victory."

When Abraham Lincoln was elected president in the fall of 1860 on a platform that promised to prevent the further spread of slavery, Emerson supported him vigorously both in his lectures and in his political essays. This support was not without risk. Conservative reactionaries were incensed that the nation was obviously drifting towards civil war, and they held abolitionists responsible. Some abolitionists, like Wendell Phillips, had taken to carrying a pistol for personal protection. Despite threats of violence, when Phillips asked Emerson to speak at the annual meeting of the Massachusetts Anti-Slavery Society in January of 1860, he accepted. The evening proved to be a disaster. The crowd had been infiltrated by pro-slavery rowdies who booed and shouted as Emerson attempted to speak, forcing him to conclude abruptly. Soon the rabble rousers grew even more unruly and threatening until finally the police swept in and cleared the galleries. Emerson was undaunted. In reflecting on that memorable evening later in his journals, he says boldly, *"If I were dumb, yet I would have gone & mowed & muttered or made signs."* Truth will not be silenced.

Throughout the Civil War that followed Lincoln's election, Emerson served as the conscience of the Union. He never wavered in his faith in democracy, even as the nation was tearing itself apart. In his 1863 address, ***"Fortune of the Republic,"*** he insisted that the democratic voice of the people in the free North must be trusted. *"In each new threat of faction,"* he observed, *"the ballot of the people has been beyond expectation right and decisive." "The instinct of the people,"* he insisted, *"is right."* Ultimately, this faith proved well-placed. The south was eventually defeated, and a new period of equal rights dawned in America. The passage of the 13th, 14th, and 15th Amendments to the Constitution destroyed slavery forever, guaranteed equal protection under the law to all citizens, and enfranchised all adult males, regardless of race. These Amendments, collectively, constituted the greatest expansion of freedom in America since the Revolution. In Emerson's view, they were all the products of the great Soul manifesting itself in the heroic actions of those who found the courage to oppose an oppressive and immoral status quo. These were, indeed, people of character.

In the post-war years, Emerson continued to support liberal causes. In an address at Harvard, appropriately titled *"Progress of Culture,"* delivered in July of 1867, he celebrated the *"fusion of races and religions"* in America, and the freedom of movement that allowed *"every wanderer to choose his climate and government."* Emerson also gave special notice to *"the new claim of woman to a political status."* He saw this development as *"an honorable testimony to the civilization which has given her a civil status new in history."* At that time, woman's suffrage was almost as controversial as abolition had been earlier. For some time the women of America had looked to Emerson for support of their cause. While in the 1850s he had spoken, with some reservation, for full enfranchisement of women, in the post-war period he threw his support unambiguously behind their effort.

In a speech delivered in Boston at a gathering of the New England Woman's Suffrage Association, in May 1869, he declared, *"The claim now pressed by woman is a claim for nothing less than all, than her share in all. She asks for her property; she asks for her rights, for her vote; she asks for her share in education, for her share in all the institutions of society, for her half of the whole world; and to this she is entitled."* At the same meeting, he accepted the vice-presidency of the New England Woman's Suffrage Association.

Most of us will not be called upon to fight in a civil war, or mount the barricades in a violent protest, but we do live in a society where we are called upon to make choices regarding how our society will be governed. Whether we are inclined to the liberal or conservative side on any issue, it is imperative that we make our voices heard in the context of constructive and rational discourse. We must participate in the system. If we do, it will work. If we don't, it will fail. It has stumbled in the recent past and the nation and the world have suffered as a result. It was not blind fear that led us to an unnecessary war. It was the reluctance of many to question the presumed wisdom of the few. Emerson reminds us that, individually we are prone to make mistakes, but collectively we possess the wisdom that can help us to avoid them. Democracy is not fool proof. Mistakes will be made, even under the best of circumstances. But democracy has a built-in mechanism for self-correction. It is the will of the people. However, it only works when the people are informed, engaged, and active. As Emerson well knew, indifference and complacency are more deadly to a democracy than any external threat of terrorism.

CHAPTER FIVE: FATE AND POWER

Dealing with Life's Limitations; Bearing Up Under the Weight of the World; Preserving Personal Freedom; Developing Personal Power.

One of the most baffling conundrums of the human condition concerns the relationship between fate and free will. Most of us acknowledge that there are many elements of our existence that we simply have no control over. They are the "givens" of life. Our sex, race, ethnicity, physical talents (or lack thereof), temperaments and personalities, and a host of other factors that impact our lives were determined at the time of our birth. We also had no choice regarding the time and place of our birth, the society into which we are born, or the economic status of our parents. And yet all of these things greatly impact our lives and affect our ability act in the world.

Collectively, these factors often appear to determine our "fate," that is our destiny, in the world. I say "appear to determine" because most of us acknowledge that we also possess free will, that is, the freedom to make choices. These choices also impact what happens to us. Sometimes it's difficult to determine the relationship between these apparently contradictory elements in our lives. To what extent must we accept fate, that is "things as they are," and simply go with the flow? And to what extent are we able to resist fate, and to make an effort to change things in our own lives and in the world around us? Without free will, there can be no virtue and no honor. There would also be no sin, no infamy. How can you applaud or condemn a person who had no choice in acting this way or that? Obviously, free will is necessary, along with the power to enforce it. But where do we draw the line between what we can do and what we can't do? Emerson tackles this very conundrum in one of his later and most provocative essays titled, *"Fate."* This work has a long background that involves Emerson's private and public life in the 1850s.

Emerson's Truth, Emerson's Wisdom

In 1860, on the eve of the Civil War, Emerson published a collection of essays that he called **Conduct of Life**. It's an apt title. Having lived through a decade of tension, turmoil, and violence generated primarily by the slavery issue, it seemed that the world he once knew was rapidly self-destructing. As noted in the previous chapter, he had also suffered through the personal humiliation of being booed, hissed, harassed, and publicly castigated because of his stand against slavery and social injustice. His compatriot in the cause, Wendell Phillips, had taken to carrying a pistol for personal protection. He was also accompanied by a bodyguard when he went out in public. Emerson's friend, Senator Charles Sumner of Massachusetts, had been nearly beaten to death on the floor of the United States Senate in the spring of 1856 by a Representative from South Carolina who took umbrage at his criticisms of slaveholders. It would take him three years to recover from his wounds.

In the meantime, guerilla warfare had broken out in "Bleeding Kansas" between pro and anti-slavery forces. John Brown was a fierce and determined leader of a group of Kansas freedom fighters and someone that Emerson knew personally from his visits to Concord. Brown had recently been captured, tried, and executed for treason by the federal government following his failed raid on the federal arsenal at Harper's Ferry, Virginia. To make matters worse, a major financial panic occurred in 1857. As usual in America's "boom and bust" economy, the panic threw people out of work, precipitated bankruptcies, and filled many hearts with anxiety regarding the future.

In this context, Emerson felt tasked to explain how his philosophy of irresistible progress and personal empowerment could possibly be valid. So much of life seemed to be dictated by colossal events and developments that were beyond the control of individuals. Under conditions like these, how could people manage their lives? How could they live in the world? How could they even begin to address the overwhelming problems of their private lives while the world itself was flying apart? Everywhere one looked it seemed that *"Things are in the saddle and ride mankind,"* as Emerson himself had observed many years before. Since then, matters had only gotten worse. Much worse.

Fate and Power

The bard was challenged but undaunted. There was an answer. It is an answer that serves us as well now as it did then. He begins his essay *"Fate,"* the first essay of the collection, by noting that *"the question of the times [has] resolved itself into a practical question of the conduct of life. How shall I live?"* Most lives, indeed, appear to be dominated by *"fate,"* which he defines as *"the laws of the world,"* that is to say, things as they are. Fate is everything that we cannot control. The world is filled with powerful and intimidating forces, both natural and manmade. These encroach upon our lives, limit our possibilities, and circumscribe our personal freedom. As a result, circumstances seem often to dictate our lives. But Emerson is not willing to accept this dictation. Instead, he calls upon a significant counterforce, which is "the power of character."

But if there be irresistible dictation, this dictation understands itself. If we must accept Fate, we are not less compelled to affirm liberty, the significance of the individual, the grandeur of duty, the power of character. This is true, and that other is true. But our geometry cannot span these extreme points and reconcile them. What to do? By obeying each thought frankly, by harping, or, if you will, pounding on each string, we learn at last its power. By the same obedience to other thoughts we learn theirs, and then comes some reasonable hope of harmonizing them. We are sure that, though we know not how, necessity does comport with liberty, the individual with the world, my polarity with the spirit of the times. The riddle of the age has for each a private solution. If one would study his own time, it must be by this method of taking up in turn each of the leading topics which belong to our scheme of human life, and by firmly stating all that is agreeable to experience on one, and doing the same

> *justice to the opposing facts in the others, the true limitations will appear. Any excess of emphasis on one part would be corrected, and a just balance would be made.*

Before elaborating on this counterforce, Emerson acknowledges the reality of "fate" as a significant limiting force in human affairs. In the first part of his essay, he considers all of those things that seem to limit, restrict, and determine our lives. These are all indicative of "foreordained fate," or things as they are, things that we cannot change.

> *But let us honestly state the facts. Our America has a bad name for superficialness. Great men, great nations, have not been boasters and buffoons, but perceivers of the terror of life, and have manned themselves to face it. The Spartan, embodying his religion in his country, dies before its majesty without a question. The Turk, who believes his doom is written on the iron leaf in the moment when he entered the world, rushes on the enemy's sabre with undivided will. The Turk, the Arab, the Persian, accepts the foreordained fate:—*
>
> *"On two days, it steads not to run*
> *from thy grave,*
> *The appointed, and the unappointed*
> *day;*
>
> *On the first, neither balm nor*
> *physician can save,*
> *Nor thee, on the second, the Universe*
> *slay."*
>
> *The Hindoo under the wheel is as firm. Our Calvinists in the last generation had something of the same dignity. They*

Fate and Power

felt that the weight of the Universe held them down to their place. What could they do? Wise men feel that there is something which cannot be talked or voted away,—a strap or belt which girds the world:—

"The Destinee, ministre general,
That executeth in the world over al,
The purveiance that God hath seen
    beforne,
So strong it is, that though the world had
    sworne
The contrary of a thing by yea or nay,
Yet sometime it shall fallen on a day
That falleth not oft in a thousand yeer;
For certainly, our appetités here,
Be it or warre, or pees, or hate, or love,
All this is ruled by the sight above."

    CHAUCER: The Knighte's Tale.

The Greek Tragedy expressed the same sense.

"Whatever is fated that will take place.
The great immense mind of Jove is not to be transgressed."

Emerson's Truth, Emerson's Wisdom

NATURAL FORCES THAT LIMIT OUR FREEDOM

Some religions promise a special, divine exemption from the ravages of fate, which are reserved for those not deemed "elect," but nature will not be fooled by a "pistareen -Providence" [i.e. a god whose favor can be bought] and promises of special exemptions. She treats us all the same, and often harshly. Natural disasters like hurricane Katrina, or the recent devastating earthquake in Haiti, offer powerful and painful proof that we are not the masters of our fates. Even prayers will not protect you when the ordained moment arrives. At times, "Providence has a wild, rough, incalculable road to its end."

Savages cling to a local god of one tribe or town. The broad ethics of Jesus were quickly narrowed to village theologies, which preach an election or favoritism. And now and then an amiable parson, like Jung Stilling or Robert Huntington, believes in a pistareen-Providence, which, whenever the good man wants a dinner, makes that somebody shall knock at his door and leave a half-dollar. But Nature is no sentimentalist,—does not cosset [i.e. pet] or pamper us. We must see that the world is rough and surly, and will not mind drowning a man or a woman, but swallows your ship like a grain of dust. The cold, inconsiderate of persons, tingles your blood, benumbs your feet, freezes a man like an apple. The diseases, the elements, fortune, gravity, lightning, respect no persons. The way of Providence is a little rude. The habit of snake and spider, the snap of the tiger and other leapers and bloody jumpers, the crackle of the bones of his prey in the coil of the anaconda,—these are in the system, and our habits are like theirs.

Fate and Power

You have just dined, and however scrupulously the slaughter-house is concealed in the graceful distance of miles, there is complicity, expensive races,—race living at the expense of race. The planet is liable to shocks from comets, perturbations [i.e. disturbances] from planets, rendings from earthquake and volcano, alterations of climate, precessions of equinoxes. Rivers dry up by opening of the forest. The sea changes its bed. Towns and counties fall into it. At Lisbon an earthquake killed men like flies. At Naples three years ago ten thousand persons were crushed in a few minutes. The scurvy at sea, the sword of the climate in the west of Africa, at Cayenne, at Panama, at New Orleans, cut off men like a massacre. Our western prairie shakes with fever and ague. The cholera, the small-pox, have proved as mortal to some tribes as a frost to the crickets, which, having filled the summer with noise, are silenced by a fall of the temperature of one night. Without uncovering what does not concern us, or counting how many species of parasites hang on a bombyx [i.e. a silkworm] or groping after intestinal parasites or infusory biters, or the obscurities of alternate generation,—the forms of the shark, the labrus, the jaw of the sea-wolf paved with crushing teeth, the weapons of the grampus, and other warriors hidden in the sea, are hints of ferocity in the interiors of nature. Let us not deny it up and down. Providence has a wild, rough, incalculable road to its end, and it is of no use to try to whitewash its huge, mixed instrumentalities, or to dress up that terrific benefactor in a clean shirt and white neck-cloth of a student in divinity.

Will you say, the disasters which threaten mankind are exceptional, and one need not lay his account for cataclysms every day? Aye, but what happens once may happen again, and so long as these strokes are not to be parried [i.e. deflected] by us they must be feared.

THE INFLUENCE OF FATE IN OUR PERSONAL LIVES

Our lives are also greatly influenced by other unalter-able givens including our own *"temperaments,"* that is, our personalities. As any parent of more than one child knows, just because children are derived from the same gene pool and are raised in the same environment does not mean that their personalities will be similar. In fact, just the opposite appears to be true. And so it seems that personalities are determined at the moment of birth and are not simply the product of our own will.

Some people are by nature quiet and contemplative. Others are outspoken and demonstrative, and so on. Additionally, there are other powerful forces that we are subject to, including natural instincts like sex drive and other elements that are encoded in our genetic structure. Some of these genetic codes dictate a specific physical characteristic while others provide special or unique talents or abilities. All of them obviously have a considerable impact on our lives. It is rather remarkable here how Emerson's insights about characteristics that are inherited have been confirmed by the relatively recent discovery of the presence in all of us of a specific and unique "genetic code."

> ***But these shocks and ruins are less destructive to us than the stealthy power of other laws which act on us daily. An expense of ends to means is fate;— organization tyrannizing over character. The menagerie, or forms and powers of the spine, is a book of fate; the bill of the bird, the skull of the snake, determines tyrannically its limits. So is the scale of races, of temperaments; so is sex; so is climate; so is the reaction of talents imprisoning the vital power in certain directions. Every spirit makes its house; but afterwards the house confines the spirit.***

Emerson's Truth, Emerson's Wisdom

In Emerson's time, pseudo-scientists known as phrenologists believed that the shape of the skull revealed character because it followed the convolutions of the brain, which was the source of personality. Others at that time, like now, believed that certain physical characteristics, inherited from parents and family and manifest at birth, serve to determine the future. Thus, the son of a laborer, it was thought, will never be *"a poet or a prince."* One's physical appearance, it was presumed, reflects traits of character. Some of these, in turn, are derived from our *"progenitors,"* drawn up, as it were, through the roots of our family tree.

The gross lines are legible to the dull; the cab-man is phrenologist so far, he looks in your face to see if his shilling is sure. A dome of brow denotes one thing, a pot-belly another; a squint, a pug-nose, mats of hair, the pigment of the epidermis, betray character. People seem sheathed in their tough organization. Ask Spurzheim, ask the doctors, ask Quetelet if temperaments decide nothing?—or if there be anything they do not decide? Read the description in medical books of the four temperaments and you will think you are reading your own thoughts which you had not yet told. Find the part which black eyes and which blue eyes play severally in the company. How shall a man escape from his ancestors, or draw off from his veins the black drop which he drew from his father's or his mother's life? It often appears in a family as if all the qualities of the progenitors were potted in several jars,—some ruling quality in each son or daughter of the house; and sometimes the unmixed temperament, the rank unmitigated elixir, the family vice is drawn off in a separate individual and the others are proportionally relieved. We sometimes see a change of expression in our companion and say his father or his mother comes to the windows of his eyes, and sometimes a remote relative. In different hours a man represents each of several of his ancestors, as if there were seven or eight of us rolled up in each man's skin,—seven or eight ancestors at least; and they constitute the variety of notes for that new piece of music which his life is. At the corner of the street you read the possibility of each passenger in the facial angle, in the complexion, in the depth of his eye. His parentage determines it. Men are what their mothers made them. You may as well ask a loom which weaves huckabuck [i.e. a rough cloth] why it does not make cashmere, as expect poetry from this engineer, or a chemical discovery from that jobber. Ask the digger in the ditch to explain Newton's laws; the fine organs of his brain have been pinched by overwork and squalid poverty from father to son for a hundred years. When each comes forth from his mother's womb, the gate of gifts closes behind him. Let him value his hands and feet, he has but one pair. So he has but one future, and that is already pre-determined in his lobes and described in that little fatty face, pig-eye, and squat form. All the privilege and all the legislation of the world cannot meddle or help to make a poet or a prince of him.

Jesus said, "When he looketh on her, he hath committed adultery." But he is an adulterer before he has yet looked on the woman, by the superfluity of animal and the defect of thought in his constitution. Who meets him, or who meets her, in the street, sees that they are ripe to be each other's victim.

Occasionally, an aberrant gene appears that deviates from the family norm and leads to a *"superior individual."* But this comes as mere chance and cannot be willed. So the reign of fate appears to be undisturbed.

In certain men digestion and sex absorb the vital force, and the stronger these are, the individual is so much weaker. The more of these drones perish, the better for the hive. If, later, they give birth to some superior individual, with force enough to add to this animal a new aim and a complete apparatus to work it out, all the ancestors are gladly forgotten. Most men and most women are merely one couple more. Now and then one has a new cell or camarilla [i.e. a small chamber] opened in his brain,—an architectural, a musical, or a philological knack; some stray taste or talent for flowers, or chemistry, or pigments, or story-telling; a good hand for drawing, a good foot for dancing, an athletic frame for wide journeying, etc.—which skill nowise alters rank in the scale of nature, but serves to pass the time; the life of sensation going on as before. At last these hints and tendencies are fixed in one or in a succession. Each absorbs so much food and force as to become itself a new centre. The new talent draws off so rapidly the vital force that not enough remains for the animal functions, hardly enough for health; so that in the second generation, if the like genius appear, the health is visibly deteriorated and the generative force impaired.

Fate and Power

Even our social and political views are influenced by our personalities and so it may be determined at birth whether we shall grow up to be conservatives or liberals, Whigs or Free-Soilers. It may be that this innate tendency is warped for a time and the conservative will show liberal qualities. Eventually, however, the dominate trait will reassert itself. What's born in the bone will, finally, come out in the flesh.

People are born with the moral or with the material bias;—uterine brothers with this diverging destination; and I suppose, with high magnifiers, Mr. Frauenhofer or Dr. Carpenter might come to distinguish in the embryo, at the fourth day,—this is a Whig, and that a Free-soiler.

It was a poetic attempt to lift this mountain of Fate, to reconcile this despotism of race with liberty, which led the Hindoos to say, "Fate is nothing but the deeds committed in a prior state of existence." I find the coincidence of the extremes of Eastern and Western speculation in the daring statement of Schelling, "There is in every man a certain feeling that he has been what he is from all eternity, and by no means became such in time." To say it less sublimely,—in the history of the individual is always an account of his condition, and he knows himself to be a party to his present estate.

A good deal of our politics is physiological. Now and then a man of wealth in the heyday of youth adopts the tenet of broadest freedom. In England there is always some man of wealth and large connection, planting himself, during all his years of health, on the side of progress, who, as soon as he begins to die, checks his forward play, calls in his troops and becomes conservative. All conservatives are such from personal defects. They have been effeminated by position or nature, born halt and blind, through luxury of their parents, and can only, like invalids, act on the defensive. But strong natures, backwoodsmen, New Hampshire giants, Napoleons, Burkes, Broughams, Websters, Kossuths, are inevitable patriots, until their life ebbs and their defects and gout, palsy and money, warp them.

The strongest idea incarnates itself in majorities and nations, in the healthiest and strongest. Probably the election goes by avoirdupois weight, and if you could weigh bodily the tonnage of any hundred of the Whig and the Democratic party in a town on the Dearborn balance, as they passed the hay-scales, you could predict with certainty which party would carry it. On the whole it would be rather the speediest way of deciding the vote, to put the selectmen or the mayor and aldermen at the hay-scales.

FATE AND THE TYRANNY OF CIRCUMSTANCE

In addition to the apparent tyranny of genetic determinism, our lives often seem hedged in by the specific circumstances of our existence. An Einstein born in a ghetto or the deep jungles of the Amazon is unlikely to become the author of Relativity Theory. Emerson saw the influence of *"circumstance"* manifested everywhere in the natural world. It points us in one direction and impedes us in all others, *"like the locomotive, strong enough on its track but can do nothing but mischief off of it."* You might say that at times our lives appear to be "railroaded" by circumstance.

In science we have to consider two things: power and circumstance. All we know of the egg, from each successive discovery, is, another vesicle [i.e. cell]; and if, after five hundred years you get a better observer or a better glass, he finds, within the last observed, another. In vegetable and animal tissue it is just alike, and all that the primary power or spasm operates is still vesicles, vesicles. Yes,—but the tyrannical Circumstance! A vesicle in new circumstances, a vesicle lodged in darkness, Oken thought, became animal; in light, a plant. Lodged in the parent animal, it suffers changes which end in unsheathing miraculous capability in the un-altered vesicle, and it unlocks itself to fish, bird, or quadruped, head and foot, eye and claw. The Circumstance is Nature. Nature is what you may do. There is much you may not. We have two things,—the circumstance, and the life. Once we thought positive power was all. Now we learn that negative power, or circumstance, is half. Nature is the tyrannous circumstance, the thick skull, the sheathed snake, the ponderous, rock-like jaw; necessitated activity; violent direction; the conditions of a tool, like the locomotive, strong enough on its track, but which can do nothing but mischief off of it; or skates, which are wings on the ice but fetters on the ground.

Race, Emerson believed, is also an element of fate. How the world sees you influences how the world treats you. Racism and ethnocentrism, unfortunately, were an inescapable part of Emerson's world, as of ours. In his day, race and ethnicity were virtually synonymous. Native Americans, Negroes, and Irish, especially, were the victims of negative stereotyping. Frequently, this negativity was extended to anyone who was not Anglo-Saxon.

The book of Nature is the book of Fate. She turns the gigantic pages,—leaf after leaf,—never re-turning one. One leaf she lays down, a floor of granite; then a thousand ages, and a bed of slate; a thousand ages, and a measure of coal; a thousand ages, and a layer of marl and mud: vegetable forms appear; her first misshapen animals, zoöphyte, trilobium, fish; then, saurians— rude forms, in which she has only blocked her future statue, concealing under these un-wieldy monsters the fine type of her coming king. The face of the planet cools and dries, the races meliorate, and man is born. But when a race has lived its term, it comes no more again.

The population of the world is a conditional population; not the best, but the best that could live now; and the scale of tribes, and the steadiness with which victory adheres to one tribe and defeat to another, is as uniform as the superposition of strata. We know in history what weight belongs to race. We see the English, French, and Germans planting themselves on every shore and market of America and Australia, and monopolizing the commerce of these countries. We like the nervous and victorious habit of our own branch of the family. We follow the step of the Jew, of the Indian, of the Negro. We see how much will has been expended to extinguish the Jew, in vain. Look at the unpalatable conclusions of Knox, in his Fragment of Races;—a rash and unsatisfactory writer, but charged with pungent and unforgettable truths. "Nature respects race, and not hybrids." "Every race has its own habitat." "Detach a colony from the race, and it deteriorates to the crab." See the shades of the picture. The German and Irish millions, like the Negro, have a great deal of guano in their destiny. They are ferried over the Atlantic and carted over America, to ditch and to drudge, to make corn cheap and then to lie down prematurely to make a spot of green grass on the prairie.

Emerson's Truth, Emerson's Wisdom

STATISTICS AND THE TYRANNY OF CHANCE

Even the laws of statistics, a relatively new science in Emerson's day and an inescapably important element in our own, seems to reinforce the limiting power of fate. We have all asked ourselves at various times, "What are the chances that a person like me could become a successful singer? entertainer? athlete? medical doctor? college professor? businessperson? entrepreneur? Senator? President? etc. The answer is often small, slim, or none. The numbers, it seems, are overwhelmingly against us, and the numbers, we are told, don't lie. Exceptional people do emerge occasionally, but their appearance is both ordained and severely limited by statistical probability. The chances of any one of us becoming a new Copernicus, or Newton, or Bach appears to be remote to the point of impossibility. And yet, these figures will come forth, predictably.

> *One more fagot [i.e. element] of these adamantine bandages is the new science of Statistics. It is a rule that the most casual and extraordinary events, if the basis of population is broad enough, become matter of fixed calculation. It would not be safe to say when a captain like Bonaparte, a singer like Jenny Lind, or a navigator like Bowditch would be born in Boston; but, on a population of twenty or two hundred millions, something like accuracy may be had.*

"The air," it seems, is filled with inventions and inventors. It is a matter of fate as to where and when a particular one shall emerge. Emerson's point here is that there are, strictly speaking, no self-made men. Their coming was predictable and inevitable.

> *'T is frivolous to fix pedantically the date of particular inventions. They have all been invented over and over fifty times. Man is the arch machine of which*

Fate and Power

all these shifts drawn from himself are toy models. He helps himself on each emergency by copying or duplicating his own structure, just so far as the need is. 'T is hard to find the right Homer, Zoroaster, or Menu; harder still to find the Tubal Cain, or Vulcan, or Cadmus, or Copernicus, or Fust, or Fulton; the indisputable inventor. There are scores and centuries of them. "The air is full of men." This kind of talent so abounds, this constructive tool-making efficiency, as if it adhered to the chemic atoms; as if the air he breathes were made of Vaucansons, Franklins, and Watts.

Doubtless in every million there will be an astronomer, a mathematician, a comic poet, a mystic. No one can read the history of astronomy without perceiving that Copernicus, Newton, Laplace, are not new men, or a new kind of men, but that Thales, Anaximenes, Hipparchus, Empedocles, Aristarchus, Pythagoras, OEnipodes, had anticipated them; each had the same tense geometrical brain, apt for the same vigorous computation and logic; a mind parallel to the movement of the world. The Roman mile probably rested on a measure of a degree of the meridian. Mahometan and Chinese know what we know of leap-year, of the Gregorian calendar, and of the precession of the equinoxes. As in every barrel of cowries [i.e. shell fish] brought to New Bedford there shall be one orangia, so there will, in a dozen millions of Malays and Mahometans, be one or two astronomical skulls. In a large city, the most casual things, and things whose beauty lies in their casualty, are produced as punctually and to order as the baker's muffin for breakfast. Punch [a British satirical magazine] makes exactly one capital joke a week; and the journals contrive to furnish one good piece of news every day.

There are various other statistically limiting factors in life such as disease and accidents. All of us, especially as we grow older, calculate our chances of developing cancer, Parkinson's, Alzheimer's, or any number of other diseases, maladies, or sicknesses. They are an inescapable part of the human condition, and it would be foolish to deny the possibilities. Consequently, as we get older conversations with our peers and siblings inevitably turn more and more into information exchanges on aches, pains, symptoms, tests, and treatments. We find ourselves lingering a bit longer over the obituary page in our morning newspaper. One account describes the passing of a person younger than ourselves and suddenly we have the sinking feeling that we're living on borrowed time. Alternately, the death of a man who lived past ninety convinces us that there's still a long road ahead. It's like dancing around lightening strikes. So far we've managed to elude the *"mechanical exactness"* of an equation that can have only one result. Everyone must die, but in the meantime, we try to *"keep afloat alone,"* for as long as we can.

And not less work the laws of repression, the penalties of violated functions. Famine, typhus, frost, war, suicide and effete [i.e. worn out] races must be reckoned calculable parts of the system of the world. These are pebbles from the mountain, hints of the terms by which our life is walled up, and which show a kind of mechanical exactness, as of a loom or mill in what we call casual or fortuitous events.

The force with which we resist these torrents of tendency looks so ridiculously inadequate that it amounts to little more than a criticism or protest made by a minority of one, under compulsion of millions. I seemed in the height of a tempest to see men over-board struggling in the waves, and driven about here and there. They glanced intelligently at each other, but 't was little they could do for one another; 't was much if each could keep afloat alone. Well, they had a right to their eye-beams, and all the rest was Fate.

ACKNOWLEDGING THE LIMITATIONS OF FATE

As difficult as it may seem, especially for a people who are raised to believe that all things are possible, the limitations of fate must be acknowledged and taken into account as we measure the calculus of our lives.

We cannot trifle with this reality, this cropping-out in our planted gardens of the core of the world. No picture of life can have any veracity that does not admit the odious facts. A man's power is hooped in by a necessity which, by many experiments, he touches on every side until he learns its arc.

The element running through entire nature, which we popularly call Fate, is known to us as limitation. Whatever limits us we call Fate. If we are brute and barbarous, the fate takes a brute and dreadful shape. As we refine, our checks become finer. If we rise to spiritual culture, the antagonism takes a spiritual form. In the Hindoo fables, Vishnu follows Maya through all her ascending changes, from insect and crawfish up to elephant; whatever form she took, he took the male form of that kind, until she became at last woman and goddess, and he a man and a god. The limitations refine as the soul purifies, but the ring of necessity is always perched at the top.

When the gods in the Norse heaven were unable to bind the Fenris Wolf with steel or with weight of mountains,—the one he snapped and the other he spurned with his heel,—they put round his foot a

Fate and Power

> *limp band softer than silk or cobweb, and this held him; the more he spurned it the stiffer it drew. So soft and so stanch is the ring of Fate. Neither brandy, nor nectar, nor sulphuric ether, nor hell-fire, nor ichor, nor poetry, nor genius, can get rid of this limp band. For if we give it the high sense in which the poets use it, even thought itself is not above Fate; that too must act according to eternal laws, and all that is wilful and fantastic in it is in opposition to its fundamental essence.*

Finally, Emerson observes that Fate also possesses a moral dimension where *"Fate is a vindicator."* In other words, what goes around, comes around. The moral laws are like the laws of physics. For every action there is an equal and opposite reaction.

> *And last of all, high over thought, in the world of morals, Fate appears as vindicator, levelling the high, lifting the low, requiring justice in man, and always striking soon or late when justice is not done. What is useful will last, what is hurtful will sink. "The doer must suffer," said the Greeks; "you would soothe a Deity not to be soothed." "God himself cannot procure good for the wicked," said the Welsh triad. "God may consent, but only for a time," said the bard of Spain. The limitation is impassable by any insight of man. In its last and loftiest ascensions, insight itself and the freedom of the will is one of its obedient members. But we must not run into generalizations too large, but show the natural bounds or essential distinctions, and seek to do justice to the other elements as well.*

Emerson's Truth, Emerson's Wisdom

POWER VS. FATE

As Emerson makes clear, Fate can be an intimidating and awesome force in our lives. But we are not consigned to it wholly. *"For, though Fate is immense, so is power, which is the other fact in the dual world, immense."* This immense power belongs to us, both individually and collectively. In the second part of his essay, Emerson examines the implications of Power.

Thus we trace Fate in matter, mind, and morals; in race, in retardations of strata, and in thought and character as well. It is everywhere bound or limitation. But Fate has its lord; limitation its limits,—is different seen from above and from below, from within and from without. For though Fate is immense, so is Power, which is the other fact in the dual world, immense. If Fate follows and limits Power, Power attends and antagonizes Fate. We must respect Fate as natural history, but there is more than natural history. For who and what is this criticism that pries into the matter? Man is not order of nature, sack and sack, belly and members, link in a chain, nor any ignominious baggage; but a stupendous antagonism, a dragging together of the poles of the Universe. He betrays his relation to what is below him,—thick-skulled, small-brained, fishy, quadrumanous, quadruped ill-disguised, hardly escaped into biped,—and has paid for the new powers by loss of some of the old ones. But the lightning which explodes and fashions planets, maker of planets and suns, is in him. On one side elemental order, sandstone and granite, rock-ledges, peat-bog, forest, sea and shore; and on the other part thought, the spirit which composes and decomposes nature,—here they are, side by side, god and devil, mind and matter, king and conspirator, belt and spasm, riding peacefully together in the eye and brain of every man.

It is the power of the Over-Soul, the "great Soul," that is the source of our freedom. Those who speak of limitations such as "destiny, their birth-star, etc.," place far too much emphasis on the forces outside of themselves while ignoring the immense power within. We have free will, and free will would be meaningless without the power to make choices in our lives.

Nor can he blink the freewill. To hazard the contradiction,—freedom is necessary. If you please to plant yourself on the side of Fate, and say, Fate is all; then we say, a part of Fate is the freedom of man. Forever wells up the impulse of choosing and acting in the soul. Intellect annuls Fate. So far as a man thinks, he is free. And though nothing is more disgusting than the crowing about liberty by slaves, as most men are, and the flippant mistaking for freedom of some paper preamble like a Declaration of Independence or the statute right to vote, by those who have never dared to think or to act,—yet it is wholesome to man to look not at Fate, but the other way: the practical view is the other. His sound relation to these facts is to use and command, not to cringe to them. "Look not on Nature, for her name is fatal," said the oracle. The too much contemplation of these limits induces meanness. They who talk much of destiny, their birth-star, etc., are in a lower dangerous plane, and invite the evils they fear.

Emerson's Truth, Emerson's Wisdom

Truly "heroic" people, those who recognize and seize upon their own unique talents and potential, are able to use Fate to their advantage in remarkable ways. The same awesome, natural power that is manifest *"in a river, an oak, or a mountain"* is manifest in humanity.

I cited the instinctive and heroic races as proud believers in Destiny. They conspire with it; a loving resignation is with the event. But the dogma makes a different impression when it is held by the weak and lazy. 'T is weak and vicious people who cast the blame on Fate. The right use of Fate is to bring up our conduct to the loftiness of nature. Rude and invincible except by themselves are the elements. So let man be. Let him empty his breast of his windy conceits, and show his lordship by manners and deeds on the scale of nature. Let him hold his purpose as with the tug of gravitation. No power, no persuasion, no bribe shall make him give up his point. A man ought to compare advantageously with a river, an oak, or a mountain. He shall have not less the flow, the expansion, and the resistance of these.

FATE AS A SOURCE OF PERSONAL STRENGTH AND COURAGE

While Fate may appear to some to be a limiting force that intimidates and weakens us, looked at another way, it can also be a source of fortitude and courage.

'T is the best use of Fate to teach a fatal courage. Go face the fire at sea, or the cholera in your friend's house, or the burglar in your own, or what danger lies in the way of duty,—knowing you are guarded by the cherubim of Destiny. If you believe in Fate to your harm, believe it at least for your good.

For if Fate is so prevailing, man also is part of it, and can confront fate with fate. If the Universe have these savage accidents, our atoms are as savage in resistance. We should be crushed by the atmosphere, but for the reaction of the air within the body. A tube made of a film of glass can resist the shock of the ocean if filled with the same water. If there be omnipotence in the stroke, there is omnipotence of recoil.

The power that we enjoy comes from aligning ourselves with the divine force of goodness and life that animates our world. It is by this alignment with the good that we naturally seek to live noble and dignified lives. When we are thus aligned, the force of fate becomes the horse that we ride or the ship that we sail. It is our thought and intuition that reveal this liberating truth to us. We shall know the truth, and the truth shall make us free. We experience new life with each successive revelation. The laws that govern the universe are the source of our strength as they act through us and we through them.

1. But Fate against Fate is only parrying and defence: there are also the

> noble creative forces. The revelation of Thought takes man out of servitude into freedom. We rightly say of ourselves, we were born and afterward we were born again, and many times. We have successive experiences so important that the new forgets the old, and hence the mythology of the seven or the nine heavens. The day of days, the great day of the feast of life, is that in which the inward eye opens to the Unity in things, to the omnipresence of law:—sees that what is must be and ought to be, or is the best. This beatitude dips from on high down on us and we see. It is not in us so much as we are in it. If the air come to our lungs, we breathe and live; if not, we die. If the light come to our eyes, we see; else not. And if truth come to our mind we suddenly expand to its dimensions, as if we grew to worlds. We are as law-givers; we speak for Nature; we prophesy and divine.

It is possible to experience this liberating power as intellectual exhilaration.

> This insight throws us on the party and interest of the Universe, against all and sundry; against ourselves as much as others. A man speaking from insight affirms of himself what is true of the mind [i.e. the soul]: seeing its immortality, he says, I am immortal; seeing its invincibility, he says, I am strong. It is not in us, but we are in it. It is of the maker, not of what is made. All things are touched and changed by it. This uses and is not used. It distances those who share it from those who share it not. Those who share it not are flocks and herds. It dates

Fate and Power

from itself; not from former men or better men, gospel, or constitution, or college, or custom. Where it shines, Nature is no longer intrusive, but all things make a musical or pictorial impression. The world of men show like a comedy without laughter: populations, interests, government, history; 't is all toy figures in a toy house. It does not overvalue particular truths. We hear eagerly every thought and word quoted from an intelletual man. But in his presence our own mind is roused to activity, and we forget very fast what he says, much more interested in the new play of our own thought than in any thought of his. 'T is the majesty into which we have suddenly mounted, the impersonality, the scorn of egotisms, the sphere of laws, that engage us. Once we were stepping a little this way and a little that way; now we are as men in a balloon, and do not think so much of the point we have left, or the point we would make, as of the liberty and glory of the way.

Comprehending the unifying force of life and our relation to it becomes a source of transcendent power.

Just as much intellect as you add, so much organic power. He who sees through the design, presides over it, and must will that which must be. We sit and rule, and, though we sleep, our dream will come to pass. Our thought, though it were only an hour old, affirms an oldest necessity, not to be separated from thought, and not to be separated from will. They must always have coexisted. It apprises us of its sovereignty and godhead, which refuse to be severed from it. It is not mine or thine, but the will of all mind. It is poured into the souls of all men, as the soul itself which constitutes them men. I know not whether there be, as is alleged, in the upper region of our atmosphere, a permanent westerly current which carries with it all atoms which rise to that height, but I see that when souls reach a certain clearness of perception they accept a knowledge and motive above selfishness. A breath of will blows eternally through the universe of souls in the direction of the Right and Necessary. It is the air which all intellects inhale and exhale, and it is the wind which blows the worlds into order and orbit.

Thought dissolves the material universe by carrying the mind up into a sphere where all is plastic [i.e. capable of being shaped, pliable]. Of two men, each obeying his own thought, he whose thought is deepest will be the strongest character. Always one man more than another represents the will of Divine Providence to the period.

Fate and Power

WILL POWER AND INTUITION

We become aware of truth through intuition as well as thought. Emerson calls this *"moral sentiment"* because it is perceived as a feeling. When you know for a certainty what is right and true, *"you cannot choose but [to] believe in unlimited power."* What you are feeling is the force of the great Soul that is the ultimate power and lawgiver. *"Each pulse from that heart is an oath from the Most High."* Of course, these intuitions of truth are only worthwhile if we have the courage to act on them. *"There can be no driving force except through the conversion of the man into his will."* We must believe in what we know to be the true and proper course for us to follow. This, then, becomes the faith that can move mountains.

> *2. If thought makes free, so does the moral sentiment. The mixtures of spiritual chemistry refuse to be analyzed. Yet we can see that with the perception of truth is joined the desire that it shall prevail; that affection is essential to will. Moreover, when a strong will appears, it usually results from a certain unity of organization, as if the whole energy of body and mind flowed in one direction. All great force is real and elemental. There is no manufacturing a strong will. There must be a pound to balance a pound. Where power is shown in will, it must rest on the universal force. Alaric and Bonaparte must believe they rest on a truth, or their will can be bought or bent. There is a bribe possible for any finite will. But the pure sympathy with universal ends is an infinite force, and cannot be bribed or bent. Whoever has had experience of the moral sentiment cannot choose but believe in unlimited power. Each pulse from that heart is an oath from the Most High. I know not what the word sublime means, if it be not the*

intimations, in this infant, of a terrific force. A text of heroism, a name and anecdote of courage, are not arguments but sallies of freedom. One of these is the verse of the Persian Hafiz, "'Tis written on the gate of Heaven, 'Woe unto him who suffers himself to be betrayed by Fate!'" Does the reading of history make us fatalists? What courage does not the opposite opinion show! A little whim of will to be free gallantly contending against the universe of chemistry.

But insight is not will, nor is affection will. Perception is cold, and goodness dies in wishes. As Voltaire said, 't is the misfortune of worthy people that they are cowards; "un des plus grands malheurs des honnêtes gens c'est qu'ils sont des lâches." There must be a fusion of these two to generate the energy of will. There can be no driving force except through the conversion of the man into his will, making him the will, and the will him. And one may say boldly that no man has a right perception of any truth who has not been reacted on by it so as to be ready to be its martyr.

Fate and Power

DISCOVERING THE HEROIC IN EVERYDAY LIFE

By connecting with the divinity within, we empower ourselves. This necessarily involves an exercise of the "will" whereby we plant ourselves firmly on our own instincts and follow wherever they may lead. Sometimes this can result in a "heroic" action. A savior, a dynamic reformer can emerge in the most unlikely circumstances when a true soul is prompted to "stand against Fate." A good example of this is Rosa Parks. On December 1, 1955 this ordinary, diminutive African-American seamstress refused to give up her seat to a white man on a bus in Montgomery, Alabama, even though the segregation laws at the time required her to do so. Her act of civil disobedience was undoubtedly based on a "moral sentiment," the feeling that these racist laws were clearly unjust and immoral. Segregation had been a way of life in Montgomery, and many other places, since the end of the Civil War. It was as real and as formidable as a brick wall. To oppose such laws was considered by most to be an act of futility that was certain to bring only suffering and pain. What could one, average, tired, middle-aged black woman possibly hope to accomplish by opposing this awesome giant? As it turns out, quite a bit.

In her refusal to accept this cruel and unjust dictate of "Fate," that is, things as they are, Rosa Parks asserted the countervailing power of eternal justice. This power resided within her, as it does in us. It manifests itself in those who are open to its call as a powerful stirring of the great Soul within. This stirring, this agitation of the spirit, fortifies our will and moves us to higher levels of personal courage. Her act of spontaneous defiance brought Rosa Parks into alignment with the divine power of the universe. That power is immense, stronger than the collective weight of hundreds of years of racial oppression and bigotry. By yoking this intuition of truth to her will, Rosa Parks, many say, helped to precipitate the modern civil rights movement in America.

This movement eventually destroyed a once mighty fortress of "fate" and thereby made possible in our own time what was unthinkable to most then, the election of an African-

American president. She refused to "be betrayed by Fate" because she knew that she possessed a greater power. Rosa Parks thus became a hero and a model to all those who yearned for justice in an oppressive world. Her example inspired thousands to follow suit. We all have access to the same spirit that empowered Rosa Parks. We, too, can accomplish a great deal in our lives, even if it seems that "fate" is against us. As Emerson insists, we have to have faith in the power of the divinity that is within us.

The one serious and formidable thing in nature is a will. Society is servile from want of will, and therefore the world wants saviours and religions. One way is right to go; the hero sees it, and moves on that aim, and has the world under him for root and support. He is to others as the world. His approbation is honor; his dissent, infamy. The glance of his eye has the force of sun-beams. A personal influence towers up in memory only worthy, and we gladly forget numbers, money, climate, gravitation, and the rest of Fate.

Many people sense the power of the great Soul within them, but this private feeling is rarely translated into specific action in the "real world," where, it appears, we are prone to *"believe a malignant energy rules."* The truth, however, is that this divine force *is "everywhere and always."* Those who chose to deny this will eventually *"run against it and themselves."*

We can afford to allow the limitation, if we know it is the meter of the growing man. We stand against Fate, as children stand up against the wall in their father's house and notch their height from year to year. But when the boy grows to man, and is master of the house, he pulls down that wall and builds a new and bigger. 'T is only a question of time. Every brave youth is in training to ride

Fate and Power

and rule this dragon. His science is to make weapons and wings of these passions and retarding forces. Now whether, seeing these two things, fate and power, we are permitted to believe in unity? The bulk of mankind believe in two gods. They are under one dominion here in the house, as friend and parent, in social circles, in letters, in art, in love, in religion; but in mechanics, in dealing with steam and climate, in trade, in politics, they think they come under another; and that it would be a practical blunder to transfer the method and way of working of one sphere into the other. What good, honest, generous men at home, will be wolves and foxes on 'Change! [i.e. the stock exchange] *What pious men in the parlor will vote for what reprobates at the polls! To a certain point, they believe themselves the care of a Providence. But in a steamboat, in an epidemic, in war, they believe a malignant energy rules.*

But relation and connection are not somewhere and sometimes, but everywhere and always. The divine order does not stop where their sight stops. The friendly power works on the same rules in the next farm and the next planet. But where they have not experience they run against it and hurt themselves. Fate then is a name for facts not yet passed under the fire of thought; for causes which are unpenetrated.

Like Rosa Parks, we all face challenges of one sort or another that seem to block our way to greater success in life. Often we feel weak, timid, and virtually powerless against the forces of fate that are ranged against us. These might take the form of hypercritical friends, relatives, or even members of our immediate family, people who are inclined to tell us what we can or cannot do, what is within our reach, and what is far beyond it. Sometimes this intimidation comes from bosses or teachers or supervisors, people who believe they know better than we the full extent of our powers and potential. In Emerson's time, these limitations were especially acute for African Americans, Native Americans, Irish and Asian immigrants, and women.

All of these groups were narrowly circumscribed by someone else's notion of what their proper role should be, what the limits of their abilities and talents were. Emerson refused to accept the dictates of this "establishment" mentality. Everywhere he looked, he saw a power that could transform people and nations, if they would only open themselves to it. As Rosa Parks has demonstrated, it is our character that determines our fortunes, not Fate. There are more possibilities in life than we are willing to acknowledge or attempt. The most crippling limitations are those that we place upon ourselves. For Emerson, all things are possible. Every force that opposes us can also be made to serve us. The enormous progress of humankind from the beginnings of human history to the present moment testify to this fact. We have extended our reach from the darkness of caves to touch the brilliance of the stars, which today serve to guide our navigation through the heavens themselves, and beyond. For a person in proper alignment with the power of the universe, not even the sky is a limit, for *"there's nothing he will not make his carrier."*

> *But every jet of chaos which threatens to exterminate us is convertible by intellect into wholesome force. Fate is unpenetrated causes. The water drowns ship and sailor like a grain of dust. But learn to swim, trim your bark, and the wave which drowned it will be cloven by it and carry it like its own foam, a plume and a power. The cold is inconsiderate of persons, tingles your blood, freezes a man like a dew-drop. But learn to skate, and the ice will give you a graceful, sweet, and*

Fate and Power

poetic motion. The cold will brace your limbs and brain to genius, and make you foremost men of time. Cold and sea will train an imperial Saxon race, which nature cannot bear to lose, and after cooping it up for a thousand years in yonder England, gives a hundred Englands, a hundred Mexicos. All the bloods it shall absorb and domineer: and more than Mexicos, the secrets of water and steam, the spasms of electricity, the ductility of metals, the chariot of the air, the ruddered balloon are awaiting you.

The annual slaughter from typhus far exceeds that of war; but right drainage destroys typhus. The plague in the sea-service from scurvy is healed by lemon juice and other diets portable or procurable; the depopulation by cholera and small-pox is ended by drainage and vaccination; and every other pest is not less in the chain of cause and effect, and may be fought off. And whilst art draws out the venom, it commonly extorts some benefit from the vanquished enemy. The mischievous torrent is taught to drudge for man; the wild beasts he makes useful for food, or dress, or labor; the chemic explosions are controlled like his watch. These are now the steeds on which he rides. Man moves in all modes, by legs of horses, by wings of wind, by steam, by gas of balloon, by electricity, and stands on tiptoe threatening to hunt the eagle in his own element. There's nothing he will not make his carrier.

Steam was till the other day the devil which we dreaded. Every pot made by any human potter or brazier had a *hole in its cover, to let off the enemy, lest he should lift pot and roof and carry the house away. But the Marquis of Worcester, Watt, and Fulton bethought themselves that where was power was not devil, but was God; that it must be availed of, and not by any means let off and wasted. Could he lift pots and roofs and houses so handily? He was the workman they were in search of. He could be used to lift away, chain and compel other devils far more reluctant and dangerous, namely, cubic miles of earth, mountains, weight or resistance of water, machinery, and the labors of all men in the world; and time he shall lengthen, and shorten space.*

Fate and Power

NATURAL POWER AND POLITICAL FREEDOM

In addition to the freedom wrought through the power of science, Emerson reminds us that our personal freedom came when the masses recognized and acted upon the political power that was naturally theirs. The result was the birth of democracy in America.

> *It has not fared much otherwise with higher kinds of steam. The opinion of the million was the terror of the world, and it was attempted either to dissipate it, by amusing nations, or to pile it over with strata of society,—a layer of soldiers, over that a layer of lords, and a king on the top; with clamps and hoops of castles, garrisons, and police. But sometimes the religious principle would get in and burst the hoops and rive every mountain laid on top of it. The Fultons and Watts of politics, believing in unity, saw that it was a power, and by satisfying it (as justice satisfies everybody), through a different disposition of society,—grouping it on a level instead of piling it into a mountain,—they have contrived to make of this terror the most harmless and energetic form of a State.*

At times, it seems that the *"lesson of Fate"* is oppressive, but for every limitation there is an opposing strength and so the two are inevitably *"reconciled"* in the unity that is life.

> *Very odious, I confess, are the lessons of Fate. Who likes to have a dapper phrenologist [i.e. one who reads character in the shape of the skull] pronouncing on his fortunes? Who likes to believe that he has, hidden in his skull, spine, and pelvis, all the vices of a Saxon*

or Celtic race, which will be sure to pull him down,—with what grandeur of hope and resolve he is fired,—into a selfish, huckstering, servile, dodging animal? A learned physician tells us the fact is invariable with the Neapolitan, that when mature he assumes the forms of the unmistakable scoundrel. That is a little overstated,—but may pass.

But these are magazines and arsenals. A man must thank his defects, and stand in some terror of his talents. A transcendent talent draws so largely on his forces as to lame him; a defect pays him revenues on the other side. The sufferance which is the badge of the Jew, has made him, in these days, the ruler of the rulers of the earth. If Fate is ore and quarry, if evil is good in the making, if limitation is power that shall be, if calamities, oppositions, and weights are wings and means,—we are reconciled.

PROGRESS IS THE DICTATE OF FATE

The necessary tendency of things is to improve. This is yet another positive aspect of Fate. Progress is inevitable, as the arc of history shows.

> *Fate involves the melioration. No statement of the Universe can have any soundness which does not admit its ascending effort. The direction of the whole and of the parts is toward benefit, and in proportion to the health. Behind every individual closes organization; before him opens liberty,—the Better, the Best. The first and worse races are dead. The second and imperfect races are dying out, or remain for the maturing of higher. In the latest race, in man, every generosity, every new perception, the love and praise he extorts from his fellows, are certificates of advance out of fate into freedom. Liberation of the will from the sheaths and clogs of organization which he has outgrown, is the end and aim of this world. Every calamity is a spur and valuable hint; and where his endeavors do not yet fully avail, they tell as tendency. The whole circle of animal life—tooth against tooth, devouring war, war for food, a yelp of pain and a grunt of triumph, until at last the whole menagerie, the whole chemical mass is mellowed and refined for higher use—pleases at a sufficient perspective.*

There is a great unity in life that derives from the conjunction of opposites. Each person is part and parcel of the world and ideally forms a seamless relationship with it. The energy of the divine flows through all and empowers our course in life, as we co-operate with it. Thus, *"Life works both voluntarily and supernaturally in its neighborhood."*

But to see how fate slides into freedom and freedom into fate, observe how far the roots of every creature run, or find if you can a point where there is no thread of connection. Our life is consentaneous [i.e. simultaneous] and far-related. This knot of nature is so well tied that nobody was ever cunning enough to find the two ends. Nature is intricate, overlapped, interweaved and endless. Christopher Wren said of the beautiful King's College chapel, that "if anybody would tell him where to lay the first stone, he would build such another." But where shall we find the first atom in this house of man, which is all consent, inosculation [i.e. the passing of one thing into another] and balance of parts?

The web of relation is shown in habitat, shown in hibernation. When hibernation was observed, it was found that whilst some animals became torpid in winter, others were torpid in summer: hibernation then was a false name. The long sleep is not an effect of cold, but is regulated by the supply of food proper to the animal. It becomes torpid when the fruit or prey it lives on is not in season, and regains its activity when its food is ready.

Eyes are found in light; ears in auricular air; feet on land; fins in water; wings in air; and each creature where it was meant to be, with a mutual fitness. Every zone has its own Fauna. There is adjustment between the animal and its food, its parasite, its enemy. Balances are kept. It is not allowed to diminish in numbers, nor to exceed. The like adjustments exist for man. His food is cooked when he arrives; his coal in the pit; the house ventilated; the mud of the deluge dried; his companions arrived at the same hour, and awaiting him with love, concert, laughter and tears. These are coarse adjustments, but the invisible are not less. There are more belongings to every creature than his air and his food. His instincts must be met, and he has predisposing power that bends and fits what is near him to his use. He is not possible until the invisible things are right for him, as well as the visible. Of what changes then in sky and earth, and in finer skies and earths, does the appearance of some Dante or Columbus apprise us!

How is this effected? Nature is no spendthrift, but takes the shortest way to her ends. As the general says to his soldiers, *"If you want a fort, build a fort,"* so nature makes every creature do its own work and get its living,—is it planet, animal or tree. The planet makes itself. The animal cell makes itself;—then, what it wants. Every creature, wren or dragon, shall make its own lair. As soon as there is life, there is self-direction and absorbing and using of material. Life is freedom,—life in the direct ratio of its amount. You may be sure the new-born man is not inert. Life works both voluntarily and supernaturally in its neighborhood. Do you suppose he can be estimated by his weight in pounds, or that he is contained in his skin,—this reaching, radiating, jaculating [i.e. darting] fellow? The smallest candle fills a mile with its rays, and the papillae of a man run out to every star.

There is a coherent force at work in the world that insures necessary things get done. The progress of humanity is the result of the divine current that flows through history and seeks higher and ever higher levels of perfection, which results in both scientific and social progress.

When there is something to be done, the world knows how to get it done. The vegetable eye makes leaf, pericarp, root, bark, or thorn, as the need is; the first cell converts itself into stomach, mouth, nose, or nail, according to the want; the world throws its life into a hero or a shepherd, and puts him where he is wanted. Dante and Columbus were Italians, in their time; they would be Russians or Americans to-day. Things ripen, new men come. The adaptation is not capricious. The ulterior aim, the purpose beyond itself, the correlation by which planets subside and crystallize, then animate beasts and men,—will not stop but will work into finer particulars, and from finer to finest.

We all have a positive role in the march of human progress, but we must exert ourselves in order to play it. Events are not *"arbitrary and independent of actions."* They are all the products of *"cause and effect,"* and they await our active input.

The secret of the world is the tie between person and event. Person makes event, and event person. The "times," "the age," what is that but a few profound persons and a few active persons who epitomize the times?—Goethe, Hegel, Metternich, Adams, Calhoun, Guizot, Peel, Cobden, Kossuth, Rothschild, Astor,

Brunel, and the rest. The same fitness must be presumed between a man and the time and event, as between the sexes, or between a race of animals and the food it eats, or the inferior races it uses. He thinks his fate alien, because the copula is hidden. But the soul contains the event that shall befall it; for the event is only the actualization of its thoughts, and what we pray to ourselves for is always granted. The event is the print of your form. It fits you like your skin. What each does is proper to him. Events are the children of his body and mind. We learn that the soul of Fate is the soul of us, as Hafiz sings,—

*"Alas! till now I had not known,
My guide and fortune's guide are one."*

All the toys that infatuate men and which they play for,—houses, land, money, luxury, power, fame, are the selfsame thing, with a new gauze or two of illusion overlaid. And of all the drums and rattles by which men are made willing to have their heads broke, and are led out solemnly every morning to parade,—the most admirable is this by which we are brought to believe that events are arbitrary and independent of actions. At the conjuror's, we detect the hair by which he moves his puppet, but we have not eyes sharp enough to descry the thread that ties cause and effect.

Nature suits us for the work we are to do and by doing it we reap *"the fruit of [our] character."* In this way, we create our own world and are reconciled to it.

Nature magically suits the man to his fortunes, by making these the fruit of his character. Ducks take to the water, eagles to the sky, waders to the sea margin, hunters to the forest, clerks to counting-rooms, soldiers to the frontier. Thus events grow on the same stem with persons; are sub-persons. The pleasure of life is according to the man that lives it, and not according to the work or the place. Life is an ecstasy. We know what madness belongs to love,—what power to paint a vile object in hues of heaven. As insane persons are indifferent to their dress, diet, and other accommodations, and as we do in dreams, with equanimity, the most absurd acts, so a drop more of wine in our cup of life will reconcile us to strange company and work. Each creature puts forth from itself its own condition and sphere, as the slug sweats out its slimy house on the pear-leaf, and the woolly aphides on the apple perspire their own bed, and the fish its shell. In youth we clothe ourselves with rainbows and go as brave as the zodiac. In age we put out another sort of perspiration,— gout, fever, rheumatism, caprice, doubt, fretting and avarice.

In the final analysis, Emerson believes that natural limitations are not bad. The order of nature is such so that it might serve our needs. Absolute freedom is an absurdity. If every person had the freedom and the power to *"derange the order of nature, who would accept the gift of life?"* We should not feel oppressed or intimidated by the structure of the world we face. Its structure is our structure. The world is infused with the same dynamic spirit that is within us, and its tendency is towards the good and the just. But this goodness and justice require our active co-operation.

The secret of success in life lies in recognizing and using the tremendous and unique power that is ours. As Emerson told

Fate and Power

the students at Harvard many years earlier, *"This time, like all times, is a perfectly good one if we know what to do with it."* He always did. In light of all this, rather than grousing at those things that are fixed and determined we should *"build altars to the Beautiful Necessity"* that both guides and informs our lives and the world about us. We were born to live, not to cringe. We were born to embrace our fate, not hide from it. Our power is dynamic, immediate, and real. It is up to us to use it.

> **Let us build altars to the Beautiful Necessity. If we thought men were free in the sense that in a single exception one fantastical will could prevail over the law of things, it were all one as if a child's hand could pull down the sun. If in the least particular one could derange the order of nature,—who would accept the gift of life?**
>
> **Let us build altars to the Beautiful Necessity, which secures that all is made of one piece; that plaintiff and defendant, friend and enemy, animal and planet, food and eater are of one kind. In astronomy is vast space but no foreign system; in geology, vast time but the same laws as to-day. Why should we be afraid of Nature, which is no other than "philosophy and theology embodied"? Why should we fear to be crushed by savage elements, we who are made up of the same elements? Let us build to the Beautiful Necessity, which makes man brave in believing that he cannot shun a danger that is appointed, nor incur one that is not; to the Necessity which rudely or softly educates him to the perception that there are no contingencies; that Law rules throughout existence; a Law which is not intelligent but intelligence;—not personal nor impersonal—it disdains**

words and passes understanding; it dissolves persons; it vivifies nature; yet solicits the pure in heart to draw on all its omnipotence.

A FINAL THOUGHT: Often it may seem that our world is spinning out of control. Or worse yet, that it has never been under control. We live in fear of war, terrorist attacks, inflation, a declining economy, and job loss. The "good life," which is everyone's American dream, appears to be a distant and increasingly impossible goal for ourselves and our children. Just maintaining a decent standard of living may seem at times almost impossible. These concerns are real and largely unavoidable. They are part of modern life, and they present an ongoing and daunting challenge. At times our problems may seem so large that they threaten to overwhelm us. Our personal resources and abilities appear puny and inadequate.

Sometimes, we're tempted just to give up the struggle, to resign ourselves to fate and to accept the inevitable defeat. "Que sera, sera." What will be, will be. It is certainly true that if we throw our hands up and resign ourselves to fate, fate will accept our resignation. We can just let things slide, take it on the chin, watch the cookie crumble. Unfortunately, as tempting as this philosophy of resignation may be at times, it's a formula for disaster. It's also unnecessary. Emerson assures us that we can take charge of our lives. We have much more power in our corner than we realize. While fate is most certainly a major force in our reality, it is not the only force. *"If you believe in Fate to your harm, believe it at least for your good."* We have the power of the great Soul within us, and that makes all the difference.

CHAPTER SIX: WEALTH AND SUCCESS

You were Born to be Rich; The Responsibilities of Wealth; Intellect, Imagination, and Creativity

Emerson was a social liberal but an economic conservative, at least by today's standards. He believed in laissez-faire economics, which he learned about from Adam Smith's classic, *The Wealth of Nations* (1776). He lived through what was probably the most dramatic and important period of change in the American economy, a transition in the first half of the nineteenth century from agricultural subsistence and barter to a market economy. In *"Wealth,"* another essay from **Conduct of Life** *(1860)*, Emerson describes this transition.

> *When men now alive were born, the farm yielded everything that was consumed on it. The farm yielded no money, and the farmer got on without. If he fell sick, his neighbors came in to his aid; each gave a day's work, or a half day; or lent his yoke of oxen, or his horse, and kept his work even; hoed his potatoes, mowed his hay, reaped his rye; well knowing that no man could afford to hire labor without selling his land. In autumn a farmer could sell an ox or a hog and get a little money to pay taxes withal. Now, the farmer buys almost all he consumes,— tin-ware, cloth, sugar, tea, coffee, fish, coal, railroad tickets and newspapers.*

Emerson believed that everyone was born to be rich. His idea of riches, however, did not mean merely the accumulation of obscene levels of material property. Rather, he believed that every individual was born with the potential to contribute in a unique way to the "common wealth" of humanity. This potential for productivity is both a gift and an obligation that derives from the great Soul within us. It is our special share of the divine power that is at work in the world and in us. When we exercise our particular creative potential to the fullest, we literally enrich the world. Some of us may become creative entrepreneurs, like Bill Gates or Warren Buffet. Or we might become famous entertainers, movie stars, singers, or even authors. Others might become sports stars, or political leaders.

Such outstanding people obviously make notable contributions to the common wealth, thereby enriching our lives as well as their own in a number of ways. Theses exceptional individuals are but the tip of the iceberg, however. It is the people who will never rise to the level of public prominence, the laborers, clerks, nurses, janitors, jailors, technicians, and teachers, as well as a myriad of others, who constitute the greater part of the treasure of our society. They are the pistons that power the engine of wealth. Without them, there would be no one to build and buy the entrepreneurs' latest product, no audiences for the actors and the singers, no readers for the authors' books, and no fans to applaud the sports stars. Ultimately, we are all important, each in our own way.

Emerson believed that the success of a commonwealth depends on each of us finding our proper vocation, our calling, and then pursuing that calling to the greatest of our ability. We all have the power to generate wealth. Because this power derives from the infinite energy of the Over-Soul, its potential is unlimited— our potential is unlimited. But most of us have yet to learn how to tap this great power within. However, many others before us, people no smarter than we, obviously figured it out. A myriad of stories have been told of poor, tired, hungry, and oppressed immigrants who, upon reaching these shores, flourished. From the Pilgrims to the present day, this saga has been repeated endlessly. Hector St. Jean de Crevecoeur, an immigrant himself, described this uniquely American phenomenon, in his book, **Letters from an American Farmer** (1782).

Wealth and Success

In this great American asylum, the poor of Europe have by some means met together, and in consequence of various causes; to what purpose should they ask one another what countrymen they are? Alas, two thirds of them had no country. Can a wretch who wanders about, who works and starves, whose life is a continual scene of sore affliction or pinching penury; can that man call England or any other kingdom his country? A country that had no bread for him, whose fields procured him no harvest, who met with nothing but the frowns of the rich, the severity of the laws, with jails and punishments; who owned not a single foot of the extensive surface of this planet? No! urged by a variety of motives, here they came. Every thing has tended to regenerate them; new laws, a new mode of living, a new social system; here they are become men: in Europe they were as so many useless plants, wanting vegetative mould, and refreshing showers; they withered, and were mowed down by want, hunger, and war; but now by the power of transplantation, like all other plants they have taken root and flourished! Formerly they were not numbered in any civil lists of their country, except in those of the poor; here they rank as citizens. By what invisible power has this surprising metamorphosis been performed? By that of the laws and that of their industry.

The transformation or rebirth that Crevecoeur described in the eighteenth century is the same phenomenon that Emerson encouraged and applauded in the nineteenth. These humble people who were nothing in their homelands, became creative, energetic, and productive citizens of the new commonwealth that was emerging in the New World. Their hidden potential was released, and they were transformed. The same phenomenon can occur to each of us, whether we are immigrants or natives, if we would only choose to see our world and ourselves in a new light. Most of us go through life accepting the limitations that others have placed upon us. But there is another self within that is far greater. We just have to discover it and release its power. Emerson's fellow Transcendentalist and probably his closest friend, Henry Thoreau, promoted the same notion of self-creation or re-creation. In **Walden** (1854) he states the following.

> *"Direct your eye right inward, and you'll find*
> *A thousand regions in your mind*
> *Yet undiscovered. Travel them, and be*
> *Expert in home-cosmography."*

> What does Africa — what does the West stand for? Is not our own interior white on the chart? black though it may prove, like the coast, when discovered. Is it the source of the Nile, or the Niger, or the Mississippi, or a Northwest Passage around this continent, that we would find? Are these the problems which most concern mankind? Is Franklin the only man who is lost, that his wife should be so earnest to find him? Does Mr. Grinnell know where he himself is? Be rather the Mungo Park, the Lewis and Clark and Frobisher, of your own streams and oceans; explore your own higher latitudes— with shiploads of preserved meats to support you, if they be necessary; and pile the empty cans sky-high for a sign. Were preserved meats invented to preserve meat merely? Nay, be a Columbus to whole new continents and worlds within you, opening new channels, not of trade, but of thought. Every man is the lord of a realm beside which the earthly empire of the Czar is but a petty state, a hummock left by the ice. Yet some can be patriotic who have no self-respect, and sacrifice the greater to the less. They love the soil which makes their graves, but have no sympathy with the spirit which may still animate their clay. Patriotism is a maggot in their heads. What was the meaning of that South-Sea Exploring Expedition, with all its parade and expense, but an indirect recognition of the fact that there are

Wealth and Success

continents and seas in the moral world to which every man is an isthmus or an inlet, yet unexplored by him, but that it is easier to sail many thousand miles through cold and storm and cannibals, in a government ship, with five hundred men and boys to assist one, than it is to explore the private sea, the Atlantic and Pacific Ocean of one's being alone.

The result of such exploration could very well be the discovery of that special gift, inclination, talent, or idea which will be the source of our personal success and personal wealth, as well as the continuing advancement of society.

Emerson believed that the progress of humankind from Cro-Magnon man to the present is a manifestation of the creative power of wealth. Primitive, underdeveloped societies are by definition poor. Progressive societies are wealthy. Wealthy societies tend to be freer and more democratic while poor societies tend to be autocratic and repressive. For Emerson, prosperity always follows freedom because only in a free society are the natural wealth-creating energies of the people allowed full reign. The Soviet Union was never a truly prosperous country because its people and their creativity were repressed. During the Cold War, Germany was divided. East Germany was a totalitarian, Communist state. West Germany was a democracy. East Germany was an economic disaster. West Germany was an economic powerhouse. East Germany produced a car known as the Trabant, which achieved a dubious distinction as one of the worst cars of all time. It was so poorly constructed that it was a matter of luck if the finished product actually would start when it reached the end of the assembly line. Meanwhile, West Germany gave the world Porsches, Mercedes, and BMWs.

Currently, we have a similar but even more extreme example on the Korean peninsula. South Korea is democratic and prosperous. North Korea is ruled by a maniacal dictator, Kim Jong-il. That nation is in the throes of a new Dark Ages. Teetering on starvation on a massive scale, North Korea's only reliable source of income is money that it extorts from the Free World in an effort to halt its nuclear weapons program. The lesson in all of these cases is that freedom is a prerequisite to the generation of wealth because, as Emerson well understood, under circumstances of repression, the creative soul of humanity, the great Soul, is stifled. All forms of creativity then suffer, not just wealth production.

Because of this fact, China is now at a cross roads. After decades of harsh repression and strict economic controls that strangled creativity of every sort, the Chinese economy has suddenly come to life. By relaxing strictures on the people's entrepreneurial spirit and allowing a modicum of capitalistic enterprise to emerge, the country has made tremendous economic gains in a very short time. However, because, as Emerson insists, one freedom always leads in another by the hand, China inevitably will have to allow greater political and intellectual freedom if prosperity there is to continue. You cannot foster cutting-edge development while censoring the internet.

In his own time, Emerson saw a perfect example of the linkage of freedom and prosperity in comparing the Free States of the North with the slave-holding South. According to data provided by the census of 1860, the Free States showed a flourishing economy and general prosperity. Everywhere, hard work and creative enterprise led to the creation of wealth in a free market society. In the conservative South, by contrast, while elite members of the slave-holding class enjoyed great wealth and comfort, the vast majority of white southerners remained poor. Black slaves, whose labor provided the underpinnings of the wealthy elite, suffered even more.

Additionally, the institutions that constitute the very back-bone of civilization, such as primary and secondary schools, colleges and libraries, a free press, lyceums for public lectures, etc., were few and far between. Literacy rates were dismal. As Emerson well knew, a society that ignores or denies the dictates of moral law and the demands of social justice, a society that stifles the natural creativity of the majority of its population, a society that refuses to grant dignity and honor to the endeavors of free labor, cannot prosper. It will eventually collapse under the weight of its own contradictions. It is simply out of synch with the laws that govern the universe.

Wealth and Success

PERSONAL PRODUCTIVITY IS THE KEY TO WEALTH

At the outset of his essay *"Wealth,"* Emerson points out that the key to *"common wealth"* is the productivity of individuals.

As soon as a stranger is introduced into any company, one of the first questions which all wish to have answered, is, How does that man get his living? And with reason. He is no whole man until he knows how to earn a blameless livelihood. Society is barbarous until every industrious man can get his living without dishonest customs.

Every man is a consumer, and ought to be a producer. He fails to make his place good in the world unless he not only pays his debt but also adds something to the common wealth. Nor can he do justice to his genius without making some larger demand on the world than a bare subsistence. He is by constitution expensive, and needs to be rich.

Wealth has its source in applications of the mind to nature, from the rudest strokes of spade and axe up to the last secrets of art. Intimate ties subsist between thought and all production; because a better order is equivalent to vast amounts of brute labor. The forces and the resistances are nature's, but the mind acts in bringing things from where they abound to where they are wanted; in wise combining; in directing the practice of the useful arts, and in the creation of finer values by fine art, by eloquence, by song, or the reproductions of memory. Wealth is in applications of mind to nature; and the art of getting rich consists not in industry, much less in saving, but in a better order, in timeliness, in being at the right spot. One man has stronger arms or longer legs; another sees by the course of streams and growth of markets where land will be wanted, makes a clearing to the river, goes to sleep and wakes up rich. Steam is no stronger now than it was a hundred years ago; but is put to better use. A clever fellow was acquainted with the expansive force of steam; he also saw the wealth of wheat and grass rotting in Michigan. Then he cunningly screws on the steam-pipe to the wheat-crop. Puff now, O Steam! The steam puffs and expands as before, but this time it is dragging all Michigan at its back to hungry New York and hungry England. Coal lay in ledges under the ground since the Flood, until a laborer with pick and windlass brings it to the surface. We may well call it black diamonds. Every basket is power and civilization. For coal is a portable climate. It carries the heat of the tropics to Labrador and the polar circle; and it is the means of transporting itself whithersoever it is wanted. Watt and Stephenson whispered in the ear of mankind their secret, that a half-ounce of coal will draw two tons a mile, and coal carries coal, by rail and by boat, to make Canada as warm as Calcutta; and with its comfort brings its industrial power.

To foster the pursuit of common wealth, nature imbues us with *"wants"* as well as a compelling desire to express

Wealth and Success

ourselves creatively. We strive to be productive. For the creative person, *"The world is his tool-chest."*

Wealth begins with these articles of necessity. And here we must recite the iron law which nature thunders in these northern climates. First she requires that each man should feed himself. If happily his fathers have left him no inheritance, he must go to work, and by making his wants less or his gains more, he must draw himself out of that state of pain and insult in which she forces the beggar to lie. She gives him no rest until this is done; she starves, taunts and torments him, takes away warmth, laughter, sleep, friends and daylight, until he has fought his way to his own loaf. Then, less peremptorily but still with sting enough, she urges him to the acquisition of such things as belong to him. Every warehouse and shop-window, every fruit-tree, every thought of every hour opens a new want to him which it concerns his power and dignity to gratify. It is of no use to argue the wants down: the philosophers have laid the greatness of man in making his wants few, but will a man content himself with a hut and a handful of dried pease? He is born to be rich. He is thoroughly related; and is tempted out by his appetites and fancies to the conquest of this and that piece of nature, until he finds his well-being in the use of his planet, and of more planets than his own. Wealth requires, besides the crust of bread and the roof,—the freedom of the city, the freedom of the earth, travelling, machinery, the benefits of science, music and fine arts, the best culture and the best company. He is the rich man who can

> *avail himself of all men's faculties. He is the richest man who knows how to draw a benefit from the labors of the greatest number of men, of men in distant countries and in past times. The same correspondence that is between thirst in the stomach and water in the spring, exists between the whole of man and the whole of nature. The elements offer their service to him. The sea, washing the equator and the poles, offers its perilous aid and the power and empire that follow it,—day by day to his craft and audacity. "Beware of me," it says, "but if you can hold me, I am the key to all the lands." Fire offers, on its side, an equal power. Fire, steam, lightning, gravity, ledges of rock, mines of iron, lead, quicksilver, tin and gold; forests of all woods; fruits of all climates; animals of all habits; the powers of tillage; the fabrics of his chemic laboratory; the webs of his loom; the masculine draught of his locomotive, the talismans of the machine-shop; all grand and subtile things, minerals, gases, ethers, passions, war, trade, government,—are his natural play-mates, and according to the excellence of the machinery in each human being is his attraction for the instruments he is to employ. The world is his tool-chest, and he is successful, or his education is carried on just so far, as is the marriage of his faculties with nature, or the degree in which he takes up things into himself.*

If wealth is power, and power properly used is a positive moral force that improves the human condition, then the opposite is also true. Namely, *"Poverty demoralizes."* Ben Franklin made the same point when he observed that it's difficult to make an empty purse stand upright. Our recent experience

Wealth and Success

with Enron, the Bernard Maddox affair, the obscene levels of compensation for mediocre CEOs and so-called "money managers," and other such scandals, proves Emerson's point that *"in failing circumstances, no man can be relied upon to kept his integrity"* and that *"the habit of expense"* can be the undoing of the most successful businessperson. Wealth gotten immorally, or excessive compensation that has not been truly earned, or gross self-indulgence will ultimately impoverish the offender and destroy *"fellow-feeling of any kind."*

> *The subject of economy mixes itself with morals, inasmuch as it is a peremptory point of virtue that a man's independence be secured. Poverty demoralizes. A man in debt is so far a slave, and Wall Street thinks it easy for a millionaire to be a man of his word, a man of honor, but that in failing circumstances no man can be relied on to keep his integrity. And when one observes in the hotels and palaces of our Atlantic capitals the habit of expense, the riot of the senses, the absence of bonds, clanship, fellow-feeling of any kind,—he feels that when a man or a woman is driven to the wall, the chances of integrity are frightfully diminished; as if virtue were coming to be a luxury which few could afford, or, as Burke said, "at a market almost too high for humanity." He may fix his inventory of necessities and of enjoyments on what scale he pleases, but if he wishes the power and privilege of thought, the chalking out his own career and having society on his own terms, he must bring his wants within his proper power to satisfy.*

We must earn what we get, honestly, through hard and virtuous work. We have the right to be proud of *"any human work which is well done,"* no matter how basic it might be.

The manly part is to do with might and main what you can do. The world is full of fops [i.e. fancy fools] who never did anything and who had persuaded beauties and men of genius to wear their fop livery; and these will deliver the fop opinion, that it is not respectable to be seen earning a living; that it is much more respectable to spend without earning; and this doctrine of the snake will come also from the elect sons of light; for wise men are not wise at all hours, and will speak five times from their taste or their humor, to once from their reason. The brave workman, who might betray his feeling of it in his manners, if he do not succumb in his practice, must replace the grace or elegance forfeited, by the merit of the work done. No matter whether he makes shoes, or statues, or laws. It is the privilege of any human work which is well done to invest the doer with a certain haughtiness. He can well afford not to conciliate, whose faithful work will answer for him. The mechanic at his bench carries a quiet heart and assured manners, and deals on even terms with men of any condition. The artist has made his picture so true that it disconcerts criticism. The statue is so beautiful that it contracts no stain from the market, but makes the market a silent gallery for itself.

Wealth and Success

THE CREATION OF WEALTH REQUIRES VISION AND ENTHUSIASM

Creative people are often speculators whose vision extends far beyond the narrow confines of the horizon. Often, people of this sort are deemed a bit mad. But this kind of creativity is the essence of true progress. It is through the efforts of these visionaries that the resources of the planet are made to serve the greater good of humanity. *"Their speculative genius is the madness of the few for the gain of the world."* These are the business men and women, the inventors and venture capitalists, who create real wealth, not the paper pyramids made up of esoteric financial instruments like "derivatives" and other such fraudulent nonsense. In distressing economic times (like the present), it is clear that America must get back to the economic principles that first made it great and powerful, the universal principles that Emerson describes here as being rooted in human nature. The value of wealth lies in the creation of general prosperity, not ostentatious, narrow, and self-indulgent consumption.

Society in large towns is babyish, and wealth is made a toy. The life of pleasure is so ostentatious that a shallow observer must believe that this is the agreed best use of wealth, and, whatever is pretended, it ends in cosseting [i.e. pampering*]. But if this were the main use of surplus capital, it would bring us to barricades, burned towns and tomahawks, presently. Men of sense esteem wealth to be the assimilation of nature to themselves, the converting of the sap and juices of the planet to the incarnation and nutriment of their design. Power is what they want, not candy;—power to execute their design, power to give legs and feet, form and actuality to their thought; which, to a clear-sighted man, appears the end for which the universe exists, and all its* *resources might be well applied. Columbus thinks that the sphere is a problem for practical navigation as well as for closet geometry, and looks on all kings and peoples as cowardly landsmen until they dare fit him out. Few men on the planet have more truly belonged to it. But he was forced to leave much of his map blank. His successors inherited his map, and inherited his fury to complete it.*

So the men of the mine, telegraph, mill, map and survey,—the monomaniacs who talk up their project in marts and offices and entreat men to subscribe:— how did our factories get built? how did North America get netted with iron rails, except by the importunity of these orators who dragged all the prudent men in? Is party the madness of many for the gain of a few? This speculative genius is the madness of a few for the gain of the world. The projectors are sacrificed, but the public is the gainer. Each of these idealists, working after his thought, would make it tyrannical, if he could. He is met and antagonized by other speculators as hot as he. The equilibrium is preserved by these counter-actions, as one tree keeps down another in the forest, that it may not absorb all the sap in the ground. And the supply in nature of railroad-presidents, copper-miners, grand-junctioners, smoke-burners, fire-annihilators, etc., is limited by the same law which keeps the proportion in the supply of carbon, of alum, and of hydrogen.

The rich have access to more power and potential than others, but they also have a greater obligation as a result, *"for he*

Wealth and Success

is the rich man in whom the people are rich." Wealth should be employed by those who know how to use it for the common benefit of humanity.

> *To be rich is to have a ticket of admission to the master-works and chief men of each race. It is to have the sea, by voyaging; to visit the mountains, Niagara, the Nile, the desert, Rome, Paris, Constantinople; to see galleries, libraries, arsenals, manufactories. The reader of Humboldt's Cosmos follows the marches of a man whose eyes, ears and mind are armed by all the science, arts and implements which mankind have anywhere accumulated, and who is using these to add to the stock. So it is with Denon, Beckford, Belzoni, Wilkinson, Layard, Kane, Lepsius and Livingstone. "The rich man," says Saadi, "is everywhere expected and at home." The rich take up something more of the world into man's life. They include the country as well as the town, the ocean-side, the White Hills, the Far West and the old European homesteads of man, in their notion of available material. The world is his who has money to go over it. He arrives at the seashore and a sumptuous ship has floored and carpeted for him the stormy Atlantic, and made it a luxurious hotel, amid the horrors of tempests. The Persians say, "'T is the same to him who wears a shoe, as if the whole earth were covered with leather."*

Although riches are often described by moralists as the root of all evil, if people everywhere gave up the pursuit of wealth, "moralists would rush to rekindle at all hazards this love of power in the people, lest civilization should be undone." It is not a bad thing to wish to improve your material life and thereby further the progress of mankind. Hospitals, schools, and museums are built with money as well as banks and corporations.

Kings are said to have long arms, but every man should have long arms, and should pluck his living, his instruments, his power and his knowing, from the sun, moon and stars. Is not then the demand to be rich legitimate? Yet I have never seen a rich man. I have never seen a man as rich as all men ought to be, or with an adequate command of nature. The pulpit and the press have many commonplaces denouncing the thirst for wealth; but if men should take these moralists at their word and leave off aiming to be rich, the moralists would rush to rekindle at all hazards this love of power in the people, lest civilization should be undone. Men are urged by their ideas to acquire the command over nature. Ages derive a culture from the wealth of Roman Caesars, Leo Tenths, magnificent Kings of France, Grand Dukes of Tuscany, Dukes of Devonshire, Townleys, Vernons and Peels, in England; or whatever great proprietors. It is the interest of all men that there should be Vaticans and Louvres full of noble works of art; British Museums, and French Gardens of Plants, Philadelphia Academies of Natural History, Bodleian, Ambrosian, Royal, Congressional Libraries. It is the interest of all that there should be Exploring Expeditions; Captain Cooks to voyage round the world, Rosses, Franklins, Richardsons and Kanes, to find the magnetic and the geographic poles. We are all richer for the measurement of a degree of latitude on the earth's surface.

Wealth and Success

Our navigation is safer for the chart. How intimately our knowledge of the system of the Universe rests on that!—and a true economy in a state or an individual will forget its frugality in behalf of claims like these.

Whilst it is each man's interest that not only ease and convenience of living, but also wealth or surplus product should exist somewhere, it need not be in his hands. Often it is very undesirable to him. Goethe said well, "Nobody should be rich but those who understand it." Some men are born to own, and can animate all their possessions. Others cannot: their owning is not graceful; seems to be a compromise of their character; they seem to steal their own dividends. They should own who can administer, not they who hoard and conceal; not they who, the greater proprietors they are, are only the greater beggars, but they whose work carves out work for more, opens a path for all. For he is the rich man in whom the people are rich, and he is the poor man in whom the people are poor; and how to give all access to the masterpieces of art and nature, is the problem of civilization. The socialism of our day has done good service in setting men on thinking how certain civilizing benefits, now only enjoyed by the opulent, can be enjoyed by all.

Emerson's Truth, Emerson's Wisdom

YOU WERE BORN TO BE RICH

Riches only come to those who work hard. Most middle-class Americans today do not think of themselves as rich, but in comparison to Americans who lived in Emerson's time, or those who lived only a hundred years ago, they certainly are. The profusion of luxuries that we now take for granted, such as central heating, electric lights, hot and cold running water (and indoor plumbing), washing machines and clothes dryers, televisions, iPods, cell phones, Blackberries, personal computers, DVD players, automobiles, access to air travel, and a thousand other such things, were virtually unknown to our immediate ancestors. And they are still unknown today in most of the Third World. That we should possess all of these comforts, all of this luxury, all of this wealth, and all of this power is now a normal expectation for most of us. From some perspectives, this development may seem simply miraculous, but it's not "magic" that brought all this wealth and laid it at our door steps. It was the hard work and ingenuity of all those who preceded us. Power generates more power. Wealth generates more wealth. As the Marseilles banker observes here, wealth is *"a mass, is an immense centre of motion, but it must be begun, [and] it must be kept up."*

Man was born to be rich, or inevitably grows rich by the use of his faculties; by the union of thought with nature. Property is an intellectual production. The game requires coolness, right reasoning, promptness and patience in the players. Cultivated labor drives out brute labor. An infinite number of shrewd men, in infinite years, have arrived at certain best and shortest ways of doing, and this accumulated skill in arts, cultures, harvestings, curings, manufactures, navigations, exchanges, constitutes the worth of our world to-day.

Commerce is a game of skill, which every man cannot play, which few men can play well. The right merchant is one

Wealth and Success

who has the just average of faculties we call common-sense; a man of a strong affinity for facts, who makes up his decision on what he has seen. He is thoroughly persuaded of the truths of arithmetic. There is always a reason, in the man, for his good or bad fortune, and so in making money. Men talk as if there were some magic about this, and believe in magic, in all parts of life. He knows that all goes on the old road, pound for pound, cent for cent,—for every effect a perfect cause,—and that good luck is another name for tenacity of purpose. He insures himself in every transaction, and likes small and sure gains. Probity [i.e. honesty] and closeness to the facts are the basis, but the masters of the art add a certain long arithmetic. The problem is to combine many and remote operations with the accuracy and adherence to the facts which is easy in near and small transactions; so to arrive at gigantic results, without any compromise of safety. Napoleon was fond of telling the story of the Marseilles banker who said to his visitor, surprised at the contrast between the splendor of the banker's château and hospitality and the meanness of the counting-room in which he had seen him,—"Young man, you are too young to understand how masses are formed; the true and only power, whether composed of money, water or men; it is all alike; a mass is an immense centre of motion, but it must be begun, it must be kept up:"—and he might have added that the way in which it must be begun and kept up is by obedience to the law of particles.

Success consists in close appliance to the laws of the world, and since those laws are intellectual and moral, an intellectual and moral obedience. Political Economy is as good a book wherein to read the life of man and the ascendency of laws over all private and hostile influences, as any Bible which has come down to us.

Money is representative, and follows the nature and fortunes of the owner. The coin is a delicate meter of civil, social and moral changes. The farmer is covetous of his dollar, and with reason. It is no waif [i.e. something found] to him. He knows how many strokes of labor it represents. His bones ache with the days' work that earned it. He knows how much land it represents;—how much rain, frost and sunshine. He knows that, in the dollar, he gives you so much discretion and patience, so much hoeing and threshing. Try to lift his dollar; you must lift all that weight. In the city, where money follows the skit of a pen or a lucky rise in exchange, it comes to be looked on as light. I wish the farmer held it dearer, and would spend it only for real bread; force for force.

THE IMPORTANCE OF MORALITY TO ECONOMICS

The value of money increases as civilization advances. This money then supports further progress, which, in turn, increases its value, and so forth. Morality is also essential to economic health. Immorality corrupts the whole system. Even today, especially in countries such as Russia and Columbia, and more recently, Mexico, investors are disinclined to invest because the rule of law is eroded by bribes, intimidation, shady dealings, and violent crime. Again, Emerson finds this moral principle manifest in nature, even among apple trees.

Every step of civil advancement makes every man's dollar worth more. In California, the country where it grew,— what would it buy? A few years since, it would buy a shanty, dysentery, hunger, bad company and crime. There are wide countries, like Siberia, where it would buy little else today than some petty mitigation of suffering. In Rome it will buy beauty and magnificence. Forty years ago, a dollar would not buy much in Boston. Now it will buy a great deal more in our old town, thanks to railroads, telegraphs, steamers, and the contemporaneous growth of New York and the whole country. Yet there are many goods appertaining to a capital city which are not yet purchasable here, no, not with a mountain of dollars. A dollar in Florida [largely undeveloped in Emerson's time] is not worth a dollar in Massachusetts. A dollar is not value, but representative of value, and, at last, of moral values. A dollar is rated for the corn it will buy, or to speak strictly, not for the corn or house-room, but for Athenian corn, and Roman house-room,— for the wit, probity and power which we

> *eat bread and dwell in house to share and exert. Wealth is mental; wealth is moral. The value of a dollar is, to buy just things; a dollar goes on increasing in value with all the genius and all the virtue of the world. A dollar in a university is worth more than a dollar in a jail; in a temperate, schooled, law-abiding community than in some sink of crime, where dice, knives and arsenic are in constant play.*

As we have learned most recently and painfully, dishonesty in the marketplace erodes the stability of the entire society.

> *The Bank-Note Detector [used to detect counterfeit currency] is a useful publication. But the current dollar, silver or paper, is itself the detector of the right and wrong where it circulates. Is it not instantly enhanced by the increase of equity? If a trader refuses to sell his vote, or adheres to some odious right, he makes so much more equity in Massachusetts; and every acre in the state is more worth, in the hour of his action. If you take out of State Street the ten honestest merchants and put in ten roguish persons controlling the same amount of capital, the rates of insurance will indicate it; the soundness of banks will show it; the highways will be less secure; the schools will feel it, the children will bring home their little dose of the poison; the judge will sit less firmly on the bench, and his decisions be less upright; he has lost so much support and constraint, which all need; and the pulpit will betray it, in a laxer rule of life. An apple-tree, if you take out every day for a number of days a load of loam and put in a load of sand about its roots, will find it out.*

Wealth and Success

An apple-tree is a stupid kind of creature, but if this treatment be pursued for a short time I think it would begin to mistrust something. And if you should take out of the powerful class engaged in trade a hundred good men and put in a hundred bad, or, what is just the same thing, introduce a demoralizing institution, would not the dollar, which is not much stupider than an apple-tree, presently find it out? The value of a dollar is social, as it is created by society. Every man who removes into this city with any purchasable talent or skill in him, gives to every man's labor in the city a new worth. If a talent is anywhere born into the world, the community of nations is enriched; and much more with a new degree of probity. The expense of crime, one of the principal charges of every nation, is so far stopped. In Europe, crime is observed to increase or abate with the price of bread. If the Rothschilds [Europe's most famous financiers] at Paris do not accept bills [i.e. paper currency], the people at Manchester, at Paisley, at Birmingham are forced into the highway, and landlords are shot down in Ireland. The police-records attest it. The vibrations are presently felt in New York, New Orleans and Chicago. Not much otherwise the economical power touches the masses through the political lords. Rothschild refuses the Russian loan [to finance military operations], and there is peace and the harvests are saved. He takes it, and there is war and an agitation through a large portion of mankind, with every hideous result, ending in revolution and a new order.

REGULATION AND NATURAL LAW IN THE MARKETPLACE

Because Emerson believed that economics and trade were subject to natural laws that were self-enforcing, he argues that, as far as possible, government should not interfere with the process of wealth creation, other than establishing *"equal laws [to] secure life and property."* As we have all recently learned, when rules are broken and principles compromised, the entire economic system is imperiled. There must be some reasonable regulation to insure the game is played fairly and honestly.

Wealth brings with it its own checks and balances. The basis of political economy is non-interference. The only safe rule is found in the self-adjusting meter of demand and supply. Do not legislate. Meddle, and you snap the sinews with your sumptuary laws. Give no bounties, make equal laws, secure life and property, and you need not give alms. Open the doors of opportunity to talent and virtue and they will do themselves justice, and property will not be in bad hands. In a free and just commonwealth, property rushes from the idle and imbecile to the industrious, brave and persevering.

The laws of nature play through trade, as a toy-battery exhibits the effects of electricity. The level of the sea is not more surely kept than is the equilibrium of value in society by the demand and supply; and artifice or legislation punishes itself by reactions, gluts and bankruptcies. The sublime laws play indifferently through atoms and galaxies. Whoever knows what happens in the getting and spending of a loaf of bread and a pint of beer, that no wishing will change the rigorous limits of pints and penny loaves; that for all that is consumed so much less remains in the basket and pot, but what is gone out of these is not wasted, but well spent, if it nourish his body and enable him to finish his task;—knows all of political economy that the budgets of empires can teach him. The interest of petty economy is this symbolization of the great economy; the way in which a house and a private man's methods tally with the solar system and the laws of give and take, throughout nature; and however wary we are of the falsehoods and petty tricks which we suicidally play off on each other, every man has a certain satisfaction whenever his dealing touches on the inevitable facts; when he sees that things themselves dictate the price, as they always tend to do, and, in large manufactures, are seen to do. Your paper is not fine or coarse enough,—is too heavy, or too thin. The manufacturer says he will furnish you with just that thickness or thinness you want; the pattern is quite indifferent to him; here is his schedule;—any variety of paper, as cheaper or dearer, with the prices annexed. A pound of paper costs so much, and you may have it made up in any pattern you fancy.

Self-regulation of the market is inevitable in a free economy.

There is in all our dealings a self-regulation that supersedes chaffering [i.e. bargaining]. You will rent a house, but must have it cheap. The owner can reduce the rent, but so he incapacitates himself from making proper repairs, and the tenant gets not the house he would have, but a worse one; besides that a relation a little injurious is established between landlord and tenant. You dismiss your laborer, saying, "Patrick, I shall send for you as soon as I cannot do without you." Patrick goes off contented, for he knows that the weeds will grow with the potatoes, the vines must be planted, next week, and however unwilling you may be, the canteloupes, crook-necks and cucumbers will send for him. Who but must wish that all labor and value should stand on the same simple and surly market? If it is the best of its kind, it will. We must have joiner, locksmith, planter, priest, poet, doctor, cook, weaver, ostler; each in turn, through the year.

If a St. Michael's pear sells for a shilling, it costs a shilling to raise it. If, in Boston, the best securities offer twelve per cent. for money, they have just six per cent. of insecurity. You may not see that the fine pear costs you a shilling, but it costs the community so much. The shilling represents the number of enemies the pear has, and the amount of risk in ripening it. The price of coal shows the narrowness of the coal-field, and a compulsory confinement of the miners to a certain district. All salaries are reckoned on contingent as well as on actual services. "If the wind were always southwest by west," said the skipper, "women might take ships to sea." One might say that all things are of one price; that nothing is cheap or dear, and that the apparent disparities that strike us are only a shopman's trick of concealing the damage in your bargain. A youth coming into the city from his native New

Hampshire farm, with its hard fare still fresh in his remembrance, boards at a first-class hotel, and believes he must somehow have outwitted Dr. Franklin and Malthus, for luxuries are cheap. But he pays for the one convenience of a better dinner, by the loss of some of the richest social and educational advantages. He has lost what guards! what incentives! He will perhaps find by and by that he left the Muses at the door of the hotel, and found the Furies inside. Money often costs too much, and power and pleasure are not cheap. The ancient poet said, "The gods sell all things at a fair price."

Emerson's Truth, Emerson's Wisdom

EQUIPPING YOURSELF FOR SUCCESS

Emerson concludes his essay with some practical advice on how we should conduct ourselves as we search out our own way to wealth. He first reminds us that we all have a certain talent or inclination that makes us useful to society. To apply this talent we must equip ourselves properly. This may mean buying the appropriate tools or acquiring the appropriate education. Every person must do *"that which he was created to do."*

> **1. The first of these measures is that each man's expense must proceed from his character.** As long as your genius buys, the investment is safe, though you spend like a monarch. Nature arms each man with some faculty which enables him to do easily some feat impossible to any other, and thus makes him necessary to society. This native determination guides his labor and his spending. He wants an equipment of means and tools proper to his talent. And to save on this point were to neutralize the special strength and helpfulness of each mind. Do your work, respecting the excellence of the work, and not its acceptableness. This is so much economy that, rightly read, it is the sum of economy. Profligacy [i.e. wastefulness] consists not in spending years of time or chests of money,—but in spending them off the line of your career. The crime which bankrupts men and states is jobwork;—declining from your main design, to serve a turn here or there. Nothing is beneath you, if it is in the direction of your life; nothing is great or desirable if it is off from that. I think we are entitled here to draw a straight line and say that society can never prosper but must always be bankrupt, until every

Wealth and Success

man does that which he was created to do.

Emerson also distinguishes between pride in being what we are and vanity, which is trying to be what we are not.

Spend for your expense, and retrench [i.e. reduce] the expense which is not yours. Allston the painter was wont to say that he built a plain house, and filled it with plain furniture, because he would hold out no bribe to any to visit him who had not similar tastes to his own. We are sympathetic, and, like children, want everything we see. But it is a large stride to independence, when a man, in the discovery of his proper talent, has sunk the necessity for false expenses. As the betrothed maiden by one secure affection is relieved from a system of slaveries,— the daily inculcated necessity of pleasing all,—so the man who has found what he can do, can spend on that and leave all other spending. Montaigne said, "When he was a younger brother, he went brave in dress and equipage, but afterward his château and farms might answer for him." Let a man who belongs to the class of nobles, those namely who have found out that they can do something, relieve himself of all vague squandering on objects not his. Let the realist not mind appearances. Let him delegate to others the costly courtesies and decorations of social life. The virtues are economists, but some of the vices are also. Thus, next to humility, I have noticed that pride is a pretty good husband. A good pride is, as I reckon it, worth from five hundred to fifteen hundred a year. Pride is handsome, economical; pride eradicates

> *so many vices, letting none subsist but itself, that it seems as if it were a great gain to exchange vanity for pride. Pride can go without domestics, without fine clothes, can live in a house with two rooms, can eat potato, purslain, beans, lyed corn, can work on the soil, can travel afoot, can talk with poor men, or sit silent well contented in fine saloons. But vanity costs money, labor, horses, men, women, health and peace, and is still nothing at last; a long way leading nowhere. Only one draw-back; proud people are intolerably selfish, and the vain are gentle and giving.*

If your calling is to be an artist or a philosopher, you best avoid activities that require hard, physical labor.

> *Art is a jealous mistress, and if a man have a genius for painting, poetry, music, architecture or philosophy, he makes a bad husband and an ill provider, and should be wise in season and not fetter himself with duties which will embitter his days and spoil him for his proper work. We had in this region, twenty years ago, among our educated men, a sort of Arcadian fanaticism, a passionate desire to go upon the land and unite farming to intellectual pursuits. Many effected their purpose and made the experiment, and some became downright plough-men; but all were cured of their faith that scholarship and practical farming (I mean, with one's own hands) could be united.*

> *With brow bent, with firm intent, the pale scholar leaves his desk to draw a freer breath and get a juster statement of*

Wealth and Success

his thought, in the garden-walk. He stoops to pull up a purslain or a dock that is choking the young corn, and finds there are two; close behind the last is a third; he reaches out his hand to a fourth, behind that are four thousand and one. He is heated and un-tuned, and by and by wakes up from his idiot dream of chickweed and red-root, to remember his morning thought, and to find that with his adamantine purposes he has been duped by a dandelion. A garden is like those pernicious machineries we read of every month in the newspapers, which catch a man's coat-skirt or his hand and draw in his arm, his leg and his whole body to irresistible destruction. In an evil hour he pulled down his wall and added a field to his homestead. No land is bad, but land is worse. If a man own land, the land owns him. Now let him leave home, if he dare. Every tree and graft, every hill of melons, row of corn, or quickset hedge; all he has done and all he means to do, stand in his way like duns, when he would go out of his gate. The devotion to these vines and trees he finds poisonous. Long free walks, a circuit of miles, free his brain and serve his body. Long marches are no hardship to him. He believes he composes easily on the hills. But this pottering in a few square yards of garden is dispiriting and drivelling. The smell of the plants has drugged him and robbed him of energy. He finds a catalepsy [i.e. a suspension of sensation] *in his bones. He grows peevish and poor-spirited. The genius of reading and of gardening are antagonistic, like resinous and vitreous electricity. One is concentrative in sparks and shocks; the other is diffuse strength;*

so that each disqualifies its workman for the other's duties.

An engraver, whose hands must be of an exquisite delicacy of stroke, should not lay stone walls. Sir David Brewster gives exact instructions for microscopic observation: "Lie down on your back, and hold the single lens and object over your eye," etc., etc. How much more the seeker of abstract truth, who needs periods of isolation and rapt concentration and almost a going out of the body to think!

Emerson's second point is good advice for Americans who are subject to the temptation of spending beyond their means, which is much easier to do now in the age of the credit card than it was in Emerson's day. Unless they are coupled with prudent restraint, *"bigger incomes do not help anybody."*

2. Spend after your genius, and by system. Nature goes by rule, not by sallies and saltations [i.e. leaps]. There must be system in the economies. Saving and un-expensiveness will not keep the most pathetic family from ruin, nor will bigger incomes make free spending safe. The secret of success lies never in the amount of money, but in the relation of income to outgo; as, after expense has been fixed at a certain point, then new and steady rills of income, though never so small, being added, wealth begins. But in ordinary, as means increase, spending increases faster, so that large incomes, in England and elsewhere, are found not to help matters;—the eating quality of debt does not relax its voracity. When the cholera is in the potato, what is the use of planting larger crops? In England, the richest country in the universe, I was assured by shrewd observers that great lords and ladies had no more guineas to give away than other people; that liberality with money is as rare and as immediately famous a virtue as it is here. Want is a growing giant whom the coat of Have was never large enough to cover. I remember in Warwickshire to have been shown a fair manor, still in the same name as in Shakspeare's time. The rent-roll I was told is some fourteen thousand pounds a year; but when the second son of the late proprietor was born, the father was perplexed how to provide for him. The eldest son must inherit the manor; what to do with this supernumerary [i.e. extra]? He was advised to breed him for the Church and to settle him in the rectorship which was in the gift of the family; which was done. It is a general rule in that country that bigger incomes do not help anybody. It is commonly observed that a sudden wealth, like a prize drawn in a lottery or a large bequest to a poor family, does not permanently enrich. They have served no apprenticeship to wealth, and with the rapid wealth come rapid claims which they do not know how to deny, and the treasure is quickly dissipated.

A system must be in every economy, or the best single expedients are of no avail. A farm is a good thing when it begins and ends with itself, and does not need a salary or a shop to eke it out. Thus, the cattle are a main link in the chain-ring. If the non-conformist or aesthetic farmer leaves out the cattle and does not also leave out the want which the cattle must supply, he must fill the gap by begging or stealing. When men now alive were born, the farm yielded everything that was consumed on it. The farm yielded no money, and the farmer got on without. If he fell sick, his neighbors came in to his aid; each gave a day's work, or a half day; or lent his yoke of oxen, or his horse, and kept his work even; hoed his potatoes, mowed his hay, reaped his rye; well knowing that no man could afford to hire labor without selling his land. In autumn a farmer could sell an ox or a hog and get a little money to pay taxes withal. Now, the farmer buys almost all he consumes,—tinware, cloth, sugar, tea, coffee, fish, coal, railroad tickets and newspapers.

DEVELOPING YOUR TRUE VOCATION

We must have a natural affinity for the work we do in order to be truly successful at it. A city man doesn't make a good farmer, and vice versa.

A master in each art is required, because the practice is never with still or dead subjects, but they change in your hands. You think farm buildings and broad acres a solid property; but its value is flowing like water. It requires as much watching as if you were decanting wine from a cask. The farmer knows what to do with it, stops every leak, turns all the streamlets to one reservoir and decants wine; but a blunderhead comes out of Cornhill, tries his hand, and it all leaks away. So is it with granite streets or timber townships as with fruit or flowers. Nor is any investment so permanent that it can be allowed to remain without incessant watching, as the history of each attempt to lock up an inheritance through two generations for an unborn inheritor may show.

When Mr. Cockayne [i.e. a city dweller] takes a cottage in the country, and will keep his cow, he thinks a cow is a creature that is fed on hay and gives a pail of milk twice a day. But the cow that he buys gives milk for three months; then her bag dries up. What to do with a dry cow? who will buy her? Perhaps he bought also a yoke of oxen to do his work; but they get blown [i.e. swollen] and lame. What to do with blown and lame oxen? The farmer fats his after the spring work is done, and kills them in the fall. But how can Cockayne, who has no pastures, and leaves his cottage daily in the cars at business hours, be bothered with fatting and killing oxen? He plants trees; but there must be crops, to keep the trees in ploughed land. What shall be the crops? He will have nothing to do with trees, but will have grass. After a year or two the grass must be turned up and ploughed; now what crops? Credulous Cockayne!

Emerson's third point is that we should learn by observing others. Whatever our function in life, there's a right way and a wrong way to do it. The foolish insist on their own way, while the wise are willing to learn from others and from the nature of the thing itself. Like the surveyor who realized that the best way to route the railroad was to follow the river (since water always flows along the path of least resistance) the wise know that there are natural laws everywhere that we can learn from. Like the cows in Boston who first mapped the streets, and the Native Americans whose trails became the basis for civilized roads, we must learn to follow the lay of the land and to listen to the voice of experience. As Emerson observes, *"Nature has her own best mode of doing each thing, and she has somewhere told it plainly."*

3. Help comes in the custom of the country, and the rule of Impera parendo [Latin: to dominate by submitting]. The rule is not to dictate nor to insist on carrying out each of your schemes by ignorant wilfulness, but to learn practically the secret spoken from all nature, that things themselves refuse to be mis-managed, and will show to the watchful their own law. Nobody need stir hand or foot. The custom of the country will do it all. I know not how to build or to plant; neither how to buy wood, nor what to do with the house-lot, the field, or the wood-lot, when bought. Never fear; it is all settled how it shall be, long beforehand, in the custom of the country,—whether to sand or whether to clay it, when to plough, and how to dress, whether to grass or to corn; and you cannot help or hinder it. Nature has her own best mode of doing each thing, and she has somewhere told it plainly, if we will keep our eyes and ears open. If not, she will not be slow in undeceiving us when we prefer our own way to hers. How often we must remember the art of the surgeon, which, in replacing the broken bone, contents itself with releasing the parts from false position; they fly into place by the action of the muscles. On this art of nature all our arts rely.

Of the two eminent engineers in the recent construction of railways in England, Mr. Brunel went straight from terminus to terminus, through mountains, over streams, crossing highways, cutting ducal estates in two, and shooting through this man's cellar and that man's attic window, and so arriving at his end, at great pleasure to geometers, but with cost to his company. Mr. Stephenson on the contrary, believing that the river knows the way, followed his valley as implicitly as our Western Railroad follows the Westfield River, and turned out to be the safest and cheapest engineer. We say the cows laid out Boston. Well, there are worse surveyors. Every pedestrian in our pastures has frequent occasion to thank the cows for cutting the best path through the thicket and over the hills; and travellers and Indians know the value of a buffalo-trail, which is sure to be the easiest possible pass through the ridge.

When a citizen fresh from Dock Square or Milk Street comes out and buys land in the country, his first thought is to a fine outlook from his windows; his library must command a western view; a sunset every day, bathing the shoulder of Blue Hills, Wachusett, and the peaks of Monadnoc and Uncanoonuc. What, thirty acres, and all this magnificence for fifteen hundred dollars! It would be cheap at fifty thousand. He proceeds at once, his eyes dim with tears of joy, to fix the spot for his corner-stone. But the man who is to level the ground thinks it will take many hundred loads of gravel to fill the hollow to the road. The stone-mason who should build the well thinks he shall have to dig forty feet; the baker doubts he shall never like to drive up to the door; the practical neighbor cavils at the position of the barn; and the citizen comes to know that his predecessor the farmer built the house in the right spot for the sun and wind, the spring, and water-drainage, and the convenience to the pasture, the garden, the field and the road. So Dock Square yields the point, and things have their own way. Use has made the farmer wise, and the foolish citizen learns to take his counsel. From step to step he comes at last to surrender at discretion. The farmer affects to take his orders; but the citizen says, You may ask me as often as you will, and in what ingenious forms, for an opinion concerning the mode of building my wall, or sinking my well, or laying out my acre, but the ball will rebound to you. These are matters on which I neither know nor need to know anything. These are questions which you and not I shall answer.

Wealth and Success

The principle of right way/wrong way applies even to our domestic lives and family relations and routines.

> *Not less within doors a system settles itself paramount and tyrannical over master and mistress, servant and child, cousin and acquaintance. 'T is in vain that genius or virtue or energy of character strive and cry against it. This is fate. And 't is very well that the poor husband reads in a book of a new way of living, and resolves to adopt it at home; let him go home and try it, if he dare.*

We must also work carefully and constantly toward that which we hope to accomplish in life, and not jump from one thing to another, which only scatters our force. The rule of thumb is, concentrate.

> *4. Another point of economy is to look for seed of the same kind as you sow, and not to hope to buy one kind with another kind. Friendship buys friendship; justice, justice; military merit, military success. Good husbandry finds wife, children and house-hold. The good merchant, large gains, ships, stocks and money. The good poet, fame and literary credit; but not either, the other. Yet there is commonly a confusion of expectations on these points. Hotspur lives for the moment, praises himself for it, and despises Furlong, that he does not. Hotspur of course is poor, and Furlong a good provider. The odd circumstance is that Hotspur thinks it a superiority in himself, this improvidence, which ought to be rewarded with Furlong's lands.*

THE SPIRITUAL VALUE OF WORK

Emerson believed that when we apply ourselves to what we do with both heart and soul, the divine spirit within acts through us. This, in turn, imparts a spiritual quality to all that we do. Our work is our way of rendering divine service to the human family, and its effect is thereby multiplied many fold. The result is *"man raised to his highest power."* Doing business with your soul reveals the soul of business. Our inner, spiritual world is reflected in the outer world and what we do in it. Hence, *"whatever we do must always have a higher aim."*

I have not at all completed my design. But we must not leave the topic without casting one glance into the interior recesses. It is a doctrine of philosophy that man is a being of degrees; that there is nothing in the world which is not repeated in his body, his body being a sort of miniature or summary of the world; then that there is nothing in his body which is not repeated as in a celestial sphere in his mind; then, there is nothing in his brain which is not repeated in a higher sphere in his moral system.

5. Now these things are so in nature. All things ascend, and the royal rule of economy is that it should ascend also, or, whatever we do must always have a higher aim. Thus it is a maxim that money is another kind of blood, Pecunia alter sanguis: or, the estate of a man is only a larger kind of body, and admits of regimen analogous to his bodily circulations. So there is no maxim of the merchant which does not admit of an extended sense, e. g., "Best use of money is to pay debts;" "Every business by itself;" "Best time is present time;" "The right investment is in tools of your trade;" and the like. The counting-room maxims liberally expounded are laws of the universe. The merchant's economy is a coarse symbol of the soul's economy. It is to spend for power and not for pleasure. It is to invest income; that is to say, to take up particulars into generals; days into integral eras—literary, emotive, practical—of its life, and still to ascend in its investment. The merchant has but one rule, absorb and invest; he is to be capitalist; the scraps and filings must be gathered back into the crucible; the gas and smoke must be burned, and earnings must not go to increase expense, but to capital again. Well, the man must be capitalist. Will he spend his income, or will he invest? His body and every organ is under the same law. His body is a jar in which the liquor of life is stored. Will he spend for pleasure? The way to ruin is short and facile. Will he not spend but hoard for power? It passes through the sacred fermentations, by that law of nature whereby everything climbs to higher platforms, and bodily vigor becomes mental and moral vigor. The bread he eats is first strength and animal spirits; it becomes, in higher laboratories, imagery and thought; and in still higher results, courage and endurance. This is the right compound interest; this is capital doubled, quadrupled, centupled; man raised to his highest power.

The true thrift is always to spend on the higher plane; to invest and invest, with keener avarice, that he may spend in spiritual creation and not in augmenting animal existence. Nor is the man enriched, in repeating the old experiments of animal sensation; nor unless through new powers and ascending pleasures he knows himself by the actual experience of higher good to be already on the way to the highest.

THE SOURCES OF SUCCESS

Wealth and success go hand in hand. Emerson provides further insights into how individuals can achieve success in life in his essay titled *"Success."* He begins with the observation that even at that time, 1858, Americans were making their mark in the world because democracy and freedom naturally stimulated a multitude of energies and potentials. Everyone, Emerson observes, possesses a special talent, *"some triumphant superiority"* that contributes to their personal success while also enriching the larger community. He provides numerous examples of successful individuals.

Our American people cannot be taxed with slowness in performance or in praising their performance. The earth is shaken by our engineries. We are feeling our youth and nerve and bone. We have the power of territory and of seacoast, and know the use of these. We count our census, we read our growing valuations, we survey our map, which becomes old in a year or two. Our eyes run approvingly along the lengthened lines of railroad and telegraph. We have gone nearest to the Pole. We have discovered the Antarctic continent. We interfere in Central and South America, at Canton and in Japan; we are adding to an already enormous territory. Our political constitution is the hope of the world, and we value ourselves on all these feats.

'T is the way of the world; 't is the law of youth, and of unfolding strength. Men are made each with some triumphant superiority, which, through some adaptation of fingers or ear or eye or ciphering or pugilistic or musical or literary craft, enriches the community with a new art; and not only we, but all

men of European stock, value these certificates. Giotto could draw a perfect circle: Erwin of Steinbach could build a minster; Olaf, king of Norway, could run round his galley on the blades of the oars of the rowers when the ship was in motion; Ojeda could run out swiftly on a plank projected from the top of a tower, turn round swiftly and come back; Evelyn writes from Rome: "Bernini, the Florentine sculptor, architect, painter and poet, a little before my coming to Rome, gave a public opera, where-in he painted the scenes, cut the statues, invented the engines, composed the music, writ the comedy and built the theatre."

"There is nothing in war," said Napoleon, "which I cannot do by my own hands. If there is nobody to make gunpowder, I can manufacture it. The gun-carriages I know how to construct. If it is necessary to make cannons at the forge, I can make them. The details of working them in battle, if it is necessary to teach, I shall teach them. In administration, it is I alone who have arranged the finances, as you know."

It is recorded of Linnaeus, among many proofs of his beneficent skill, that when the timber in the shipyards of Sweden was ruined by rot, Linnaeus was desired by the government to find a remedy. He studied the insects that infested the timber, and found that they laid their eggs in the logs within certain days in April, and he directed that during ten days at that season the logs should be immersed under water in the docks;

which being done, the timber was found to be uninjured.

Columbus at Veragua found plenty of gold; but leaving the coast, the ship full of one hundred and fifty skilful seamen,—some of them old pilots, and with too much experience of their craft and treachery to him,—the wise admiral kept his private record of his homeward path. And when he reached Spain he told the King and Queen that "they may ask all the pilots who came with him where is Veragua. Let them answer and say if they know where Veragua lies. I assert that they can give no other account than that they went to lands where there was abundance of gold, but they do not know the way to return thither, but would be obliged to go on a voyage of discovery as much as if they had never been there before. There is a mode of reckoning," he proudly adds, "derived from astronomy, which is sure and safe to any one who understands it."

Hippocrates in Greece knew how to stay the devouring plague which ravaged Athens in his time, and his skill died with him. Dr. Benjamin Rush, in Philadelphia, carried that city heroically through the yellow fever of the year 1793. Leverrier carried the Copernican system in his head, and knew where to look for the new planet. We have seen an American woman [Harriet Beecher Stowe] write a novel of which a million copies were sold, in all languages, and which had one merit, of speaking to the universal heart, and was read with equal interest to three audiences, namely, in the *parlor, in the kitchen and in the nursery of every house. We have seen women who could institute hospitals and schools in armies. We have seen a woman who by pure song could melt the souls of whole populations. And there is no limit to these varieties of talent.*

All of these accomplishments are a reflection of the infinite capacity of the Over-Soul which underlies and assures the progress of humankind. It is not just the shakers and makers that are responsible for this remarkable development. As Emerson notes, *"Our civilization is made up of a million contributions of this kind."*

These are arts to be thankful for,— each one as it is a new direction of human power. We cannot choose but respect them. Our civilization is made up of a million contributions of this kind. For success, to be sure we esteem it a test in other people, since we do first in ourselves. We respect our-selves more if we have succeeded. Neither do we grudge to each of these benefactors the praise or the profit which accrues from his industry.

Here are already quite different degrees of moral merit in these examples. I don't know but we and our race elsewhere set a higher value on wealth, victory and coarse superiority of all kinds, than other men,—have less tranquility of mind, are less easily contented. The Saxon is taught from his infancy to wish to be first. The Norseman was a restless rider, fighter, free-booter. The ancient Norse ballads describe him as afflicted with this inextinguishable thirst of victory. The mother says to her son:—

Wealth and Success

> *"Success shall be in thy courser tall,*
> *Success in thyself, which is best of all,*
> *Success in thy hand, success in thy*
>   *foot,*
> *In struggle with man, in battle with*
>   *brute:—*
> *The holy God and Saint Drothin dear*
> *Shall never shut eyes on thy career;*
> *Look out, look out, Svend Vonved!"*

But Emerson warns that we should not overrate such triumphs. The obsession with a purely personal success leads to *"exclusion, grasping, and egotism."* We realize that things haven't changed much when he observes that *"we Americans are tainted with this insanity, as our bankruptcies and our reckless politics may show."*

> **These feats that we extol do not signify so much as we say. These boasted arts are of very recent origin. They are local conveniences, but do not really add to our stature. The greatest men of the world have managed not to want them. Newton was a great man, without telegraph, or gas, or steam-coach, or rubber shoes, or lucifer-matches, or ether for his pain; so was Shakespeare and Alfred and Scipio and Socrates. These are local conveniences, but how easy to go now to parts of the world where not only all these arts are wanting, but where they are despised. The Arabian sheiks, the most dignified people in the planet, do not want them; yet have as much self-respect as the English, and are easily able to impress the Frenchman or the American who visits them with the respect due to a brave and sufficient man.**

These feats have, to be sure, great difference of merit, and some of them involve power of a high kind. But the public values the invention more than the inventor does. The inventor knows there is much more and better where this came from. The public sees in it a lucrative secret. Men see the reward which the inventor enjoys, and they think, 'How shall we win that?' Cause and effect are a little tedious; how to leap to the result by short or by false means? We are not scrupulous. What we ask is victory, without regard to the cause; after the Rob Roy rule, after the Napoleon rule, to be the strongest to-day,—the way of the Talleyrands, prudent people, whose watches go faster than their neighbors', and who detect the first moment of decline and throw themselves on the instant on the winning side. I have heard that Nelson used to say, "Never mind the justice or the impudence, only let me succeed." Lord Brougham's single duty of counsel is, "to get the prisoner clear." Fuller says 't is a maxim of lawyers that "a crown once worn cleareth all defects of the wearer thereof." Rien ne réussit mieux que le succès. [Nothing succeeds like success.] *And we Americans are tainted with this insanity, as our bankruptcies and our reckless politics may show. We are great by exclusion, grasping and egotism. Our success takes from all what it gives to one. 'T is a haggard, malignant, careworn running for luck.*

Egotism is a kind of buckram [i.e. a heavy fabric used for stiffening] *that gives momentary strength and concentration to men, and seems to be much used in*

Nature for fabrics in which local and spasmodic energy is required. I could point to men in this country, of indispensable importance to the carrying on of American life, of this humor, whom we could ill spare; any one of them would be a national loss. But it spoils conversation. They will not try conclusions with you. They are ever thrusting this pampered self between you and them. It is plain they have a long education to undergo to reach simplicity and plain-dealing, which are what a wise man mainly cares for in his companion. Nature knows how to convert evil to good; Nature utilizes misers, fanatics, show-men, egotists, to accomplish her ends; but we must not think better of the foible for that. The passion for sudden success is rude and puerile, just as war, cannons and executions are used to clear the ground of bad, lumpish, irreclaimable savages, but always to the damage of the conquerors.

TRUE SUCCESS REQUIRES HARD WORK AND PATIENCE

Our efforts to succeed in the world require a real exertion of our natural and unique powers. It requires hard work and personal authenticity. There is no substitute for this. It can't be done on credit, but in Emerson's time, as in our own, many people tried. Delayed gratification, unfortunately, has never been a popular ideal in America. Pretense, self-promotion, and pure fluff are often substituted for real quality and talent, with predictably disastrous consequences.

I hate this shallow Americanism which hopes to get rich by credit, to get knowledge by raps on midnight tables, to learn the economy of the mind by phrenology, or skill without study, or mastery without apprenticeship, or the sale of goods through pretending that they sell, or power through making believe you are powerful, or through a packed jury or caucus, bribery and "repeating" votes, or wealth by fraud. They think they have got it, but they have got something else,—a crime which calls for another crime, and another devil behind that; these are steps to suicide, infamy and the harming of mankind. We countenance each other in this life of show, puffing, advertisement and manufacture of public opinion; and excellence is lost sight of in the hunger for sudden performance and praise.

Emerson offers his *"first rule for success"* using the example of one of his favorite artists, Michael Angelo, who learned early in life that his success or failure depended entirely on himself.

There was a wise man, an Italian artist, Michel Angelo, who writes thus of

Wealth and Success

himself: "Meanwhile the Cardinal Ippolito, in whom all my best hopes were placed, being dead, I began to understand that the promises of this world are for the most part vain phantoms, and that to confide in one's self, and become something of worth and value, is the best and safest course." Now, though I am by no means sure that the reader will assent to all my propositions, yet I think we shall agree in my first rule for success,—that we shall drop the brag and the advertisement, and take Michel Angelo's course, "to confide in one's self, and be something of worth and value."

We should all concentrate on our own special talent or inclination and avoid dispersing our energies by attempting to be a jack-of-all-trades. When necessary, we should employ others to do what they were born to do, while we do our own special thing. *"Doing your own work"* is an authentic form of self-reliance, but most are afraid to assert themselves and prefer to do what others have done before them. As Emerson observes, *"nothing is more rare in any man than an act of his own."*

Each man has an aptitude born with him. Do your work. I have to say this often, but Nature says it oftener. 'T is clownish to insist on doing all with one's own hands, as if every man should build his own clumsy house, forge his hammer, and bake his dough; but he is to dare to do what he can do best; not help others as they would direct him, but as he knows his helpful power to be. To do otherwise is to neutralize all those extraordinary special talents distributed among men. Yet whilst this self-truth is essential to the exhibition of the world and to the growth and glory of each mind, it is rare to find a man who believes his own thought or who speaks that which he was created to say. As nothing astonishes men so much as common sense and plain dealing, so nothing is more rare in any man than an act of his own. Any work looks wonderful to him, except that which he can do. We do not believe our own thought; we must serve somebody; we must quote somebody; we dote on the old and the distant; we are tickled by great names; we import the religion of other nations; we quote their opinions; we cite their laws. The gravest and learnedest courts in this country shudder to face a new question, and will wait months and years for a case to occur that can be tortured into a precedent, and thus throw on a bolder party the onus of an initiative. Thus we do not carry a counsel in our breasts, or do not know it; and because we cannot shake off from our shoes this dust of Europe and Asia, the world seems to be born old, society is under a spell, every man is a borrower and a mimic, life is theatrical and literature a quotation; and hence that depression of spirits, that furrow of care, said to mark every American brow.

THE IMPORTANCE OF SELF-TRUST

We should not be afraid of creating or developing something new, innovative, and truly unique simply because others cannot comprehend it. I'm sure that Bill Gates, Ted Turner, and Steve Jobs, along with many other truly creative individuals, met with this same resistance many times. People always applaud a material accomplishment but not the abstract and creative thinking that led to it.

Self-trust is the first secret of success, the belief that if you are here the authorities of the universe put you here, and for cause, or with some task strictly appointed you in your constitution, and so long as you work at that you are well and successful. It by no means consists in rushing prematurely to a showy feat that shall catch the eye and satisfy spectators. It is enough if you work in the right direction. So far from the performance being the real success, it is clear that the success was much earlier than that, namely, when all the feats that make our civility were the thoughts of good heads. The fame of each discovery rightly attaches to the mind that made the formula which contains all the details, and not to the manufacturers who now make their gain by it; although the mob uniformly cheers the publisher, and not the inventor. It is the dulness of the multitude that they cannot see the house in the ground-plan; the working, in the model of the projector. Whilst it is a thought, though it were a new fuel, or a new food, or the creation of agriculture, it is cried down, it is a chimera; but when it is a fact, and comes in the shape of eight per cent., ten per cent., a hundred per cent., they cry, 'It is the voice of God.'

Horatio Greenough the sculptor said to me of Robert Fulton's visit to Paris: "Fulton knocked at the door of Napoleon with steam, and was rejected; and Napoleon lived long enough to know that he had excluded a greater power than his own."

We must not be afraid to invest our time and energy in projects that we believe in and through which we express the spiritual force and creative genius that is our unique gift. When our hearts are gratified by what we do, we are always the gainers thereby. *"The sum of wisdom is, that the time is never lost that is devoted to work."* I have comforted myself several times with this thought, while working on this book, for example, and other such projects. I have no idea what, if anything, will eventually come of it. I just feel a strong sense of gratification in doing it. Also, by following the spirit wherever it might lead we live in proper alignment with *"the central intelligence which subordinates and uses all talents."* This, in itself, makes the endeavor worthwhile by imbuing it with a spiritual significance.

Is there no loving of knowledge, and of art, and of our design, for itself alone? Cannot we please ourselves with performing our work, or gaining truth and power, without being praised for it? I gain my point, I gain all points, if I can reach my companion with any statement which teaches him his own worth. The sum of wisdom is, that the time is never lost that is devoted to work. The good workman never says, 'There, that will do;' but, 'There, that is it: try it, and come again, it will last always.' If the artist, in whatever art, is well at work on his own design, it signifies little that he does not yet find orders or customers. I pronounce that young man happy who is content with having acquired the skill which he had aimed at, and waits willingly when the occasion of making it appreciated shall arrive, knowing well that it will not loiter. The time your rival spends in dressing up his work for effect, hastily, and for the market, you spend in study and experiments towards real knowledge and efficiency. He has thereby sold his picture or machine, or won the prize, or got the appointment; but you have raised yourself into a higher school of art, and a few years will show the advantage of the real master over the short popularity of the showman. I know it is a nice point to discriminate this self-trust, which is the pledge of all mental vigor and performance, from the disease to which it is allied,—the exaggeration of the part which we can play;—yet they are two things. But it is sanity to know that, over my talent or knack, and a million times better than any talent, is the central intelligence which subordinates and uses all talents; and it is only as a door into this, that any talent or the knowledge it gives is of value. He only who comes into this central intelligence, in which no egotism or exaggeration can be, comes into self-possession.

When we do what we are born to do, we are *"in harmony"* with the great Soul that is the source of *"infinite strength."* This is the ultimate source of our individual power, and it enables us to make our unique contribution to the world cheerfully. It is the action of this spiritual force that creates *"the fullness of man,"* if we are open to it. It is through the exercise of our talents that we help to illuminate the world for others.

My next point is that in the scale of powers it is not talent but sensibility which is best: talent confines, but the central life puts us in relation to all. How

Often it seems the chief good to be born with a cheerful temper and well adjusted to the tone of the human race. Such a man feels himself in harmony, and conscious by his receptivity of an infinite strength. Like Alfred, "good fortune accompanies him like a gift of God." Feel yourself, and be not daunted by things. 'T is the fulness of man that runs over into objects, and makes his Bibles and Shakespeares and Homers so great. The joyful reader borrows of his own ideas to fill their faulty outline, and knows not that he borrows and gives.

✧✧✧✧✧✧✧✧✧

The light by which we see in this world comes out from the soul of the observer. Wherever any noble sentiment dwelt, it made the faces and houses around to shine. Nay, the powers of this busy brain are miraculous and illimitable. Therein are the rules and formulas by which the whole empire of matter is worked. There is no prosperity, trade, art, city, or great material wealth of any kind, but if you trace it home, you will find it rooted in a thought of some individual man.

INTUITION AS A GUIDE

We find true guidance towards success in life by paying attention to our own intuitions, which are *"fountains of right thought."* These feelings are reflections of the *"familiar experience of every man."* By being ourselves, we will find harmony with the outer world because it resonates with the same animating spirit. If we do this consistently, we can avoid the *"cankering ambition"* to be something that we are not. True success will be found by living spontaneously *"in the happy sufficing present."*

> *The fundamental fact in our metaphysic constitution is the correspondence of man to the world, so that every change in that writes a record in the mind. The mind yields sympathyetically to the tendencies or law which stream through things and make the order of Nature; and in the perfection of this correspondence or expressiveness, the health and force of man consist. If we follow this hint into our intellectual education, we shall find that it is not propositions, not new dogmas and a logical exposition of the world that are our first need; but to watch and tenderly cherish the intellectual and moral sensibilities, those fountains of right thought, and woo them to stay and make their home with us. Whilst they abide with us we shall not think amiss. Our perception far outruns our talent. We bring a welcome to the highest lessons of religion and of poetry out of all proportion beyond our skill to teach. And, further, the great hearing and sympathy of men is more true and wise than their speaking is wont to be. A deep sympathy is what we require for any student of the mind; for the chief difference between*

> *man and man is a difference of impressionability. Aristotle or Bacon or Kant propound some maxim which is the key-note of philosophy thence-forward. But I am more interested to know that when at last they have hurled out their grand word, it is only some familiar experience of every man in the street. If it be not, it will never be heard of again.*
>
> *Ah! if one could keep this sensibility, and live in the happy sufficing present, and find the day and its cheap means contenting, which only ask receptivity in you, and no strained exertion and cankering ambition, overstimulating to be at the head of your class and the head of society, and to have distinction and laurels and consumption! We are not strong by our power to penetrate, but by our relatedness. The world is enlarged for us, not by new objects, but by finding more affinities and potencies in those we have.*

We must always be positive in our attitudes and endeavors if we wish to succeed in life. It should be a source of joy to know that our lives and our works contribute to the irresistible progress of humanity. Our system appears limited, but our aspirations are infinite. There are many more Shakespeares who are yet to be heard from.

> *One more trait of true success. The good mind chooses what is positive, what is advancing,—embraces the affirmative. Our system [presently] is one of poverty. 'Tis presumed, as I said, there is but one Shakespeare, one Homer, one Jesus,—not that all are or shall be inspired. But we must begin by affirming. Truth and goodness subsist forevermore. It is true*

Wealth and Success

there is evil and good, night and day: but these are not equal. The day is great and final. The night is for the day, but the day is not for the night. What is this immortal demand for more, which belongs to our constitution? this enormous ideal? There is no such critic and beggar as this terrible Soul. No historical person begins to content us. We know the satisfactoriness of justice, the sufficiency of truth. We know the answer that leaves nothing to ask. We know the Spirit by its victorious tone. The searching tests to apply to every new pretender are amount and quality,—what does he add? and what is the state of mind he leaves me in? Your theory is unimportant; but what new stock you can add to humanity, or how high you can carry life? A man is a man only as he makes life and nature happier to us.

We should not bother ourselves with the world's notion of success. Instead, we should maintain a positive disposition, despite all the negativity around us. We don't adorn our homes with grisly pictures of suffering and pain, and we shouldn't burden our lives with painful notions of hurt, harm, or defeat. "Don't waste yourself in rejection, nor bark against the bad, but chant the beauty of the good." The source of all such affirmation is divine love.

I fear the popular notion of success stands in direct opposition in all points to the real and wholesome success. One adores public opinion, the other private opinion; one fame, the other desert; one feats, the other humility; one lucre, the other love; one monopoly, and the other hospitality of mind.

We may apply this affirmative law to letters, to manners, to art, to the decorations of our houses, etc. I do not find executions or tortures or lazar-houses, or grisly photographs of the field on the day after the battle, fit subjects for cabinet pictures. I think that some so-called "sacred subjects" must be treated with more genius than I have seen in the masters of Italian or Spanish art to be right pictures for houses and churches. Nature does not invite such exhibition. Nature lays the ground-plan of each creature accurately, sternly fit for all his functions; then veils it scrupulously. See how carefully she covers up the skeleton. The eye shall not see it; the sun shall not shine on it. She weaves her tissues and integuments of flesh and skin and hair and beautiful colors of the day over it, and forces death down underground, and makes haste to cover it up with leaves and vines, and wipes carefully out every trace by new creation. Who and what are you that would lay the ghastly anatomy bare?

Don't hang a dismal picture on the wall, and do not daub with sables and glooms in your conversation. Don't be a cynic and disconsolate preacher. Don't bewail and bemoan. Omit the negative propositions. Nerve us with incessant affirmatives. Don't waste yourself in rejection, nor bark against the bad, but chant the beauty of the good. When that is spoken which has a right to be spoken, the chatter and the criticism will stop. Set down nothing that will not help somebody;—

Wealth and Success

> *"For every gift of noble origin*
> *Is breathed upon by Hope's perpetual breath."*

The affirmative of affirmatives is love. As much love, so much perception. As caloric [i.e. heat] to matter, so is love to mind; so it enlarges, and so it empowers it. Good will makes insight, as one finds his way to the sea by embarking on a river. I have seen scores of people who can silence me, but I seek one who shall make me forget or overcome the frigidities and imbecilities into which I fall. The painter Giotto, Vasari tells us, renewed art because he put more goodness into his heads. To awake in man and to raise the sense of worth, to educate his feeling and judgment so that he shall scorn himself for a bad action, that is the only aim.

We should always do what we can to encourage hope and inspire optimism in others. The work of the cynic, unfortunately, is more easily accomplished, as most of us know by experience.

'T is cheap and easy to destroy. There is not a joyful boy or an innocent girl buoyant with fine purposes of duty, in all the street full of eager and rosy faces, but a cynic can chill and dishearten with a single word. Despondency comes readily enough to the most sanguine. The cynic has only to follow their hint with his bitter confirmation, and they check that eager courageous pace and go home with heavier step and premature age. They will themselves quickly enough give the hint he wants to the cold wretch. Which of them has not failed to please where they most wished it? or blundered where they were most ambitious of success? or found

themselves awkward or tedious or incapable of study, thought or heroism, and only hoped by good sense and fidelity to do what they could and pass unblamed? And this witty malefactor makes their little hope less with satire and skepticism, and slackens the springs of endeavor. Yes, this is easy; but to help the young soul, add energy, inspire hope and blow the coals into a useful flame; to redeem defeat by new thought, by firm action, that is not easy, that is the work of divine men.

Emerson acknowledges that the outer world is full of sound and fury and getting and spending, while the great Soul resides within. It is this inner world of the spirit that is the ultimate source of transcendent understanding and tranquility. It is here that our success in life both begins and ends. We have within ourselves the alpha and the omega, the full circle of life. This divinity within enables us to keep the trials, tribulations, and triumphs of the outer world in perspective. It is this inner voice that assures us, even when we're caught up in the trammels of our all-too-busy lives, that God is in his heaven, and in us, and all is right with the world.

We live on different planes or platforms. There is an external life, which is educated at school, taught to read, write, cipher and trade; taught to grasp all the boy can get, urging him to put himself forward, to make himself useful and agreeable in the world, to ride, run, argue and contend, unfold his talents, shine, conquer and possess.

But the inner life sits at home, and does not learn to do things, nor value these feats at all. 'T is a quiet, wise perception. It loves truth, because it is itself real; it loves right, it knows nothing else; but it makes no progress; was as wise in our first memory of it as now; is just the same now in maturity and hereafter in age, it was in youth. We have grown to manhood and womanhood; we have powers, connection, children, reputations, professions: this makes no account of them all. It lives in the great present; it makes the present great. This tranquil, well-founded, wide-seeing soul is no expressrider, no attorney, no magistrate: it lies in the sun and broods on the world. A person of this temper once said to a man of much activity, "I will pardon you that you do so much, and you me that I do nothing." And Euripides says that "Zeus hates busybodies and those who do too much."

In the final analysis, Emerson reminds us that true success in life comes from being ourselves by becoming what we were born to be and by developing the talents that were given us, however great or small. By doing this, we act in accord with the divinity within us, which is the power that animates the great world itself. If you do this, you will be happy.

EPILOGUE

Ralph Waldo Emerson died quietly in his sleep on April 27, 1882, just weeks short of his eightieth birthday. By the time of his death, he was considered a national treasure. His poems appeared in schoolbooks everywhere, and classic essays like ***"Self-Reliance"*** were widely read throughout the land. One reviewer of Emerson's writings at the time touched upon their unique nature when he observed that they were "more easily reflected upon than described, more easily felt than reflected upon." They remain so today. Some years before his death, Emerson sensed that his creative powers were waning. It was just one more inevitable element in the experience of life. As with all other such experiences, Emerson sought to find the lesson to be learned. The result of his effort is the beautiful poem ***"Terminus."*** The title is the Latin name for the Roman god of boundaries. The poem expresses Emerson's gentle acceptance of the fact that his life's work was now largely complete. It was time to take in the sails. The final port of call lies just over the horizon. Emerson's son, Edward, describes the occasion when his father first presented this poem to him.

> As we sat by the fire he read me two or three of his poems for the new May-Day volume, among them "Terminus" It almost startled me. No thought of his ageing had ever come to me, and there he sat, with no apparent abatement of bodily vigor, and young in spirit, recognizing with serene acquiescence his failing forces; I think he smiled as he read. He recognized, as none of us did, that his working days were nearly done. They lasted about five years longer, although he lived, in comfortable health, yet ten years beyond those of his activity. Almost at the time when he wrote "Terminus" he wrote in his journal:—
>
> "Within I do not find wrinkles and used heart, but unspent youth."

TERMINUS

IT is time to be old,
To take in sail:—
The god of bounds,
Who sets to seas a shore,
Came to me in his fatal rounds,
And said: 'No more!
No farther shoot
Thy broad ambitious branches, and thy root.
Fancy departs: no more invent;
Contract thy firmament
To compass of a tent.
There's not enough for this and that,
Make thy option which of two;
Economize the failing river,
Not the less revere the Giver,
Leave the many and hold the few.
Timely wise accept the terms,
Soften the fall with wary foot;
A little while
Still plan and smile,
And,—fault of novel germs,—
Mature the unfallen fruit.
Curse, if thou wilt, thy sires,
Bad husbands of their fires,
Who, when they gave thee breath,
Failed to bequeath
The needful sinew stark as once,
The Baresark marrow to thy bones,
But left a legacy of ebbing veins,
Inconstant heat and nerveless reins,—
Amid the Muses, left thee deaf and dumb,
Amid the gladiators, halt and numb.'
As the bird trims her to the gale,
I trim myself to the storm of time,
I man the rudder, reef the sail,
Obey the voice at eve obeyed at prime:
'Lowly faithful, banish fear,
Right onward drive unharmed;
The port, well worth the cruise, is near,
And every wave is charmed.

www.ingramcontent.com/pod-product-compliance
Lightning Source LLC
Chambersburg PA
CBHW071648160426
43195CB00012B/1395